ADVANCES IN
LIBRARY ADMINISTRATION
AND ORGANIZATION

Volume 7 • 1988

ADVANCES IN LIBRARY ADMINISTRATION AND ORGANIZATION

A Research Annual

Editors: **GERARD B. McCABE**
Director of Libraries
Clarion University of Pennsylvania

BERNARD KREISSMAN
University Librarian, Emeritus
University of California, Davis

VOLUME 7 • 1988

 JAI PRESS INC.

Greenwich, Connecticut   *London, England*

CONTENTS

INTRODUCTION

Opening volume 7, the editors are pleased to present a research paper by Joy M. Greiner of the University of Southern Mississippi. This paper, based on an earlier research effort on the same subject, male and female public library directors, notes some interesting facts: salaries of recent appointees as public library directors do not differ significantly; the salary gap between men and women public library directors is decreasing; participatory management is gaining; and the dual career structure is changing. All are very welcome trends in the library profession. Specifically written for ALAO, this paper should be of interest to all readers.

Raymond D. Fisher, an English librarian, informs us of British library practice in serving off-campus students. This editor has a serious interest in off-campus library service and welcomed the opportunity to learn more about practice in Great Britain. After hearing Raymond Fisher speak at the Off-Campus Library Services Conference II in Knoxville, Tennessee, in April 1985, he was asked very quickly to write a paper describing such services in Great Britain, and now the result is here.

Also a pleasure is the welcome return of Priscilla C. Yu to this series with another important paper on library practice in China. Her report of research sponsored by the Council on Library Resources should be of interest to librarians who someday may visit China to offer professional assistance and advice to our Chinese colleagues.

Several years ago, David Kaser was asked to keep ALAO in mind for a paper on library buildings. He did, and now we publish his review of the evaluation of academic library buildings.

ALAO is eclectic in its approach to subject matter, and for some time we sought writing on school libraries. P. Diane Snyder of the editor's own university responded. Another multiauthored paper by Nancy Mitchell-Tapping, Valerie Lepus, Rashelle S. Karp, and Bernard S. Schlessinger, presents a bibliographic review of a core collection for a special library, confirming ALAO's continuing interest in well-prepared subject bibliographies.

Many librarians, most notably those who are associated with colleges and universities where ALA-accredited library schools are located, receive invitations to teach occasionally. Barbara I. Dewey and J. Louise Malcomb have looked into the question of compensation and observe some interesting conclusions.

Delmus E. Williams also returns to this series with a study of the regional accrediting process and its potential impact on change in academic libraries.

Of interest to public librarians responsible for selecting fiction for their libraries will be Judith L. Palmer's study of *Library Journal* and *Booklist*.

Eugene R. Hanson writes of new technology in academic libraries and foresees the eventual installation of online catalogs in virtually all libraries by the twenty-first century.

Nahla Natour and As'ad M. Abdul-Rahman, from Jordan, discuss activities in their country that led to the development of a unique public library and describe some of its services.

Volume 7 is yours to enjoy.

Gerard B. McCabe
Series Editor

A COMPARATIVE STUDY OF THE MANAGEMENT STYLES AND CAREER PROGRESSION PATTERNS OF RECENTLY APPOINTED MALE AND FEMALE PUBLIC LIBRARY ADMINISTRATORS (1983–1987)

Joy M. Greiner

INTRODUCTION

Appropriate management behaviors have been identified in the areas of business and industry and have primarily been associated with male role models. Although librarianship is considered a female profession, historically males, who

Advances in Library Administration and Organization,
Volume 7, pages 1–27.
Copyright © 1988 by JAI Press Inc.
All rights of reproduction in any form reserved.
ISBN: 0-89232-817-7

are in the minority, have held the majority of administrative positions. The lack of males in librarianship was cited in the Williamson Report in 1923 as detrimental to the profession.[1] When referring to library professionals, Williamson consistently used the masculine pronoun, and when referring to clerical training and duties, he used the feminine pronoun.[2] In the 1950s and 1960s, males were actively recruited specifically for library administration.

Kathleen Heim contended that while legally women may have an equal opportunity with men to achieve the higher echelons of library work, sociologically they do not. She attributes this inequity in part to women trying to conform against their natures to male models of leadership. In addition, Heim asserts that women are disproportionately represented professionally and fail to make an impact on the scholarly world by publishing.[3]

In May 1983, a study was conducted to investigate the status and career development opportunities of male and female public library directors. The directors of all public libraries in the continental United States serving populations of 100,000 or more were mailed questionnaires designed for the collection of data relating to career progression patterns, salaries and library support levels, as well as educational, professional, and experiential characteristics.[4]

Following the same profile, in January 1987, individuals identified in the *American Library Directory* 1986 as having replaced the directors listed in the *American Library Directory* 1982 were asked to participate in an update and potential reevaluation of the current state of public library administration by providing data that would enable an assessment of the situation.

The primary focus of this study is the management behaviors of public library directors, both male and female, who assumed their positions between 1983 and 1987. Leadership styles, professional association activities, and publishing records were the principal areas of investigation, along with mentoring and networking. The developmental career patterns of these administrators were also examined. This study continued the 1983 investigation of the professional development of male and female public library administrators.

The background and development of role definition based on gender is documented in library literature. Examples are available from the early days of the profession when inequities in status and remuneration were perceived as quite normal and even justifiable. A dual career structure was identified in the 1950s, followed by the heightened awareness of disparities that has prevailed since the mid-1960s.

In 1877 Justin Winsor, at the Conference of Librarians in London, reflected the current attitudes toward the appropriate role of women as librarians: "In American libraries we set a high value on women's work. They soften our atmosphere, they lighten our labour, they are equal to our work, and for the money they cost . . . they are infinitely better than equivalent salaries will produce by the other sex."[5]

In a study of public library personnel reported in 1952, Alice Bryan introduced the concept of a dual career structure for librarians, according to sex.[6] From a basic sample of 2,395 public librarians in public libraries serving populations of 250,000 or more, the following data were compiled: 92 percent of the sample were women, 91 percent of the professional staffs were women, and 93 percent of the subprofessional staffs were women. All of the top administrators were men, and only 4 percent of the women, as compared with 15 percent of the men, were head librarians or first-line assistants to the chief.[7]

In 1971, Helen Lowenthal continued this discussion on the dual career structure, characterizing the professional hierarchy in librarianship as one that recruited for two different levels: selecting men for the fewer positions at the top and women for the greater number of positions at the lower levels.[8]

Similarly, Janet Friedman described the situation in which males were younger and less experienced but were paid higher salaries in higher-level positions than females. She also pointed out that male librarians usually hire other males as their chief administrative associates, leaving only middle management positions for female professionals who conversely do not provide that same kind of support for other females.[9]

In 1971 Ruth Kay Maloney conducted a study to determine whether there were significant differences in the profiles of current public library directors as compared with earlier leaders in public libraries. The population consisted of the directors of twenty-six municipal libraries listed in the 1967 *Bowker Annual,* all of which served populations of 500,000 or more for the years 1969, 1950, and 1930. The characteristics of age, sex, tenure, professional training, pattern of professional career development, and participation in the American Library Association were studied. Maloney determined that two patterns of professional advancement had emerged by 1950: internal advancement and advancement through the top positions in progressively larger libraries. Interestingly, her study did not find any correlation between the sex of the director (which included seven females in 1950 and two in 1969) and the pattern of advancement. The only major trend that the investigator was able to identify was a decrease in the number of women directors in large municipal libraries from 1930 to 1969.[10]

Reflecting the feminist issues of the late 1970s, Kathleen Weibel directed the interests of women in the profession inward. She recommended the transition of librarianship from a "feminized" profession to a "feminist" one. As Dee Garrison discerned, "Feminist in this sense would mean a commitment of both male and female librarians to the development of role-free human beings and to a transformation of our concept of power: cooperation, compassion, and humanism rather than aggression, dominance and hierarchy."[11]

Darlene E. Weingand introduced the pragmatic dimension, postulating that almost all of the problems that women face in the marketplace of jobs are determined by the real economic structures of society, not by sexual discrimination as such. Wages are given based on the perceived importance of the work and the need of the wage earner.[12]

Patricia Schuman seems to have reconciled these positions in her 1984 article, stating that women lack structural power—the power to change and improve institutions and society—and economic power. She suggested that power be redefined as the ability to get cooperation. Given that definition, women will have power when they can gain access to resources, information, and support and when they mobilize these effectively to get things done. She identified networking, consciousness raising, organized action, and pressure to change existing structures and laws as valuable tools for effecting change.[13]

In the earlier examination of salaries, library support, and career development paths of public library administrators, Joy Greiner found the career advancement for males and females in public libraries similar to those in academic and research libraries, in professional associations, and in related predominantly female professions. Male directors received higher salaries and higher support for their libraries than did female directors. Female directors were older than their male counterparts, and a significantly higher number were single. They were more likely to have advanced through one library or system, while males moved to higher positions from one library to another. Females were less likely than males to have an advanced degree beyond the master's in library science (M.L.S.) and less likely to have published in the professional literature.[14]

In 1985, six recently appointed top-level women managers from academic and public libraries, a state library, and a library school were interviewed by Susan Brandehoff. She sought to examine their perceptions of personal career paths and planning, management styles and philosophies, as well as their ideas concerning networking, mentors, and professional education. Elizabeth K. Gay, Central Library director for the Los Angeles Public Library, identified a present management goal as that of developing other people. When asked if men and women were different administrative types, Gay suggested that women were better able to deal with details and interpersonal conflict, but she did not see good organizational and people skills as gender related.[15]

Judy K. Rule, director of the Cabell County, West Virginia, public library, perceived personal and professional goals to be closely related. Rule also cited female attention to detail and categorized men as more theoretical and women as more practical.[16]

The roles of networking and mentors were described as important in the career development of the women interviewed, although the mentors were not necessarily in libraries in each case. Gay stated that mentor relationships and networking require maintaining a sophisticated balance of independence and support.[17] Linda Beaupre, associate director of General Libraries at the University of Texas at Austin, listed participation in professional associations as helpful in network development and emphasized that networks should not be gender specific.[18]

When asked if they would recommend education beyond the M.L.S. as an asset to a career in administration, Gay cited her master's degree in business administration as a definite asset. Bridget L. Lamont, director of the Illinois State Library, agreed and recommended advanced education in business, marketing, public administration, and group behavior rather than additional courses in librarianship.[19]

Overall, Brandehoff's interviews revealed that women administrators were more people oriented and more detail conscious. When asked if they subscribed to a particular management theory, individual responses showed that they perceived themselves to be strong communicators, advocates of the commonsense approach, nurturers of both professional and paraprofessional staffs, and proponents of participatory management.

Person and Ficke, in a longitudinal study, investigated the effects of a continuing education program designed to train librarians to develop management potential in women. The effects of a week of intensive, interactive sessions on the career growth of the participants were evaluated. The activities focused on the image of women in librarianship, assertiveness training, effecting change, and leadership and management skills, as well as the management potential of other women.[20] The researchers concluded three important results of the continuing education program: contributions to career advancement, contributions to the development of other women, and the development of a network.[21]

Public libraries have consistently represented a large portion of the lowest library salaries: in 1982, 42 percent;[22] in 1983, 28 percent;[23] in 1984, 39 percent; and in 1985, 35 percent.[24]

The salary survey of public library directors, annually included in *Library Journal,* reported that in 1985 the average salary of male library directors was 15 percent higher than that of female directors, compared to 18 percent in 1981. An 8.5 percent decline in the percentage of directorships held by men over the ten-year period 1975–1985 is considered indicative of a trend. Although male directors continue to receive more per capita support, the difference was perceived to be decreasing.[25]

It was reported that in 1985 there were indications of improvement of the status of women in the profession. Beginning male and female librarians reported the same median salary, $18,000. It was noted that women were in charge of the largest public libraries in the country and at the highest salary levels. Larger numbers of women were reported as entering the previously male-dominated ranks, and slightly fewer women were going into jobs that represent their traditional roles in libraries.[26]

The literature reveals both the identification of a problem and varying investigations of the situation. In accordance with the scientific method, data have been collected and analyzed, and conclusions have been formulated and reported throughout the profession. A trend appears to be developing toward qualifications other than gender as the determinants for career advancement. This study continues the examination of the patterns and behaviors for professional development in librarianship.

METHODOLOGY

In January 1987, directors appointed since 1983 to administrate public libraries in the United States serving population of 100,000 or more were identified in the

American Library Directory. [27] At that time, questionnaires were mailed to these public library administrators. The instrument was designed to investigate the management styles, as well as the educational, experiential, and professional activities of the recently appointed directors. Personal data included sex, age, and marital status. Current salaries and library support levels were studied in relation to gender and to the 1983 study of directors of large public libraries. (The questionnaire is reproduced in Appendix A.)

Library or library system data included the geographical location of the library agency and the size of the population served, in addition to the library support level. Library support level was measured by the size of the total operating budget and the size of the materials collection.

Professional career development information concerned the total years of professional library experience, the number of career interruptions, and the number of library employers. Educational background, publishing activity, professional association involvement, and initial aspirations for administration were considered. The influence of mentors, as well as the manner in which the respondent learned of the position opening, were part of the developmental pattern investigated. Examination of the position immediately previous to the present directorship concerned the job title, the length of time in the job, and the yearly salary. All of these factors, along with the age of the respondent at the time of the present appointment and the present annual salary, enabled the development of a profile of public library directors appointed in the past four years. An objective of the investigation was to assess the extent of gender as a predictor of career achievement or management behaviors.

A Likert-type scale was developed to assess management behaviors. Through responses to statements designed to elicit opinions on a continuum scale from "strongly disagree" to "strongly agree," the directors were given the opportunity to indicate their perception of their roles as administrators. Areas of interest in the management process were the individual's predominant management theory, supervisory behavior, strategy for organizational development, and political activity. The perception of the authority and of the qualifications of governing boards was explored. Overall the extent of the participative process in decision making and in routine library operations is indicated by the responses to the statements on the scale.

DATA ANALYSIS

The total population of directors appointed during the four-year period (1983–1987) was 116. Returns were received from 98 individuals, which constituted an 84.6 percent return rate. Of those, 90 (77.5 percent) were usable. One of the libraries did not have a director, two of the libraries had acting directors, and one return was a duplication. Three of the directors had been appointed prior to the

Table 1. Distribution of
Respondents, 1983

	Number	Percent
Male	189	58.88
Female	132	41.12
Total	321	100.00

identified time period, and one of the directors was in a library that served a population of fewer than 100,000.

Directors identified in the previous study of all public library directors in libraries serving populations of 100,000 or more consisted of 420 individuals: 256 (60.95 percent) males and 163 (38.81 percent) females. Usable returns were analyzed from 321 directors, constituting a response rate to the questionnaire of 76.43 percent.[28]

In that study, the ratio of directors was 58.88 percent males to 41.12 percent females, as indicated in Table 1.[29] In the present assessment of recently appointed directors, usable returns indicate that the ratio is 52.22 percent males to 47.78 percent females (Table 2). It appears that females are gaining in the achievement of top-level public library administrative positions.

Of 86 of the 90 directors appointed during the identified four-year period (1983–1987), 30 (34.9 percent) males replaced other males; 16 (18.6 percent) females replaced other females; 25 (29.1 percent) females replaced males; and 15 (17.4 percent) males replaced females. This information was not available from four of the libraries. Although 25 women replaced male directors, as compared to 15 men who replaced female directors, 30 men continued in the traditional pattern of following other men into the higher echelons of management (Table 3). The number of females either replacing males or other females totals 41. Forty-five males either replaced females or other males, which constitutes a ratio of 52.3 percent male to 47.7 percent female. This represents a difference of only 4.6 percent.

Table 2. Distribution of
Respondents, 1987

	Number	Percent
Male	47	52.22
Female	43	47.78
Total	90	100.00

Table 3.   Succession of the Directors

	Number	Percent
Males succeeded by males	30	34.88
Females succeeded by females	16	18.61
Males succeeded by females	25	29.07
Females succeeded by males	15	17.44
Total	86	100.00

Salaries

In the study conducted in 1983, males predominated in the higher than $30,000 annual salary category. Of those reporting $30,000 or less, the percentage of female directors was more than twice the percentage of male directors. Annual salaries of more than $50,000 were reported by 35 males compared to 14 females.[30]

Contrary to that 1983 study of the total population of directors of large public libraries, the male and female directors appointed during the last four years did not report significantly different salaries. The majority of salaries reported by men and women were in the $40,001–45,000 range (category 6), with the mean for men (6.97) slightly higher than that for women (6.13), indicating that more men than women were in a higher salary range ($t = 1.85$, $df = 88$, $p = .068$), though this difference of means is not significant at the .05 level. But as is shown in Table 4, 20 males, compared to 9 females, are in the $50,000 or higher salary bracket. Of these, 7 men and 6 women, or 14.89 percent of the men compared to 13.95 percent of the women, are at the $60,000 or above yearly salary level.

Table 4.   Present Salary

Category	Yearly Salary	Male Number	Male Percent	Female Number	Female Percent	Total Number	Total Percent
1	Less than $20,000	0	0.00	1	2.33	1	1.11
2	$20,000–25,000	0	0.00	1	2.33	1	1.11
3	$25,001–30,000	3	6.38	4	9.30	7	7.78
4	$30,001–35,000	1	2.13	3	6.98	4	4.44
5	$35,001–40,000	9	19.15	4	9.30	13	14.44
6	$40,001–45,000	9	19.15	14	32.55	23	25.56
7	$45,001–50,000	5	10.63	7	16.28	12	13.33
8	$50,001–55,000	6	12.77	3	6.98	9	10.00
9	$55,001–60,000	7	14.89	0	0.00	7	7.78
10	Over $60,000	7	14.89	6	13.95	13	14.44
	Total	47	99.99	43	100.00	90	99.99

Population Served

There was not a significant difference in the size of the populations served by men and women directors. The majority of directors were in libraries that served populations of between 100,000 and 500,000. Thirty-five of 47 men direct these libraries, while 38 of 42 women are in the same population category (Table 5). Although 12 men, compared to 4 women, administer libraries in the 500,001 to over 1 million population range, the difference is not statistically significant at the .05 level. Of the 12 male-directed libraries serving populations over 500,000, three are in the Northeast, three are in the North Central region, and six are in the South. One of the 4 females is in the North Central region, 2 are in the South, and 1 is in the West.

Library Support

There is a significant difference between the size of the collections in libraries directed by males and those directed by females. As is shown in Table 6, the majority of the directors reported collection sizes of from 250,000 to 500,000 (category 3), with a significantly higher percentage of the men in a higher range ($t = 2.06$, $df = 86$, $p = .042$). In 88 of the libraries that reported collection size, 47 directed by men and 41 by women, the mean for male-administered libraries was 3.98 (in the 250,000–500,000 range) and in female-managed libraries 3.17 (also in the 250,000–500,000 range). The significantly larger collection size in male-managed libraries contradicts the findings in the earlier study. In that examination, collection size was the only area of library support in which there was not a significant difference for men and women directors.[31]

Career Development Patterns

From the onset of their careers, men, to a greater extent than women, wanted to be involved with library management. Thirty-five males, compared to 21

Table 5. Population Served

Population	Male		Female		Total	
	Number	Percent	Number	Percent	Number	Percent
100,000–250,000	22	46.81	30	71.43	52	58.43
250,001–500,000	13	27.66	8	19.05	21	23.60
500,001–750,000	5	10.64	3	7.14	8	8.99
750,001–1,000,000	4	8.51	0	00.00	4	4.49
Over 1,000,000	3	6.38	1	2.38	4	4.49
Total	47	100.00	42	100.00	89	100.00

Table 6.   Collection Size

Category	Size	Male Number	Male Percent	Female Number	Female Percent	Total Number	Total Percent
1	Less than 100,000	3	6.4	6	14.6	9	10.2
2	100,000–250,000	9	19.1	9	22.0	18	20.5
3	250,001–500,000	13	27.7	11	26.8	24	27.3
4	500,001–750,000	4	8.5	8	19.5	12	13.6
5	750,001–1,000,000	5	10.6	3	7.3	8	9.1
6	1,000,001–3,000,000	8	17.0	3	7.3	11	12.5
7	3,000,001–5,000,000	4	8.5	0	0.0	4	4.5
8	5,000,001–7,000,000	0	0.0	1	2.4	1	1.1
9	7,000,001–9,000,000	0	0.0	0	0.0	0	0.0
10	Over 9,000,000	1	2.1	0	0.0	1	1.1
	Total	47	99.9	41	99.9	89	99.9

females, responded that they aspired to be administrators when they entered the profession (Table 7). This represented a significant difference (chi-square = 5.95, $df = 1$, $p = .015$). In the 1983 investigation, not only did more males than females aspire to be administrators, they also predominated in the higher salary category regardless of initial aspirations.[32]

A gender relationship was not evident in the educational preparation of the directors appointed in the past four years. The M.L.S. was the highest degree reported by the majority of the administrators. Thirty-four women and 30 men were in this category. Eleven men compared to 5 women had earned both an M.L.S. and a master's degree in a subject area. It is indicative of female career planning that currently two females and two males reported doctorates either in library science or a subject area, while in the 1983 study, none of the females had completed a doctorate compared to 8 males who had earned the degree in either library science or a subject area.[33]

A significantly higher percentage of females than males reported leaves from the profession of six months or more. Of the males and females who reported

Table 7.   Aspirations for Administration

	Male Number	Male Percent	Female Number	Female Percent	Total Number	Total Percent
Yes	35	76.1	21	48.8	56	62.9
No	11	23.9	22	51.2	33	37.1
Total	46	100.0	43	100.0	89	100.0

leaves, there is not a significant difference in prior or present salary. Although more females than males reported leaves, the incidence of leaves does not appear to have made a difference in salary levels. These findings agree with a study of the relationship of job mobility and career progression conducted by Judith Braunagel.[34] This also concurs with the 1983 study of public library directors.[35]

There is no gender difference in the number of libraries in which the directors worked or in the length of time employed in each of the libraries. In the previous study, a significantly higher percentage of females reported fewer library employers, as well as longer periods of time in individual library organizations.[36]

There were no significant differences in lengths of time that males and females had spent in their prior positions. Of the 47 males and 43 females, 2 males and 2 females had been in the position prior to their present appointment for less than one year, and 7 males and 3 females had been in the previous position for ten years or more. Forty-six of the respondents had been directors in their previous positions, and 18 were assistant librarians.

Male directors reported a significantly higher previous salary than female directors (Table 8). The average salary for males was in the $26,001–30,000 range (category 5) and for females in the $22,001–$26,000 range (category 4). The mean salary of male directors was 5.89 and for females 4.81, which constituted a significant difference ($t = 2.68$, $df = 88$, $p = .009$).

Twenty-nine males and 30 females reported an influential mentor. There is a tendency of the mentor to be of the same sex as the respondent, although the difference is not statistically significant. A significant relationship was found between the sex of the mentor and the sex of the person who informed the administrators of the job opening (chi-square = 13.5, $df = 4$, $p = .009$). Directors with male mentors learned of the opportunity from males and directors with female mentors from females.

Data regarding publishing activity are displayed in Tables 9, 10, 11, and 12.

Table 8.   Salary in Prior Position

Category	Yearly Salary	Male		Female		Total	
		Number	Percent	Number	Percent	Number	Percent
1	Less than $14,000	0	0.00	4	9.30	4	4.44
2	$14,000–18,000	2	4.26	3	6.98	5	5.56
3	$18,001–22,000	2	4.26	3	6.98	5	5.56
4	$22,001–26,000	9	19.15	7	16.28	16	17.78
5	$26,001–30,000	6	12.77	8	18.60	14	15.55
6	$30,001–35,000	9	19.14	9	20.93	18	20.00
7	$35,001–40,000	5	10.63	6	13.95	11	12.22
8	Over $40,000	14	29.79	3	6.98	17	18.89
	Total	47	100.00	43	100.00	90	100.00

Table 9. Publishing Activity

Area of Publication	Male		Female		Total	
	Number	Percent	Number	Percent	Number	Percent
National	14	40.00	6	37.50	20	39.21
Regional	5	14.29	2	12.50	7	13.73
State	16	45.71	8	50.00	24	47.06
Total	35	100.00	16	100.00	51	100.00

Table 10. Prior Salary of Directors Who Have Published

Salary	Male		Female		Total	
	Number	Percent	Number	Percent	Number	Percent
$14,000–18,000	1	4.5	0	0.0	1	2.9
$18,001–22,000	1	4.5	1	8.3	2	5.9
$22,001–26,000	2	9.1	3	25.0	5	14.7
$26,001–30,000	3	13.6	1	8.3	4	11.8
$30,001–35,000	6	27.3	3	25.0	9	26.5
$35,001–40,000	2	9.1	2	16.7	4	11.8
Over $40,000	7	31.8	2	16.7	9	26.5
Total	22	99.9	12	100.0	34	100.1

Table 11. Present Salary of Directors Who Have Published

Salary	Male		Female		Total	
	Number	Percent	Number	Percent	Number	Percent
$25,001–30,000	1	4.5	1	8.3	2	5.9
$30,001–35,000	1	4.5	0	0.0	1	2.9
$35,001–40,000	5	22.7	1	8.3	6	17.6
$40,001–45,000	1	4.5	2	16.7	3	8.8
$45,001–50,000	3	13.6	3	25.0	6	17.6
$50,001–55,000	3	13.6	2	16.7	5	14.7
$55,001–60,000	4	18.2	0	00.0	4	11.8
Over $60,000	4	18.2	3	25.0	7	20.6
Total	22	99.8	12	100.0	34	99.9

Table 12.   Collection Size in Libraries Whose Directors Have Published

Size	Male Number	Male Percent	Female Number	Female Percent	Total Number	Total Percent
Less than 100,000	2	9.1	1	9.1	3	9.1
100,000–250,000	4	18.2	0	0.0	4	12.1
250,001–500,000	3	13.6	5	45.5	8	24.2
500,001–750,000	3	13.6	2	18.2	5	15.2
750,001–1,000,000	1	4.5	2	18.2	3	9.1
1,000,001–3,000,000	6	27.3	0	0.0	6	18.2
3,000,001–5,000,000	2	9.1	0	0.0	2	6.1
5,000,001–7,000,000	0	0.0	1	9.1	1	3.0
7,000,001–9,000,000	0	0.0	0	0.0	0	0.0
Over 9,000,000	1	4.5	0	0.0	1	3.0
Total	22	99.9	11	100.1	33	100.1

Directors who had published during the past five years reported higher prior salaries, higher present salaries, and larger collections. Twenty-two men and 12 women had published during the past five years. These respondents reported a significantly higher prior salary ($t = 2.15$, $df = 88$, $p = .034$), a significantly higher present salary ($t = 2.28$, $df = 88$, $p = .025$), and a significantly larger collection size ($t = 2.31$, $df = 86$, $p = .023$).

It appears to be of benefit to direct publishing activities toward the national scene. Nineteen of the directors who had published in national journals reported significantly higher salaries than those who had published in state and regional journals ($t = 2.14$, $df = 32$, $p = .040$).

There was not a significant difference between male and female membership in national, regional, or state library associations. Eighty-five of the directors belong to the American Library Association, 36 to regional associations, and 87 to state associations.

Profile of Current Directors

The ages of the male and female administrators when they achieved their present positions did not differ significantly. Over half (56.7 percent) of the recently appointed directors were between the ages of 35 and 44, while only 2 males and 1 female were in the 55 to 64 years of age category. Table 13 is a description of the age distribution of the administrators.

A significantly higher percentage of the male directors than of the female directors are married (chi-square $= 6.83$, $df = 2$, $p = .032$ level of significance). This continues the trend identified in 1983 and supports the theory that marriage is an asset for males but can be considered a disadvantage for females. The marital status of the directors is described in Table 14.

Table 13.   Age on Becoming Director

	Male		Female		Total	
Age	Number	Percent	Number	Percent	Number	Percent
25–34	13	27.66	7	16.28	20	22.22
35–44	24	51.06	27	62.79	51	56.67
45–54	8	17.02	8	18.61	16	17.78
55–64	2	4.26	1	2.32	3	3.33
Total	47	100.00	43	100.00	90	100.00

There is no significant difference in the number of years of total library experience reported by male and female librarians. The mean length of experience of the directors was 16.28 years, with a standard deviation of 5.86, and no significant difference between males and females. Total years of experience ranged from a minimum of 3 years to a maximum of 38 years (Table 15).

There was not a significant difference in the total years of professional experience reported by males and females in the study conducted in 1983, and nearly half (45.14 percent) of the directors reported 21 or more years experience. Of those, 86 were males and 58 were females (45.99 percent of the males and 43.94 percent of the females).[37]

Management Behaviors

The managers were given the opportunity to agree or disagree with statements designed to assess overall management theories, self-perception in relation to their position and to staff, as well as specific attitudes toward the areas of change, nurturing, and motivation of employees.

Significant gender differences were demonstrated in responses to the management scale in the areas of staff development, interaction with funding authorities, and the perception of the role of official governing boards. A significantly higher

Table 14.   Marital Status

	Male		Female		Total	
Marital Status	Number	Percent	Number	Percent	Number	Percent
Married	38	82.61	25	58.14	63	70.79
Single	2	4.35	7	16.28	9	10.11
Divorced, widowed	6	13.04	11	25.58	17	19.10
Total	46	100.00	43	100.00	89	100.00

Table 15.   Total Experience

Years	Male		Female		Total	
	Number	*Percent*	*Number*	*Percent*	*Number*	*Percent*
1–5	0	0.00	1	2.33	1	1.11
6–10	4	8.51	1	2.33	5	5.56
11–15	22	46.81	18	41.86	40	44.44
16–20	12	25.53	16	37.21	28	31.11
21–25	6	12.77	4	9.30	10	11.11
26–30	1	2.13	3	6.98	4	4.44
31–35	0	00.00	0	00.00	0	00.00
36–40	2	4.26	0	00.00	2	2.22
Total	47	100.01	43	100.01	90	99.99

percentage of males indicated that their greatest asset was their ability to choose qualified and capable staff members ($t = 2.12$, $df = 87$, $p = .037$). A significantly higher percentage of females agreed that they are concerned about the development and growth of their subordinates ($t = 2.51$, $df = 87$, $p = .014$) and that they take advantage of training and educational opportunities that will help them better practice participative techniques ($t = 3.09$, $df = 87$, $p = .003$).

In the area of political visibility, more of the women than of the men agreed that library directors should regularly attend meetings of the county board of supervisors and/or the city council ($t = 2.05$, $df = 87$, $p = .044$).

There was consensus among the male and female administrators in their disagreement with the statements that the official library board should have total control of budgeting and personnel decisions. The majority of the directors also disagreed with the statements that board members were either educationally qualified or qualified by professional experience to make policy decisions for library agencies.

The educational qualifications of the official library board to make policy decisions for the administration of a public library were viewed more positively by the males than by the females ($t = 2.18$, $df = 87$, $p = .032$). Also, the older male directors who had spent a longer period of time in the immediately prior positions were more in agreement with the library board's authority and they perceived the qualifications of the members more positively.

Forty-eight directors, with no significant gender difference, agreed that they try to plan specifically for time to involve subordinates in decision making, that most employees are motivated by a sense of accomplishment and achievement, and that most employees would rather have more interesting jobs than a small annual financial raise in a particular year.

Of the directors who agreed that most employees would prefer a more interesting job to a small annual raise in a specific year, a majority perceived their employees to be interested in the goals of their library organization. Seventy-five percent of the directors agreed that most employees will be more effective if given broad policy guidelines rather than specific rules and regulations. Those who agree with providing training and encouragement of subordinates for involvement in the participatory process, were in the majority, with no significant gender difference.

The managers' level of security in their jobs related to their perception of their staffs and the ensuing interaction with those individuals. The directors who stated that they felt secure in their jobs also stated that their greatest asset was their ability to choose qualified and capable staff members. A higher percentage of the male directors indicated that they felt secure in their jobs and that their greatest asset was their ability to choose qualified and capable staff members. A higher percentage of female directors who stated that they felt secure in their jobs also responded that they took advantage of training and educational opportunities to enable them to practice participative techniques better.

All of the directors, male and female, who agreed that they felt secure in their jobs agreed that they tried to maintain open, candid communication with their subordinates, that they tried to plan specifically for times to involve subordinates in decision making, and that they valued suggestions from subordinates. These administrators also perceived most employees to be motivated by a sense of accomplishment and achievement.

A majority of those directors, regardless of gender, who agreed that they felt secure in their jobs agreed that they used their jobs as administrators to be team leaders rather than controllers or overseers. They perceived their employees to be interested in the goals of the library organization, and they tried to provide training and encouragement to enable subordinates to be involved in the participatory process.

Of those secure in their jobs, a majority of the administrators said that they were concerned about the professional development and growth of their subordinates. Forty men and 36 women agreed or strongly agreed with this statement.

There were no gender or age relationships among the 51 directors who agreed that they perceive their role as one of agent of change. However, 31 of those administrators disagree that as a new administrator it is advisable to target areas for change immediately. The other 20 respondents who also perceive their role as one of agent of change contend that it is advisable to target areas for change immediately.

Male directors who succeeded other male directors were more likely to initiate change immediately than female directors who succeeded either female directors or male directors (chi-square = 8.84, $df = 3$, $p = .0314$).

The responses to the statements relating to the administrative philosophies of the population of recently appointed directors indicate a trend toward gender-free management behaviors. A participative management style appears to prevail. The majority of the directors are secure in their jobs. They perceive the library staff to be interested in the goals of the organization, open lines of communications are maintained, and staff members are encouraged to participate in decision making.

CONCLUSIONS

The dual career structure reported by Bryan early in 1950 has continued to be reported by researchers through the present decade.[38] The profiles, derived from data collected in 1983, of the directors of large public libraries were gender specific. Salaries and library support levels were higher for male library directors than for female library directors. Female library directors were older, predominantly single, and more likely to have advanced through internal promotions.

In this investigation of public library directors appointed since 1983, however, similarities in career progression of males and females are at least equivalent to the differences. There was not a difference in the number of previous library employers reported or in the length of time employed in each of the libraries. Men and women had spent a comparable length of time in the immediately prior position, and their ages when they achieved the present directorship did not differ significantly. Neither was there a significant difference in the total years of library experience.

Women and men have secured positions as managers of libraries serving equivalent population sizes. Prior salary, present salary, and collection size are all highly correlated, regardless of gender.

It is of primary interest that the salaries of the directors appointed in the last four years do not differ significantly. The present equitable salaries of this portion of the population of public library administrators may indicate that the salary gap is indeed narrowing, at least for individuals assuming positions at a different level or in different library organizations. Although there is no significant difference in present salaries of male and female directors, males reported higher salaries in the immediately prior positions. This is in accord with the higher male salaries reported in 1984.

A participative management style was identified by the majority of the directors. The nurturing management behaviors indicated by the new directors, regardless of gender, suggest that women are indeed changing the workplace rather than adopting the stereotypical male role model.

It should be considered that many of the male directors who had been recruited specifically for library management are now retiring. In the 1983 study, 86 male directors reported 21 or more years of experience. It is probable that those individuals will be replaced by library administrators, women or men, who have been influenced by the advocates of gender-free professional achievement.

Publishing activity is not limited to women or men professionals. The importance to career progression of scholarly accomplishment is illustrated by the relationship of salaries and a successful publishing record.

The importance of mentoring and networking to position achievement has certainly been suggested by the significantly positive relationship between the sex of the mentor and the sex of the person who informed the respondent of the job opening. The extent of involvement and representation in professional organizations can also be influenced by the presence of an astute mentor and access to a viable network. Although there is not a gender difference in the representation of the administrators in professional organizations, the level of involvement needs to be investigated.

The purpose of this investigation of public library administration after a period of four years was to identify trends in career development and management behaviors. Women, as well as men, have recognized the importance of publishing to career achievement. Also, throughout the profession, the role of mentoring and networking is being recognized as crucial to career development. The responses from directors appointed during this time period signify an encouraging trend: that the dual career structure is being modified and that management behavior is becoming gender free.

NOTES

1. Charles C. Williamson, *A Report Prepared for the Carnegie Corporation of New York* (Metuchen, N.J.: Scarecrow Press, 1971), p. 107.

2. Ibid., p. 11.

3. Kathleen M. Heim, "Factors Contributing to a Continued Status Differentiation between Male and Female Librarians," in *Women and Library Management: Theories, Skills and Values,* ed. Darlene E. Weingand (Ann Arbor, Mich.: Pierian Press, 1982), p. 8.

4. Joy M. Greiner, "A Comparative Study of the Career Development Patterns of Male and Female Library Administrators in Large Public Libraries" (Ph.D. diss., Florida State University, 1984).

5. Anita R. Schiller, "Women in Librarianship," in Kathleen Weibel, Kathleen M. Heim, and Dianna J. Ellsworth, *The Role of Women in Librarianship, 1876–1976: The Entry, Advancement, and Struggle for Equalization in One Profession* (Phoenix: Oryx Press, 1979), p. 239.

6. Alice I. Bryan, *The Public Librarian* (New York: Columbia University Press, 1952), p. 86.

7. Ibid., pp. 29–30.

8. Helen Lowenthal, "A Healthy Anger," *Library Journal* 96 (September 1971): 2597.

9. Janet Friedman, "The Liberated Librarian," *Library Journal* 95 (May 1, 1970): 1709.

10. Ruth K. Maloney, "The 'Average' Director of a Large Public Library," *Library Journal* 96 (February 1, 1971): 443–445.

11. Dee Garrison, *Apostles of Culture* (New York: Free Press, 1979), p. 241.

12. Darlene E. Weingand, *Women and Library Management: Theories, Skills and Values* (Ann Arbor, Mich.: Pierian Press, 1982), p. x.

13. Patricia Glass Schuman, "Women, Power and Libraries," *Library Journal* 109 (January 1984): 43–47.

14. Joy M. Greiner, "A Comparative Study of the Career Development Patterns of Male and Female Library Administrators in Large Public Libraries." *Library Trends* 34 (Fall 1985): 264–280.

15. Susan Brandehoff, "Spotlight on Women Managers," *American Libraries* 16 (January 1985): 23.

16. Ibid., p. 22.

17. Ibid., p. 45.

18. Ibid., pp. 45, 46.

19. Ibid., p. 46.

20. Ruth J. Person and Eleanor R. Ficke, "A Longitudinal Study of the Outcomes of a Management Development Program for Women in Librarianship," in *Advances in Library Administration and Organization,* vol. 5 (Greenwich, CT: JAI Press, 1986), p. 2.

21. Ibid., p. 8.

22. Carol L. Learmont and Stephen Van Houten, "Placements and Salaries 1982: Slowing Down," *Library Journal* 108 (September 15, 1983): 1765, 1766.

23. Carol L. Learmont and Stephen Van Houten, "Placements and Salaries 1983: Catching Up," *Library Journal* 109 (October 1, 1984): 1810.

24. Carol Learmont and Stephen Van Houten, "Placements and Salaries 1985: Little Change," *Library Journal* 111 (October 15, 1986): 37.

25. Kay F. Jones, "Sex, Salaries, and Library Support," *Library Journal* 111 (September 1, 1986): 149.

26. "Women in Librarianship," *The ALA Yearbook of Library and Information Services,* vol. 11 (1986), p. 325.

27. *American Library Directory,* 39th ed. (New York: R. R. Bowker, 1986).

28. Greiner, "A Comparative Study" (Fall 1985), p. 261.

29. Ibid., p. 262.

30. Ibid., p. 269.

31. Ibid., pp. 276, 278.

32. Ibid., p. 272.

33. Ibid., p. 266.

34. Judith S. Braunagel, "Job Mobility as Related to Career Progression of Female Academic Librarians in the South" (Ph.D. diss., Florida State University, 1975), p. 163.

35. Greiner, "A Comparative Study" (Fall 1985), p. 272.

36. Ibid., pp. 267, 268.

37. Ibid., pp. 269.

38. Bryan, *The Public Librarian,* p. 86.

APPENDIX A

An Examination of the Advancement Patterns and Management Styles of Men and Women Assuming the Directorships of Large Public Library Units (1983–1987)

Circle the number adjacent to the appropriate answer.

Professional Career

1. What is the total number of years, including the current year, of your professional library experience?

2. In how many libraries, other than the one in which you are presently
employed, have you held professional positions, and how many years
were you in each?

Number of libraries	Number of years in each
0 No other	_____
1 One	_____
2 Two	_____/_____
3 Three	_____/_____/_____
4 Four	____/____/____/____
5 Five	___/___/___/___/___
6 Six	__/__/__/__/__/__
7 Seven	_/_/_/_/_/_/_
8 More than seven	
(please specify) _____	_____

3. From the time you accepted your first professional position in a library,
did you ever leave library work for a period of six months or more?
   1 Yes   If *Yes*, answer *4*
   2 No   If *No*, go to *5*

4. Please indicate reasons for interruptions and for how long.

Reasons for interruptions	Total leaves taken	Total years of leaves
1 To work in another field	_____	_____
2 To continue education	_____	_____
3 Personal health	_____	_____
4 Health of family members	_____	_____
5 Pregnancy or child rearing	_____	_____
6 Moved with spouse	_____	_____
7 Other reasons (please specify)	_____	_____

5. What was the job title of your position immediately prior to your present
position?

6. How long were you employed in the position immediately prior to your
present position?
   1 Less than one year

2   1–3 years
3   4–6 years
4   7–9 years
5   10 years or more

7.   Where did you learn of the opening for your present position as director?
1   Notification in mail
2   Board of trustees solicitation
3   Former director recruiting successor
4   Library school referral
5   Professional association placement
6   Published job notice
7   Notification from associate
8   Other _____ (please specify)

8.   If you learned of the position opening from another person, indicate the sex of the person.
1   Male
2   Female

9.   At what age did you become the director of the library in which you are presently employed?
1   Under 25
2   25–34
3   35–44
4   45–54
5   55–64
6   65 and over

10.   What was your yearly salary immediately prior to your present position? NOTE: Salary information will be regarded as confidential and will be used for statistical purposes only. It will not be identified with you.
1   Less than $14,000
2   $14,000–18,000
3   18,001–22,000
4   22,001–26,000
5   26,001–30,000
6   30,001–35,000
7   35,001–40,000
8   Over $40,000

11.   What is your present yearly salary?
1   Less than $20,000

```
 2   $20,000–25,000
 3    25,001–30,000
 4    30,001–35,000
 5    35,001–40,000
 6    40,001–45,000
 7    45,001–50,000
 8    50,001–55,000
 9    55,001–60,000
10   Over $60,000
```

12. When you entered the profession, did you aspire to be a library administrator?
    1 Yes
    2 No

13. Was a mentor (adviser, role model) influential in your career development?
    1 No
    2 Yes
    3 Sex of mentor
       A Male
       B Female

Library or Library System

14. What is the population served by your library or library system?
    1   100,000–250,000
    2   250,001–500,000
    3   500,001–750,000
    4   750,001–1,000,000
    5   Over 1,000,000

15. In what state is the library or library system located?

16. What is the yearly total operating budget allocated for your library or library system (include federal, state, and city allocations)?
    1   Less than $500,000
    2   $ 500,000–1,000,000
    3   1,000,001–3,000,000
    4   3,000,001–6,000,000
    5   6,000,001–9,000,000
    6   9,000,001–12,000,000

7   12,000,001–20,000,000
8   20,000,001–30,000,000
9   Over $30,000,000

17. What is the size of your total materials collection (include book volumes, periodical subscriptions, bound volumes, micromaterials, and audiovisual materials)?
1   Less than 100,000
2   100,000–250,000
3   250,001–500,000
4   500,001–750,000
5   750,001–1,000,000
6   1,000,001–3,000,000
7   3,000,001–5,000,000
8   5,000,001–7,000,000
9   7,000,001–9,000,000
10   Over 9,000,000

18. How many professionals are employed in your library or library system?
1   Less than 25
2   25–50
3   51–75
4   76–100
5   101–150
6   151–200
7   201–250
8   Over 250

19. What is the entry level salary for professionals?
1   Less than $10,000
2   $10,000–12,000
3   12,001–14,000
4   14,001–16,000
5   16,001–18,000
6   Over $18,000

Personal Data

20. Sex
1   Male
2   Female

21. Age
    1 Under 25
    2 25–34
    3 35–44
    4 45–54
    5 55–64
    6 65 and over

22. Marital status
    1 Married
    2 Single (never married)
    3 Divorced, separated, or widowed

23. Do you have children?
    1 No
    2 Yes
       How many? _____
       What are their ages? _____

24. *Highest* level of education attained (circle the category that applies to you)
    1 Bachelor's degree. List major _____
    2 Master's degree in library/information science
    3 Master's degree in subject area
    4 Master's degree in library/information science and a master's degree in a subject area
    5 Advanced certificate or specialist degree in library/information science
    6 Advanced certificate or specialist degree in a subject area
    7 Doctorate in library/information science
    8 Doctorate in a subject area
    9 Other _____ (please specify)

25. Have you published during the past five years?
    No_____
    Yes_____
                  _____ State professional journal
                  _____ Regional professional journal
                  _____ National professional journal

26. To what professional organizations do you belong?
    1 American Library Association
    2 Regional library association

3   State library association

4   Other _____ (please specify)

Management Style

Circle the number that best reflects the extent of your agreement with each of the following statements, using the scale below:

Strongly disagree (SD) = 1
Disagree (D) = 2
Neutral (N) = 3
Agree (A) = 4
Strongly Agree (SA) = 5

27.   As a new administrator, it is advisable to immediately target areas for change.

1 2 3 4 5

28.   My greatest asset is my ability to choose qualified and capable staff members.

1 2 3 4 5

29.   I prefer to directly supervise the implementation of policies and procedures.

1 2 3 4 5

30.   I perceive my role as one of agent of change.

1 2 3 4 5

31.   Library directors should be politically aggressive.

1 2 3 4 5

32.   Library directors should work behind the scenes with Friends, Boards of Trustees, etc., to bring about change.

1 2 3 4 5

33.   Library directors should regularly attend meetings of the County Board of Supervisors and/or the City Council.

1 2 3 4 5

34.   Memberships in community service clubs and/or civic groups are advantageous to the library director.

1 2 3 4 5

35. The official governing board of the library should have total control in library budgeting decisions.

1 2 3 4 5

36. The official governing board of the library should have total control in library personnel decisions.

1 2 3 4 5

37. Library board members are educationally qualified to make policy decisions for the administration of a public library.

1 2 3 4 5

38. Library board members are qualified by professional experience to make policy decisions for the administration of a public library.

1 2 3 4 5

39. I value the suggestions I receive from my subordinates.

1 2 3 4 5

40. I try to plan specifically for times to involve subordinates in decision making.

1 2 3 4 5

41. Most employees are motivated by a sense of accomplishment and achievement.

1 2 3 4 5

42. Most employees would rather have more interesting jobs than a small annual financial raise in a particular year.

1 2 3 4 5

43. I feel secure in my job.

1 2 3 4 5

44. I use my job as an administrator to be a team leader rather than a controller or overseer.

1 2 3 4 5

45. I try to provide training and encouragement to my subordinates to be involved in the participatory process.

1 2 3 4 5

46. I take advantage of training and educational opportunities that will help me better practice participative techniques.

    1 2 3 4 5

47. My employees are interested in and want to know the goals of our library organization.

    1 2 3 4 5

48. Giving greater independence to the employees in our organization would be good for the organization.

    1 2 3 4 5

49. I am concerned about the development and growth of my subordinates.
    1 2 3 4 5

50. I try to maintain open, candid communication with my subordinates.
    1 2 3 4 5

51. I try to be as concerned about maintaining my subordinates' morale and satisfaction as I am about getting our tasks accomplished.

    1 2 3 4 5

52. Most employees will be more effective if given broad policy guidelines versus specific rules and regulations to follow.

    1 2 3 4 5

LIBRARY SERVICES FOR ADULT HIGHER EDUCATION IN THE UNITED KINGDOM

Raymond K. Fisher

INTRODUCTION

This article is a critical survey of the library services currently offered to adult students in the United Kingdom pursuing formal courses of higher education. A comprehensive survey of this subject has not previously been published. After a brief description of the opportunities that exist for adults to undertake continuing education courses through universities, polytechnics, and other institutions and of the current levels of participation, the main part of the paper is an examination of the library needs of these students and the ways in which their needs are being met according to different types of institutions and different types of courses. The term *continuing education* in this context is defined as "any form of educa-

Advances in Library Administration and Organization,
Volume 7, pages 29-57.
Copyright © **1988 by JAI Press Inc.**
All rights of reproduction in any form reserved.
ISBN: 0-89232-817-7

tion, whether vocational or general, resumed after an interval following the end of continuous initial education'' (University Grants Committee, 1984, p. 1), and the term *adult* normally signifies a person 25 years or over.

With the growing importance now attached to continuing education in many countries, especially in Europe and North America, it is hoped that this paper will provide a useful basis for comparison for librarians and other practitioners working in this area outside the United Kingdom. For a useful summary of the whole field of adult education in the United Kingdom, see Jennings (1985). In this paper, we are dealing with approximately 0.5 percent of the U.K. population (Simpson, 1983, p. 103).

ADULTS IN HIGHER EDUCATION

National Bodies

The ministry responsible for all education in England is the Department of Education and Science (DES). In Wales, responsibility for adult and higher education (except universities) was passed to the Welsh Office Education Department in 1978. For Scotland, there is the Scottish Education Department, and Northern Ireland has its own Department of Education. The University Grants Committee, however, allocates central government funds to all universities in the United Kingdom. Polytechnics and colleges of higher education receive most of their funds from local education authorities (often called the public sector), and it is the local authorities that are responsible for most (nonadvanced) adult education at the local level.

The National Institute of Adult Continuing Education (England and Wales) (NIACE) exists to promote "the study and the general advancement of adult continuing education" and is pursuing specific projects through its Unit for the Development of Adult Continuing Education. NIACE possesses a reference library of adult continuing education material and operates computerized databases of bibliographical information; these servites are intended mainly for adult education practitioners and researchers. In addition, there are the Scottish Institute of Adult and Continuing Education and the Northern Ireland Council for Further and Continuing Education.

Other relevant national bodies include the British Broadcasting Corporation (BBC), which has separate Continuing Education Departments for television and for radio; the Educational Counselling and Credit Transfer Information Service (ECCTIS), which provides a public database of information on higher education throughout the United Kingdom; and the National Education Guidance Unit, which supports local providers of educational guidance.

Finally, the Library Association (LA) has a standing Sub-Committee on Libraries and Continuing Education, whose function is to monitor and review developments in this field, to raise the awareness of librarians of their own potential role in this area of work, and to issue guidelines.

In the work of most of these national bodies, there is rarely a clear-cut distinction between higher education for adults and other forms of adult education. In spite of the organizational complexity, however, it is possible to isolate particular types of institutions and particular aspects of their work as coming within our definition.

Universities

There are many different ways in which adults can participate in education at university level in the United Kingdom. These include the following:

1.   Several universities have special schemes for accepting applicants aged over 21 (with or without the standard entry qualifications) for full-time degree courses (Smithers and Griffin, 1986). These mature students currently represent about 10 percent of the total full-time undergraduate population.

2.   All universities offer part-time courses for adults. These include programs of vocational-professional-postexperience courses (mainly on campus), usually organized by the appropriate internal subject departments and also liberal adult education courses (mainly off campus) organized by extramural departments. Most of the larger universities (twenty-one of the thirty-two in England) are designated as Responsible Bodies; that is, they have departments of extramural studies (sometimes also called continuing education or adult education) that receive DES grants to provide a liberal adult education program for the general public throughout a clearly defined geographical area. Tables 1 and 2 indicate the amount and type of work being done by universities in the areas of extramural and short course provision.

In addition to these nonqualification courses, some universities offer part-time degree or diploma courses (involving mainly evening classes on campus) either through their extramural department or through the appropriate subject department or a combination of the two (see Tight 1982, 1986). Unique in the United Kingdom is London University's external degree system, which since 1858 has provided opportunities for adults to study independently for the same degrees as those taken by its internal full-time students. However, the university is an examining body only and provides no direct teaching for its external degrees. Birkbeck College (University of London) specializes in offering part-time degree courses in conventional subjects, through evening classes, for adults in employment.

3.   A small number of universities (including Exeter and Lancaster) have opened some of their regular undergraduate lectures to the general public.

4.   One of the main providers of adult higher education is the Open University, which offers opportunities for adults to study at home by distance teaching

Table 1. U.K. University Extramural and Short Course
Provision: Number of Courses and Enrollments, 1980–1985

	Number of Courses			
	Extramural Department	Extramural/ WEA[a]	Other Departments	Total
1980–1981	9,037	2,142	2,832	14,011
1981–1982	9,531	2,240	3,583	15,354
1982–1983	9,978	2,411	3,835	16,224
1983–1984	11,158	1,932	4,107	17,197
1984–1985	11,361	1,949	4,761	18,071

	Number of Enrollments			
	Extramural Department	Extramural/ WEA[a]	Other Departments	Total
1980–1981	209,392	36,567	82,590	328,549
1981–1982	222,939	37,437	100,738	361,114
1982–1983	230,792	42,259	102,513	375,564
1983–1984	253,764	32,599	117,730	404,093
1984–1985	255,710	33,825	130,309	419,844

Source: The figures are taken from the Universities Statistical Record and Universities Council for
Adult and Continuing Education (UCACE) annual reports 1980–1981 to 1984–1985.
Note: This table excludes postgraduate medical departments. The figures indicate a sharp increase
each year in the number of adults enrolled on short courses at university level and underline
the growing importance of this area of university work.
[a]Workers' Educational Association. (see p. 34)

methods. Originally offering degree courses only, it now has an expanding
program of nondegree continuing education courses. Since its foundation in
1969, the numbers of applicants for degree courses have far exceeded the number
of places available (Table 3). There are no formal entrance requirements (hence
''Open''). A general B.A. degree is obtained by passing in six credits (ordinary)
or eight credits (honors) in one of six areas: arts, education, mathematics, science, social science, and technology.

Polytechnics and Colleges of Higher Education

In the field of part-time study, the polytechnics have been more responsive to
changing needs than have the conventional universities in the sense of providing
a wider range of courses and more varied patterns of student attendance. (See
Tables 4 and 5.) They tend to have more flexible admission requirements for
mature student entry, and several have developed modular courses involving
mixed mode study. A recent notable example is North East London Poly-

Table 2.   U.K. University Extramural and
Short Course Provision: Number of
Courses and Enrollments, 1984–1985,
by Selected Institutions

University	Number of Courses	Number of Enrollments
Aberdeen	291	7,647
Belfast	422	10,637
Birmingham	1,074	26,883
Bristol	1,106	24,851
Leeds	635	17,446
London	1,144	24,138
Manchester	901	28,639
Nottingham	926	20,654
Oxford	444	10,378
Wales (Cardiff)	468	14,483

Source: These figures are taken from the UCACE annual report
1984–85 (Table 10). They do not include postgraduate
medical departments.

technic's M.A./M.Sc. by independent study. In addition, there is a wide range
of short courses mounted by polytechnics each year, on which mature students
predominate.

One of the main differences between polytechnics and universities in our
context is that the former put more emphasis on vocationally oriented subjects
(mainly in the general areas of business studies, education, mathematical sciences, and engineering), while the latter (apart from their short postexperience
courses, half of which are in medical sciences) have so far emphasized the

Table 3.   Open University:
Applications and Registrations for
Undergraduate-Level Courses
1977, 1984–1985

	Applications	Admissions
1977	49,956	20,010
1984	45,621	22,203
1985	54,371	19,623

Source: These figures are taken from Open University Reports of the Vice-Chancellor for the
years 1976, 1983, 1984.

Table 4.   Public Sector Higher Education:
Part-time Students, 1975–1983

1975	1980	1981	1982	1983
134,100	188,500	191,700	194,600	200,800

Source: DES, *Statistical Bulletin* (July 1985).

humanities and social sciences in their part-time provision. In addition, polytechnics engage in a substantial amount of nondegree or subdegree work.

Many colleges of higher education have also moved into the area of part-time
first degree courses, largely in an attempt to break away from a past concentration on teacher training. These colleges, together with many colleges of further
education, also offer access courses, designed specifically to encourage adults to
return to study and provide a preparation for courses in higher education (Lucas
and Ward, 1985).

Workers' Educational Association (WEA)

One of the main objectives of the WEA is "to stimulate and to satisfy the
demand of workers for education." It works largely through its local branches,
which organize classes in which subjects chosen by members are studied in a
systematic way. Each of its districts is recognized by the DES as a Responsible
Body and receives government grant accordingly. Most of the districts work
closely with university extramural departments and organize courses with them
through joint committees. Many WEA courses are therefore of a fairly high
academic standard and may reasonably be included in a survey of adult higher
education.

Table 5.   Part-time Students in
Polytechnics, August 1984, by Mode of
Attendance and Age

	Day Students	Evening Only
Age 25 and over	25,720	13,668
Age 65 and over	506	223
All students	48,657	18,748

Source: DES, *Statistics of Education: Further Education*
(November 1984): table F4.

Residential Adult Education

This category includes eight long-term residential colleges providing one- and two-year courses and a larger number of short-term colleges and centers offering courses lasting from one weekend to up to three weeks. Many of the courses, particularly those at the long-term colleges, are of a sufficiently high standard to be included in this survey.

General Conclusions

From this brief overview, it is clear that the opportunities for adult participation in higher education in the United Kingdom are rather fragmented. The main strength lies in the wide range of short courses available, both on and off campus, at most universities and polytechnics. At the same time, these universities have been very slow to move into part-time degree courses. The Open University has partly filled this gap, but its distance-teaching methods do not suit everyone, and it does not provide single-subject degrees. What is needed most of all is a comprehensive scheme of part-time degree courses at every university, and particularly a system in which adults can attend degree classes in off-campus locations near where they live or work. In this respect, the United Kingdom has a long way to go in comparison with the United States, Australia, and Canada, where the range of off-campus degree opportunities is wider and where the overall proportion of adult students in higher education is larger.

It follows that library services in this complex area are also rather fragmented; a simple description is not possible. I propose to look first at the library needs of adult students, then at the ways in which those needs are being met by different institutions, and finally at what is happening at the University of Birmingham as a "place-study."

LIBRARY NEEDS OF ADULT STUDENTS

Educational Information and Advice

One of the primary needs of adults wishing to undertake advanced-level study is information about what is available and advice about what to choose. For many people, the public library is the first place to go to for this kind of information. Not all adults are sure which subjects they want to learn; in addition, many have particular problems concerning cost, entry qualifications, domestic responsibilities, and transport. In an attempt to meet these needs, a number of local educational guidance units have been set up in recent years

throughout the United Kingdom, and in some cases the local public library
authority has been closely involved in this development.

Study Skills and Library Education

Another important need of many adult students before launching into higher
education is the acquisition of appropriate study skills (Smithers and Griffin,
1986, pp. 103–105). For some, it may be many years since formal study, while
others may have left school at the minimum age of 16 and had little or no
postschool education. In addition, there is no doubt that many adults are intimi-
dated when first using a large academic library; it may take several visits and
several weeks before a student is fully orientated. This is a particular problem for
part-time students, who may visit the campus only once a week.

Access to Library Materials and Facilities

For most adult students in higher education the key word in the context of
library services is *immediacy*. Many are busy people with jobs and family commitments and often with long distances to travel to their lectures. When given a
reading or writing assignment, they should not have to encounter long delays or
complicated bureaucratic procedures before they can obtain the items they require, for otherwise the disadvantages they already have are aggravated. With
regard to on-campus adult students (part time, short course, or full time), librarians should make regular assessments of need and attempt to make special
provision in terms of opening hours, reserve collections, photocopying, and
other facilities. For off-campus students, who may rarely or never visit the
university library, the aim should be to deliver materials *to* the students, either as
individuals or as groups, and to supplement this with other on-site facilities.
Distance education students need comprehensive learning packages, a great deal
of bibliographical help, and borrowing rights either at their parent institution or
at their nearest academic library.

Library needs will, of course, vary widely according to the type of subject
being studied, the location and length of the course, the teaching methods used,
and other factors. But in spite of the large number of variables, the basic principle remains: the value of a library lies in the immediacy of its service rather than
in the backup facilities to which it can give access.

In the light of this brief survey of educational opportunities and needs, let us
look now at the ways in which the different kinds of institutions are attempting to
meet the different kinds of library needs.

CURRENT LIBRARY SERVICES: ARE NEEDS BEING MET?

Educational Information and Advice

Currently about fifty educational guidance units offer information and guidance to the general public on all the educational opportunities available to adults in the area. Some of these units have built up computer data banks of information (Butler et al., 1986). But many are underfinanced, and the overall provision is patchy. The movement is, however, gathering momentum. An important recent report (UDACE, 1986) recommends an expansion of provision, to be supported and coordinated by a new national unit; government response is awaited.

The role of public libraries is seen to be particularly important in this new development. Many already participate, to a greater or lesser extent, in the work of the existing units. But in times of economic cutbacks, some public librarians are reluctant to take on new responsibilities, and some argue that giving educational advice is not a librarian's role. At least the *opportunities* are there for public librarians to be closely involved in the work of the units. For this reason, the LA's Sub-Committee on Libraries and Continuing Education is promoting a series of regional seminars designed to increase awareness of these opportunities and to promote discussion of such topics as collaboration with other institutions and the special skills needed by librarians in the work. It is hoped that all of these developments will lead to a better system of information and advice for adults wishing to undertake further learning.

Study Skills and Library Education

Study skills are taught in some of the access courses (previously mentioned) organized by local colleges. Also some universities (mainly extramural departments) offer "returning to study" or "learning to learn" courses, but again provision is patchy. The focus is usually on such activities as techniques of learning and remembering, effective reading, note taking, essay writing, and using libraries.

Librarians are occasionally involved in the planning and in some of the teaching of these courses, and clearly there should be a strong link-up with user education. But so far there is little evidence to show that universities in the United Kingdom have made any special provision to meet the orientation needs of new adult students. What is needed is a greater recognition by university librarians of the fact that there is a growing number of adult students on campus and that many of them lack library use skills.

Access to Library Materials and Facilities

Universities

Extramural courses.   The oldest form of university adult education, extramural courses, is the first to be considered. About 290,000 students attend over 13,000 courses each year (see Table 1). Because these are scattered among numerous (mainly off-campus) locations throughout the country, the organization of a library service to them presents considerable logistical problems. Most universities with extramural departments have special libraries that exist solely to serve the needs of extramural students and lecturers. The main function of these libraries is to send collections of books and other materials (book boxes) to the centers where the classes meet. Here the principle is that of immediacy: delivering materials to the classes *before* they are needed so that they are available *when* they are needed.

The normal procedure is for each lecturer to submit a syllabus and book list for his or her course; the extramural librarian decides what to buy, allocates existing stock to different classes, and so builds up a collection for each course, to be dispatched before the first meeting. The books are retained at the meeting place for the duration of the course, and students can borrow them for home reading. Mutliple copies of essential works are supplied, and supplementary titles are provided during the course as required. Some of these libraries also provide audiovisual equipment and teaching aids for the use of lecturers. Table 6 indicates the scale of operations of a selected number of extramural libraries.

In 1977 a set of minimum recommended standards for university extramural libraries was published (LA, 1977). These are still applicable, but few of the libraries listed in Table 6 meet them. In addition, most of the smaller extramural departments do not have their own libraries and rely on public library provision. But this is not satisfactory because public libraries cannot be expected to stock (or have available for long loan) the often specialized kind of material needed. An extramural library can build up a collection of books on, for example, Egyptology, and circulate them among different centers each year in a way that no other type of library can, without prejudice to other users. Among the other strengths of this kind of library are that it is geared to long loans, transport over long distances, rapid and flexible response to sudden requests, and regular contacts between librarian and lecturers. But this is a case where small is not beautiful; below a provision of about seventy-five courses a year, an extramural library is not financially justifiable.

These courses are largely liberal adult education nondegree courses of study for the general public. Some are introductory, aimed at introducing academic subjects to those who have not studied them before; others are specialized, sometimes assuming considerable knowledge on the part of the students (for

Table 6. University Extramural Libraries:
Size, Issues, and Staff, 1984–1985

University	Volumes in Stock	Courses Supplied	Books Issued to Classes	Staff
Birmingham	102,000	504	17,366	2 librarians 2 librarian assistants ½ clerical assistant (1 audiovisual technician)
Bristol	35,000	184	5,354	½ librarian ½ librarian assistant
Leeds	40,000	150	7,000	½ librarian 2 librarian assistants
London	200,000	541	21,718	1 librarian 2 librarian assistants
Manchester	40,000	112	2,373	1 librarian ½ librarian assistant
Nottingham	60,000	429	10,000	1 librarian 1 librarian assistant
Oxford	80,900	169	6,765 + 7,238 personal loans	2 librarians 1 librarian assistant

example, local history or natural history research groups or role education courses for professional groups). However, because of their different nature and because they are intended for a different public, these courses have traditionally received a library service quite separate from that of university main libraries. Ironically, therefore, even when extramural courses are held on campus, they still receive a separate class collection in the meeting room. Further, extramural students are not normally granted borrowing rights at the main library of their university because they are not fully registered university students and are not paying full-time equivalent fees. As a result, university libraries in the United Kingdom have usually had very little to do with external work (unlike the situation in the United States and Australia, for example).

The class collection–book-box system has sometimes been challenged as being out of date or ineffective (Newman, 1979; Corney, 1983, p. 21). The problem is usually seen as one of tradition versus innovation, but library problems are rarely as simple as this. Some of the arguments for and against the system are outlined below in the section on Birmingham. At this point, it is worth mentioning some of the policies recently adopted by different universities.

When the University of Liverpool's Institute of Extention Studies was amalgamated with its Faculty of Education in 1981, a review was held of the faculty's library services. A working party was set up to examine all the possibilities. It was finally agreed that the existing extension library should be retained, separate from the main faculty library, and that its core work should continue to be the supply of books and teaching materials as class sets to courses in the university's extramural teaching area. In 1984, the University of Warwick was granted Responsible Body status and assumed responsibility for part of the extramural area previously served by the University of Birmingham. It too considered all the options but finally chose to set up a separate library based on the traditional book-box system. The University of Keele for many years has had a small adult education library, operating a book-box service. In 1986, this collection was moved into the university's main library building because of pressure on teaching space. It was decided to retain the collection intact (rather than to amalgamate it with the general stock) and to continue the same service, in spite of the fact that it took up valuable reading space within the main library.

The general agreement seems to be that in the context of extramural courses, separateness is the best library model because it is seen to work and to meet general needs; however, not all universities have chosen, or been able, to maintain an extramural library. When the University of Kent became a Responsible Body in 1975, its School of Continuing Education chose not to establish its own library; the responsibility for book-box supply to extramural classes was accepted by Kent County Library. In 1985, however, the county library withdrew this service, partly because of a shortage of funds and partly because it was unhappy about this role of serving the needs of groups meeting away from libraries (at the expense of serving the individuals who come into the libraries). It is planned to disperse the county's extramural collection among its own libraries. The University of Kent therefore has no extramural library; however, it is now trying to adopt a compromise solution: its 1986–1987 publicity brochure states, "With the co-operation of the [county's] Area Librarian, the University has established a library collection in Tonbridge Public Library [to serve the University's Centre in Tonbridge]. Although primarily for the use of registered students, the collection is available to the public for reference purposes." This highlights the problem of trying to serve two kinds of public at the same time, and because there is no dedicated library, the immediacy of on-site deposit collections is lost.

Part-time Degree and Diploma Courses.   Having dealt at some length with library services to traditional (mainly off-campus) extramural courses, we now move into the gray area of part-time (mainly on-campus) award-bearing courses. These degree or diploma courses are pursued mainly through evening class teaching; they are distinguished from the short (mainly daytime) postexperience courses offered by subject departments. Their "grayness" is due to the fact that they are usually organized jointly by an extramural department and by the appropriate internal subject department, so that the students registered in them are neither fully extramural nor fully internal. As a result, such students in the past have rarely been seen as fully acceptable clientele for a university library. For example, at the University of Kent, the main library confines its role to serving full-time students (Crocker, 1985, pp. 26–27). At the University of Liverpool, the Faculty of Education's working party on library provision had to recommend (in 1983) "that students working for diplomas and certificates validated by the University should be admitted as full members of the University Library, and that this should happen as soon as possible." This kind of resistance by university libraries to admitting to their membership a new kind of university student has not been uncommon; it may be due to a genuine concern about increasing pressures on diminishing resources, but it may also indicate a general conservatism. The question is referred to again in the section on Birmingham.

It does seem, however, that the growing number of these part-time, award-bearing courses for adults on campus have a latent function in that they are closing the gap between librarians' concepts of the extramural student as "second class" (Corney, 1983) and their concept of the full-time undergraduate as their sole responsibility. Many part-time degree courses involve students coming to the university for lectures three evenings a week (and on some weekends) and undertaking reading assignments, essay writing, and, of course, examinations. For many adults, this is a heavy commitment, and it would be quite anomalous to exclude such students from membership of their university library. Although as the extramural department's students they may have access to the traditional book box, they clearly need more than this, and the signs are that these needs are at last being recognized by most university librarians; however, recognition is sometimes as far as the problem gets. Granting membership is one thing, but this may be of little use if opening and service hours remain unchanged. At Southampton University, for example, the library implications of part-time study were officially recognized by its Working Party on Continuing Education in 1979, but since then financial cuts have made access to the library even more restricted by a reduction in opening hours and some services (Corney, 1983, p. 26). Similar problems will be reported below in the section on Birmingham. The irony is that although the central government is urging the expansion of continuing education, it is not providing the additional funds needed to support it.

The Study of Adult Education.   Another area that falls between extramural and internal is the study of the subject of adult education. Several universities have responded to the need for training teachers of adults by setting up separate departments offering full-time and part-time diplomas and first and higher degrees, with their own libraries specializing in the literature of adult education. These include Bristol, Edinburgh, Glasgow, Hull, Kent, Leeds, Leicester, Liverpool, London, Manchester, Nottingham, Sheffield, Southampton, and Surrey. These adult education libraries vary in size and quality. One of the largest, at Manchester, consists of 14,000 books, 6,000 pamphlets and reports, 160 periodical title subscriptions, and 1,400 theses. The literature of adult education is a rapidly growing area, and the librarians working in this field have regular meetings to discuss bibliographical control and cooperation under the auspices of the Standing Conference on University Teaching and Research in the Education of Adults (SCUTREA).

Short Courses on Campus.   With regard to the short postexperience courses offered by individual teaching departments in most universities, there is no clearcut pattern of library service. In some cases, students get little or no time to read or to use a library during their course. But they should not for this reason be denied the opportunity of access to the departmental library or to the university library. While a small number of university libraries (including Strathclyde University in Glasgow) offer full borrowing rights to all students enrolled in postexperience vocational education, others are not so generous. A fairly typical situation exists at Birmingham, and this is described in more detail below.

London University's External Degree.   The activities described so far in this section cut across most universities; we now come to some more specialized services. London University's external degree system has about 10,000 students in the United Kingdom and a similar number overseas. The emphasis is very much on independent study, with very little provision for special tuition, and students can work largely at their own pace. Unfortunately, this independence is also applied to library services; students are encouraged to use their local resources as fully as possible and are given little guidance apart from a leaflet, *The Library Service of Great Britain.* Those who cannot gain access to, and borrowing rights from, their local academic library are therefore at a serious disadvantage. Students can use a postal service operated for them from the University's Central Library, but this is of limited scope and not heavily used because the library does not acquire multiple copies of course books and does not lend periodicals. An attempt should be made to reduce the library-related problems of independent study and to provide a more positive service.

Birkbeck College.   London University's Birkbeck College is in a different category. Because it is based largely on evening class teaching for working adults, it requires regular attendance at the college and so can offer a conventional college library service. This service is in fact of a high standard and is designed largely with the evening class student in mind; however, the college has to be confined to students living in the London area. What is needed is for other universities to establish Birkbeck-type courses and library services from within their existing institutions to serve the other regions of the country. It is therefore ironical again that at the time of writing, the very existence of Birkbeck College is being threatened by a drastic reduction in funding.

Open University.   The Open University's degree courses are highly structured correspondence courses using distance teaching methods (including radio and television broadcasts). The nature of the learning packages (course units) received on a regular basis is such that students at the first and second levels have to concentrate almost entirely on this material and have little time or need for wider reading. Third- and fourth-level students, with more project-based work, are almost certain to need library resources. It is therefore surprising that the Open University's own library serves the academic staff of the university only and offers no direct service to its students. As an alternative, some indirect help is given: guides to libraries and literature in particular subjects are produced as parts of course units and some regional guides to local resources. In addition, some help is given through individual student counseling and at study centers and summer schools. But the immediacy is lost. It has been shown (Simpson 1983, p. 108) that many Open University students are still encountering library use problems: long traveling time, high travel costs, inconvenient opening hours, difficulty in obtaining borrowing rights, and interlibrary loan delays. What is needed is either a system by which Open University students obtain automatic membership in their local academic library (if necessary, by contractual agreement) or a radical reassessment of the ways in which the Open University Library can provide direct support for its students.

Broadcasting and Public Libraries

In the context of the Open University, it is natural to mention the role of broadcasting in adult education. Apart from provision for schools, the specifically educational programs on radio and television are the responsibility of the Continuing Education Department of the BBC and the Education Departments of the independent television companies. These are, of course, not strictly higher education. Some programs, however, do treat subjects in depth and to this extent may be compared with university extramural courses. The important point here is that many such programs stimulate adults to read and to use public libraries. Some series are accompanied by a book and by other printed materials or cassettes; a few public libraries make a point of promoting the programs and the literature, but there could be more cooperation between public libraries and the broadcasting authorities in this field.

The role of public libraries in adult education in general is a large subject. It is sufficient to state here that some of the larger metropolitan libraries are a significant resource for all kinds of adult students and particularly for those working independently and also that many university extramural classes are held in public library accommodation.

Independent Study and Individual Study

Independent learning in its "pure" form is strictly outside the scope of this survey, which is concerned with formal courses of study. There are, however, some courses in higher education that are described as independent because of their emphasis on students' self-planning. Two of these courses, a diploma in higher education at North East London Polytechnic and a component of a full-time degree course at Lancaster University, have been documented by Percy and Ramsden (1980). One of the features common to the two case studies was the importance of study skills, including information retrieval and the effective use of libraries. In the former course, the planning stage lasted about four months and included workshops and seminars on information retrieval and research methods. Library education is an important component in the process of learning how to be an independent student. All students in these courses had full membership of their institutions' libraries.

A distinction needs to be made here between *independent* study and *individualized* study. The former implies a large element of student control over his or her own learning, with a minimum of dependence on teachers. The latter simply implies students working on their own (such as at home), but they may be heavily dependent on a fixed syllabus, prescribed texts, and teacher direction. Open University courses typically provide for a great deal of individual study of this latter kind. Ironically, it is these individualized students, usually at the receiving end of distance teaching methods, who are most vulnerable with regard to access to libraries.

A recent example is the master's degree by distance learning, offered by the College of Librarianship Wales for professional librarians, in the management of library and information services. In a review of the first year's experience, Sherwell (1986) writes:

> The major difficulty so far has been in gaining access to material cited on the reading lists, since little reading material is provided directly by CLW and the onus is therefore on the student. . . . The concept of distance learning is likely to have an increasing part to play in the continuing education of library and information staff in the future, as few can study full-time because of domestic or work commitments. However, if it is to be greatly extended, then thought will have to be given to providing the necessary library back-up, or alternatively to providing more of the reading material directly to students.

Once again, the immediacy is lost. It is doubly ironical when librarians themselves have problems of access to library materials. The United Kingdom has much to learn from the experience of distance education in Australia, for example, where a direct library service to individual external students is provided by such institutions as the University of Queensland, Deakin University, and the University of New South Wales.

Polytechnics

The polytechnics have traditionally taken on more part-time students than the universities (either day release or day and evening, or evening only), and about one-third of these are in degree or other advanced courses. There are similar average proportions at colleges of higher education (although among these, the course offerings are more variable) (Jennings, 1985, pp. 57–61). What is important here is that the staff of polytechnics and colleges have more readily recognized the distinctive characteristics and needs of mature adults than have internal university staff, and there is evidence of this recognition in some recent studies of library use (Pritchard and Payne, 1980; Payne, 1983a; McDowell, 1985). Over half of all part-time students at polytechnics are aged over 25; this usually implies family and work commitments, which in turn have an effect on the time available for study and for using libraries. But in spite of this recognition, Payne (1983a) concludes that there is still much to learn about the different factors that influence the levels of use of the library of any particular institution by part-time students and about how these factors interrelate; he includes among them the subject and level of study, the mode of attendance, the type of course, the attitudes of lecturers, and the methods of teaching. In the proceedings of a conference he organized at the City of London Polytechnic in 1982, Payne (1983b) reproduces the list of recommendations for future action agreed there. These deal with such topics as library opening hours and publicity, librarians' rapport with part-timers, special loan collections, and cooperation between academic and public libraries.

In a recent survey, McDowell (1985) has taken some of these topics further. Of the students at Newcastle upon Tyne whom she surveyed, 58 percent were over 25 years of age, and 84 percent were taking either degree or professional courses. Her findings underlined the fact that part-time students are not a homogeneous group; for example, one-third had done a previous course at the polytechnic, but most of the others were new to higher education and needed a basic introduction to library use. Perhaps the most significant results from her survey were:

1. That low use or nonuse of the library was related to course requirements and to the attitude of particular lecturers toward the role of wider reading and information seeking in their courses. She recommends that lecturers should be made more aware of this relationship.
2. That shortage of time is an obstacle to library use; for example, students with longer traveling time make less use of the library. She recommends that more time within course sessions be specifically designated for library use.
3. That 60 percent of students thought that they would benefit from further guidance in library use. She recommends that the library staff press for more time to be devoted to user education on part-time courses.

What is needed now is for more polytechnics to follow the lead of the City of London and Newcastle upon Tyne by carrying out surveys of their part-time student population, making recommendations on the basis of their findings, and turning these recommendations into practical measures for improvement.

The WEA and Residential Adult Education

Some WEA courses are organized in conjunction with university extramural departments and are of a comparable academic standard to "normal" extramural courses. Such classes usually receive a library service from the appropriate extramural library. Most WEA courses, however, are independently organized, and the more academic of these create problems, for the WEA has no libraries of its own, either national or regional. Some of these courses receive a book-box supply from their local public library, but the present tendency is for this kind of service, where it exists, to be withdrawn. Most WEA courses therefore have to manage as best they can, either through individual borrowings from libraries or through loans from the adult class section of the British Library Document Supply Centre (which is now too expensive for bulk loans) or through private purchase. The service to them is generally inadequate; there is considerable room for improvement.

One possible solution would be the establishment of regional libraries for adult education. I first proposed these in 1971 (Fisher, 1971), and a similar recommendation was made in the Russell report (DES, 1973). These libraries would serve all adult students on higher education courses in a region, mainly by supplying deposit collections to classes and study centers but also serving as a resource center for audiovisual teaching aids and as the main local source for the literature of adult education. They would be financed by a consortium of local organizations. Within their scope would come all university extramural and WEA courses, local authority classes where relevant, informal and self-help groups, and also Open University courses. For the last category, an individualized service could be provided in collaboration with the Open University's central library and its regional counselors. Help might also be given to students attending part-time internal courses at universities and polytechnics. Unfortunately, the Russell report appeared shortly before economic conditions in the United Kingdom took a sudden turn for the worse, and it was largely shelved; however, the concept of regional libraries in our context is still highly relevant.

Most of the long-term residential colleges for adult students, such as Coleg Harlech in Wales, Fircroft College in Birmingham, Ruskin College in Oxford, and Northern College in South Yorkshire, have their own libraries, run on conventional college lines. One of the main problems is the pressure on these libraries from resident students for very long opening hours, but few colleges can afford to staff their libraries for the long hours needed. These libraries might also benefit from the existence of regional libraries, especially for the long loan of multiple copies of texts required for particular courses.

THE UNIVERSITY OF BIRMINGHAM: THE EXPERIENCE OF ONE INSTITUTION

The final section of this paper briefly describes the continuing education activities at the University of Birmingham and examines the library services currently offered in their support. The university is a fairly typical provincial university in the industrial Midlands. In comparison with most other universities, it has a large program of continuing education courses (Table 7). The total number of students participating in any one year, therefore, is, by U.K. standards, very large, and one would expect them to have considerable impact on the university's library service.

Educational Information and Advice

Some of the students may have obtained advance information about their courses from the City of Birmingham's Adult Learner's Enquiry Centre (ALEC). This center is run by a joint committee consisting of various organizations in the city, including the university. The main inquiry point is located in the entrance hall of the large city reference library, but librarians play only a small part in its operation. The main public library branches in the city are, however, a major source of information on the university's extramural courses for the general public because they house all printed publicity for adult education.

Study Skills and Library Education

It is generally recognized that the teaching of adults requires skills rather different from those required in the teaching of younger people, and one of these is the ability to train adults how to study. Lecturers need to be aware of the problems that adult students encounter in the process of learning. For this reason, among others, the university's Department of Extramural Studies has set up an Adult Teaching Methods Discussion Group and also holds regular briefing conferences for its new part-time lecturers. The extramural library staff are involved in both of these activities. In addition, I contributed a chapter on reading (Fisher, 1985) to the department's booklet on teaching methods (Henderson, 1985) and have jointly supervised a British Library project investigating the ways in which adult students are either helped or hindered in learning through economics texts (Henderson and Hewings, 1987). These are the kinds of activities in which both teaching staff and library staff can fruitfully cooperate.

For some years, the department has offered a "learning to learn" course for the general public, and a component of this is a session on the use of libraries, given by the library staff. Trainee social workers are given a similar session in their "how to study" course before going on to full-time training. Perhaps the greatest difficulties in adjusting to academic study and library use have been encountered by the department's new part-time degree students. An end-of-year questionnaire in 1984 to the students on the English course revealed a desire for more instruction in study skills and considerable problems in using the university library (De Wit, 1985). Although these students are given a special talk and tour of the main library, this is clearly not enough. Often the times when they can visit the library (evenings and Saturdays) are those when there are fewest staff to

Table 7. University of Birmingham Continuing Education Courses and Students, 1982–1985

Faculty or Department	Number of Courses			Number of Students		
	1982–1983	1983–1984	1984–1985	1982–1983	1983–1984	1984–1985
Arts	24	24	29	800	869	1,011
Commerce and Social Science	238	276	228	5,287	6,276	4,602
Education	10	9	20	464	538	691
Extramural Studies	749	733	638	18,693	18,769	17,417
Health Services Management Centre	279	218	114	3,735	3,677	2,215
Medicine and Dentistry	166	92	156	5,445	2,908	4,992
Science and Engineering	80	74	44	1,285	1,242	974
Total	1,546	1,426	1,229	35,709	34,279	31,902

Source: University Board of Continuing Education, *Annual Report* (1986).

help. The practical implications for library staffing, if part-time students are to be given the kind of long-term orientation they need, have not yet been grasped.

Access to Library Materials and Facilities

Under this heading, the different libraries involved with adult students at Birmingham University are dealt with separately.

Extramural Library

This library was established in the late 1930s and now holds over 100,000 volumes. In 1985, the university set up a working party to examine the independent libraries on campus "to look at any overlap of provision between these libraries and the University Library, and to investigate what economies could be obtained by closer co-ordination of resources." Its recommendation on the extramural library stated, "In view of the very different nature of their operations, the Working Party feels that no advantage would be gained by either physical or administrative amalgamation with the University Library." The idea of separateness is again underlined.

The basic function of extramural libraries has already been described. At Birmingham, the library's stock of 105,000 volumes includes 5,000 music scores, 1,000 records, 2,000 maps, and multiple copies of standard texts and textbooks. In addition, it houses 30,000 slides and a large collection of audiovisual equipment. The book stock reflects the nature of the extramural program over the years; the emphasis is on the humanities (literature, history, archaeology, theology, philosophy, music, fine arts) and the social sciences (psychology, sociology, economics, politics, education), with holdings also in geology, the biological sciences, and the physical sciences.

The advantage of the book-box system is that the relevant books are available to the students at the meeting place at the time when they are needed. There is no real substitute for this immediacy of provision. It is of enormous benefit to lecturers in their teaching if they can rely on the essential texts being available in the class collection at the right time. Only in this way can they make reading an integral part of their course. The book-box system is therefore an important factor in the maintenance of academic standards in university extramural education. In addition, it is part of the process of taking the expertise and resources of the university to the public at large, the main raison d'être of an extramural department. The book-box system may be less appropriate in North America or Australia, where the tradition of liberal adult education is not so strong, but it could certainly be given more consideration by institutions planning an off-campus service than it is normally given at present.

The alleged disadvantages of this system are (1) that it narrows students' horizons and discourages them from browsing in a large library and (2) that book boxes are underused and thus uneconomical. Argument 1 misses the point of this kind of teaching, which involves planned study, not browsing. Students need specified books for a definite purpose, and it is no use offering them a wide range of other books if those they want are not there. Argument 2 is a fallacy: book boxes are underused only where they are ill prepared (not containing enough relevant books) or where the lecturer fails to make reading an integral part of the course; here it is not the system but the way it is used that is at fault.

At Birmingham, there are plans to investigate these questions further by carrying out a survey of the library needs of extramural students and lecturers. This will involve distributing sets of questionnaires to classes, with the aim of finding out students' opinions about the present service, how much use they make of the books provided, whether they use other libraries in addition, and whether they have any suggestions for improvement.

University Main Library

Birmingham is fairly typical in that the presence of adult students on the campus, whether full time or part time, has so far made little impression on the services of its main library. Their presence, however, may give rise to certain dilemmas. For example, mature students who have children to collect from school have sometimes asked if they may take overnight-loan books earlier than the norm, but the library staff are aware that granting such privileges to a few people may be disadvantaging a far greater number. The dilemma has not been resolved. A recent survey at Birmingham specifically highlighted "the problem created for some mature students by the Short Loan arrangements in the library" (Moodie, 1986, p. 7).

This is typical of the kind of problems encountered by all adult students. The library staff recognize that present opening hours do not leave much time for library use by part-time students, especially when they work full time and live some distance away. In term time, the library is open from 9 A.M. to 9 P.M. Mondays to Fridays but issues books only to 6:30 P.M. Part-time students may often be required to use the same material as full-time students, but in a competitive situation, they are less likely to be able to obtain it. Their need for more intensive library education has already been noted. In spite of these problems, it is officially stated that "the library has no extra resources to provide services to continuing education students." It may be partly because of these difficulties that adult students make relatively little use of the university's main library, as Table 8 indicates.

The low registrations for courses 5–7 in Table 8 are largely due to the fairly high dropout rate in the first year of the part-time degree course. Apart from these, the registrations are fairly high. However, although separate statistics are not kept, it is estimated that the level of borrowing by these students is low, mainly because of the difficulties already outlined. It should be remembered that

Table 8. A Selection of Continuing Education Courses, 1985–1986, and Number of Students Registered at the Main Library

Course	Department	Duration	Number of Students	Number Registered at Main Library
1. Plant genetic resources	Plant Biology	11 weeks	5	5
2. Water resources technology in developing countries	Civil Engineering	6 months	20	5
3. Educational psychology	Education	1 year	5	5
4. Advanced diploma in midwifery	Birmingham Maternity Hospital	1 year	15	15
5. Sociology year 1	Extramural Studies	1 year	27	14
6. Theology year 1	Extramural Studies	1 year	8	3
7. English year 1	Extramural Studies	1 year	30	14
8. Theology year 2	Extramural Studies	1 year	8	7
9. English year 2	Extramural Studies	1 year	9	8

Note: Courses 1–4 are short postexperience courses. For courses of fewer than six weeks, students are not entitled to library membership. Courses 5–9 are sections of the part-time degrees.

students of courses 5–9 also have access to extramural library book boxes (and direct access to the extramural library itself, although only from 9 A.M. to 5 P.M.), which to a small extent makes up for these difficulties. Students of courses 3 and 4 also have access to the appropriate faculty libraries (education and medicine).

Medical Library

A significant part of the Medical Library's services is for external users employed by the National Health Service. The library has an arrangement with the Regional Health Authority to allow all doctors working in the region to register as personal borrowers. Those who take advantage of this are likely to be attending short courses (see Table 7) and seminars, particularly those preparing for post-graduate medical qualifications. Other health service staff, including qualified nurses, are also allowed to register as borrowers. In July 1986, there were 1,640 external borrowers, representing 35 percent of the total registered users.

No special provision is made by the library for these readers in terms of book and periodical stock. It is easier for a specialized library to attempt to be reasonably comprehensive and so not to aim at any particular readership group. In addition, periodicals here are for reference only so that they are permanently available; photocopies may be made. On-line literature searches are also made, for which direct costs are charged. Opening hours are generous. The library is heavily used by internal and external members, but again one of the main difficulties for the latter may be access to the short loan collection, which contains the latest editions of the most heavily used textbooks.

Education Library

All practicing teachers who work in the surrounding area are eligible for membership in the faculty library; however, external use of the library (by locally employed teachers not on a course in the faculty) is low—typically only about twenty-five issues a month. The most intensive use is, naturally, by students on campus, mainly postgraduates and currently about 380 full time and 297 part time (the total library membership is about 3,500). As with the medical library, most of the services are aimed at all readers rather than at particular groups; however, opening hours are arranged to take into account the needs of part-time students and are therefore rather complex. In addition, books are posted to readers who live or work beyond the city boundary.

All the students attending the Faculty of Education's short continuing education courses (Table 7) are local teachers who are therefore eligible for membership in the faculty library. In fact, many of these courses are one-day (Saturday) schools, so that in practice they entail minimum library use.

One course of particular interest in this context is the two-year part-time distance teaching course for teachers of the visually handicapped leading to a diploma in special education. It is a version of the one-year course also offered. It is run very much on Open University lines: packages of materials (thirty units, supplemented by study guides, audiotapes, and readers containing important articles) posted to students by the relevant tutors and two one-week summer schools on campus. The students are spread throughout England and Wales in special schools for blind and partially sighted children. Frequent written assignments are required, and school practice supervisors are appointed regionally to help supervise students' teaching. The operation was set up to be largely independent of additional resources in order to enable the teachers to continue in their jobs in residential schools while studying. The faculty library thus has only a minor role to play in this course, and that is almost entirely restricted to use (although intensive at the time) in the summer school week. This, then, is a good example of a course designed specifically for working adults whose circumstances largely deny them the time or opportunity to use libraries.

Health Services Management Centre Library

The center offers a large number of short courses each year (Table 7), and course members consist almost entirely of National Health Service (NHS) managers. They need to have available in the building (on the outskirts of the university campus) a range of up-to-date information on both the NHS and a wide variety of related disciplines such as management techniques, quality assessment, and statistics. The material is used for both background reading for lectures and increasingly for project work and individual study programs. The library is open during office hours and also in the evenings for students in residential courses. Access is also allowed to the main library and medical library for reference only.

Special services here include literature searches, using computerized databases such as Department of Health and Social Security Data, and compilation of bibliographies. It is perhaps surprising that many course members are not familiar with using libraries for their work; the center's librarian therefore teaches the use of the library and literature searching skills to students on longer courses.

Shakespeare Institute Library

The institute is a postgraduate research center for Elizabethan studies and has a research library at Birmingham. It also organizes a large number of short courses at Stratford-upon-Avon, at both undergraduate level for groups of foreign students and at a more advanced level for teachers and other postexperience students. The Stratford courses are supported by a small permanent branch library, and students also have access (for reference only) to the specialized Shakespeare Centre Library nearby. Because of the nature of the courses, students are fully occupied with classes and theater visits rather than with written assignments, and library use is therefore low.

There is not enough space to mention all the continuing education activities at Birmingham, but the sample indicates the kind of opportunities provided for adults in the community and the related library services. There is little doubt that the most effective service is given where there is a library dedicated to a particular subject or to a particular group of people and with a librarian with special responsibility for that subject or group. Although as a result the overall service is rather fragmented, this is preferable to sole dependence on a university main library, which usually tries to be all things to all people and tends to overlook the special needs of small groups.

CONCLUSION

Common Elements

Because of the rather amorphous nature of adult and continuing education, spanning as it does so many different types of institutions and courses, it has often been difficult to focus on it as a coherent identity with reference to library services; however, there are common elements and needs that can be identified and ought to receive further attention from the library profession. These include

the need for surveys, evaluation, and guidelines, the need for more documentation and comparative studies, and a continuous assessment of the role of
technology.

The Need for Survey and Evaluation

We have seen that adult students have special but varied needs in terms of the
learning process and in terms of library use. These needs are reasonably well met
by those departments and libraries whose function it is to serve the adult community but rather less so by those that have a wider clientele. What is needed is for
all institutions that serve adult students, however small this clientele is, to carry
out surveys of these students in order to identify exactly what are the main
problems they encounter, to try to solve these problems in practical terms, and to
evaluate the effectiveness of the services provided. In particular, more should be
known about the learning and library needs of students following university short
and extramural courses, Open University courses, and London external degrees.
University libraries should look more closely at the needs of their own part-time
adult students on campus and follow the example of some polytechnics in making special provision for them. New cooperative measures, such as the regional
libraries already proposed, should be considered.

The Need for Guidelines

Some of the problems that recur are common to most adult students; they
relate mainly to time, travel, study conditions and study skills, and easy access to
library materials. There is an urgent need for some published guidelines in the
United Kingdom, similar to those for services to external students in Australia
(LAA, 1982) and for extended campus services in the United States (ACRL,
1982) but covering all types of libraries that have a responsibility for adult
continuing education. The Library Association has now completed work on such
a publication (Fisher 1988).

The Need for Documentation

The amorphous nature of adult education also creates problems in terms of
documentation, and a mechanism is needed for gathering and disseminating up-
to-date information. The Library Association has recently launched *Adult Learn-
ers and Libraries News,* which consists of short summaries of news items. Its
scope is wide, but its future uncertain. What is needed is a more specialized
publication, giving details of current practice in different institutions and the
results of recent research and surveys. Information about developments overseas
would also be of benefit, as U.K. librarians have much to learn from library

services in the United States, Canada, and Australia, particularly those to external and off-campus students.

The Role of Technology

The emphasis in this paper has been on conventional library services, as the main needs are still in this area; however, once these basic needs have been met, there is considerable scope for refining and enhancing both teaching methods and library services by the use of new technology. This is a field in which librarians and teachers can cooperate. For example the introduction of interactive videodiscs and of CD Rom (Compact Disc Read-only Memory) are likely to widen the scope for self-study and home-based study by making lectures and documents more accessible to students where they live or work. In the immediate future, the main problem will be access, but in the long term, once the systems have been established, the emphasis in library work is likely to be on service to individual students or small groups.

Two examples of recent innovations using new technology and with implications for library services may be mentioned. In the first, the University of Aston's Centre for Extension Education since 1982 has offered professional updating courses to commerce and industry through tutored video instruction. Course packages are developed by video-recording live lectures, and these are studied by small groups of employees helped by a tutor. The second is a planned link-up (from October 1987) of all the colleges of London University by a fiber optics network, for the purpose of multisite conferences by television in the area of continuing education. Such developments offer challenges to librarians relating to both off-campus services and interinstitutional services.

The Purpose of Higher Education

Finally, each generation is likely to ask the apparently naive question, ''What is higher education for?'' and must try to answer it in its own way. Librarians will also want a rationale for their work. Why do so many adults make so much effort to attend so many courses? One answer may be ''to learn or to update skills useful to society.'' But such skills may quickly become out of date again, or the needs of society may change, and such an answer may, or should, apply to only a small percentage of higher education courses. The most satisfactory answer is ''to acquire knowledge'': knowledge for its own sake arising out of simple curiosity and a basic human need to learn. If this is accepted as a fundamental reason, the librarian's role falls easily into place. Adult learning at an advanced level can represent the most satisfying environment in which a librarian can work. Serving the needs of adults who *want* to learn at an advanced academic level is one of the most rewarding experiences in our profession.

REFERENCES

Association of College and Research Libraries. 1982. "Guidelines for Extended Campus Library Services." *College and Research Libraries News* 43 (3):86–88.

Butler, L., et al. 1986. *Information and Technology in Educational Guidance*. Leicester: National Institute of Adult Continuing Education.

Corney, E. 1983. "Part-time Students and Second-class Citizens: A Preliminary Investigation of Library Facilities Available to Part-timers at the University of Southampton." In Payne, 1983b, pp. 19–27.

Crocker, C. 1985 "Report: James Cook Bicentenary Scholarship 1984–85." Unpublished manuscript. (Available from author, Deakin University, Victoria, Australia.)

Department of Education and Science. 1973. *Adult Education: A Plan for Development* [Russell report]. London: HMSO.

De Wit, P. 1985. "University Extramural Education: The Tradition and the Future." M.Ed. thesis, University of Leicester.

Fisher, R. K. 1988. *Library services for adult continuing education and independent learning: a guide*. London: Library Association Publishing.

Fisher, R. K. 1985. Reading. In Henderson, 1985, pp. 35–43.

Fisher, R. K. 1971. "Regional Libraries for Adult Education." *Journal of Librarianship* 3 (4):228–236.

Henderson, W., ed. 1985. *Teaching Academic Subjects to Adults*. Birmingham: University of Birmingham.

Henderson, W., and Hewings, A. *Reading Economics: How Text Hinders or Helps. British National Bibliography Research Fund Report. London: British Library*. 1987.

Jennings, B. 1985. *The Education of Adults in Britain: A Study of Organisation, Finance and Policy*. University of Hull, Department of Adult and Continuing Education.

Library Association. 1977. *Standards for University Extramural Libraries*. London: Library Association.

Library Association of Australia. Special Interest Group on Distance Education. 1982. *Guidelines for Library Services to External Students. Ed. C. Crocker. Ultimo (New South Wales): Library Association of Australia*.

Lucas, S., and Ward, P., eds. 1985. *A Survey of "Access" Courses in England*. University of Lancaster, School of Education.

McDowell, E. 1985. *Part-time Students and Libraries: The Results of Research Studies at Newcastle upon Tyne Polytechnic Library*. Newcastle upon Tyne Polytechnic Products Ltd.

Moodie, P. 1986. "Mature Students at Birmingham." *Teaching News* 29:5–7

Newman, M. 1979. *The Poor Cousin: A Study of Adult Education*. London: Allen and Unwin.

Payne, P. 1983a. "Determinants of Library Use by Part-time Students in Polytechnics." In Payne, 1983, pp. 53–67.

Payne, P., ed. 1983b. *The Part-time Student in the Library: Papers prepared for a Conference Held at City of London Polytechnic, April 15 and 16, 1982*. London: City of London Polytechnic.

Percy, K., and Ramsden, P. 1980. *Independent Study: Two Examples from English Higher Education*. Guildford: Society for Research into Higher Education.

Pritchard, A., and Payne, P. *Part-time Students: Their Use of a Polytechnic Library*. London: City of London Polytechnic.

Sherwell, J. "Professional Education by Distance Learning: Experience of the Master's Degree at CLW." *L.A. Record* 88(11):544.

Simpson, D. J. 1983. "Part-time Students and Their Need for Library Services." In Payne, 1983, pp. 99–112.

Smithers, A., and Griffin, A. 1986. *The Progress of Mature Students*. Manchester: Joint Matriculation Board.

Tight, M. 1982. *Part-time Degree Level Study in the United Kingdom*. Leicester: Advisory Council on Adult and Continuing Education.

Tight, M. 1986. *Part-time Degrees, Diplomas and Certificates: A Guide to Part-time Higher Education Courses at Universities, Polytechnics and Colleges*. Cambridge: Hobsons.

Unit for the Development of Adult Continuing Education. 1986. *The Challenge of Change: Developing Educational Guidance for Adults*. Leicester: National Institute for Adult Continuing Education.

University Grants Committee. 1984. *Report of the Working Party on Continuing Education*. London: UGC

FURTHER BIBLIOGRAPHY

Drodge, S. 1984. *Adult Education Library Provision*. Leicester: East Midlands Branch of the Library Association.

Fisher, R. K. 1974. *The Libraries of University Departments of Adult Education and Extramural Studies*. LA pamphlet, 36. London: Library Association.

Fisher, R. K. 1981. "Library Services for University Adult Education: A Neglected Area." *Adult Education* 53 (6):372–375.

Fisher, R. K. 1986. "Off-Campus Students and Reading: A Yardstick of Academic Standards?" In Lessin, B., ed., *Proceedings of the Off-Campus Library Services Conference, Knoxville, Tennessee, April 18–19, 1985*. Mount Pleasant: Central Michigan University Press.

Gains, D. 1978. "Libraries and Other Information Sources for Open University Students on Higher Level Courses in 1976." *Teaching at a Distance* 11:65–69.

Haworth, E. D. 1982. "Library Services to the Off-Campus and Independent Learner: A Review of the Literature." *Journal of Librarianship* 14 (3):157–175.

Jones, H. A., and Williams, K. E. 1979. *Adult Students and Higher Education*. Leicester: Advisory Council for Adult and Continuing Education.

Marsterson, W. A. J., and Wilson, T. D. 1975. "Home Based Students and Libraries." *Libri* 25 (3):213–226.

Wilson, T. D. 1978. "Learning at a Distance and Library Use: Open University Students and Libraries." *Libri* 28 (4):270–282.

CHINESE THEORIES ON COLLECTION DEVELOPMENT

Priscilla C. Yu

INTRODUCTION

This study examines the role of collection development in Chinese libraries, specifically, to what extent collection development has been discussed, whereby Chinese universities and research institutes have procured for their libraries the necessary scholarly books and journals to support teaching and research.

The study discusses the concept of coordinated cooperative collection development as a method of building academic research libraries' collections. First we will look at the way American academic libraries define this concept and then examine some of the Chinese theoretical research studies on the subject matter. Finally, we will conclude by suggesting how libraries in China might improve their skills in acquisition tasks and management.

Advances in Library Administration and Organization,
Volume 7, pages 59–72.
Copyright © 1988 by JAI Press Inc.
All rights of reproduction in any form reserved.
ISBN: 0-89232-817-7

COORDINATED AND COOPERATIVE COLLECTION DEVELOPMENT

China has the largest population in the world; it is also a developing third world nation, with many sectors in the process of modernization, all requiring large financial outlays. For a country of such magnitude, it is unlikely that academic libraries can hope to gain access to unlimited funding and an exhaustive collection. Therefore, a cooperative acquisition policy on the basis of subject specialization offers one approach to building collections. Costly duplication could be avoided, and greater coverage of titles could be expected.

In the United States, collection development came about as a result of the rapid expansion and growth of libraries after World War II; libraries were very much concerned with building and developing large collections. This expansion came to a halt in the 1970s with the freeze in financial support of higher education. With tightened library budgets, the situation was worsened by escalating prices of books and journals. No longer could individual libraries count on purchasing all the important scholarly works. The days of self-contained collections were over. Libraries were forced to determine what books and serials should be added to the collection. Libraries also realized that to meet the needs of users, currently and in the future, cooperative collection development would become a necessity.

A definition of cooperative or coordinated collection development is "cooperation, coordination, or sharing in the development and management of collection by two or more libraries entering into an agreement for this purpose."[1] Cooperation now goes hand in hand with resource sharing and networking. Local self-sufficiency has been replaced by the idea of "a service center, capable of linking users to national bibliographic files and distant collections."[2]

As a start, a library's collection should be examined closely from the users' point of view. The success of the library's collection should be focused on each library's mission and goal in meeting the institutional program needs. The term *collection development* includes the systematic planning and rational building of a collection in a cost-effective way. Collection development "includes assessing user needs, evaluating the present collection, determining selection policy, coordinating selection of items, weeding and storing parts of the collection, and planning for resource sharing."[3] An articulated collection development policy statement should be written where a library not only analyzes the needs of its primary group but also appraises the strengths and weaknesses of its collection. The American Library Association's Resources and Technical Services Division (RTSD) *Guidelines for Collection Development* is useful to libraries writing a policy statement. It outlines the basic parts of the statement that are helpful in analyzing a particular collection. Included are the clientele to be served, the subject boundaries of the collection, the kinds of programs supported, and limitations governing the selection (such as language, format, and geography). The guidebook also contains a detailed collecting code, divided by classification, to be placed according to levels of collecting density and intensity. Only when each library's commitment has been made can there be a meeting with other libraries to discuss a cooperative collection development program.

According to Duane Webster,

> Cooperative collection development is not a substitute for libraries maintaining collections sufficient to serve their primary user group. It is the infrequently used materials that best lend themselves to shared development. Since one library's infrequently used materials may be the collections most in demand at another type of library, both can benefit without adversely affecting the user.[4]

Added to that is the fact that cooperative collection development eliminates duplication and frees funds to purchase materials that might otherwise not be available. Cost-effectiveness is thus encouraged, and areas of strength are identified.

In an academic environment, the success of cooperative collecting depends on the interaction of the librarian and the teaching faculty with respect to the library's collections. From a meeting on National and Regional Aspects of Collecting and Preserving Library Materials, Warren J. Haas reported:

> A reliable inventory of distinctive subject collections throughout the nation is required so that each participating library might make informed decisions concerning its own practices. The same information, current and readily available, is important to scholars for their own work and as they, in cooperation with librarians, monitor the performance of research libraries in building and maintaining collections of lasting importance and providing the necessary coverage of current materials.[5]

Even in a developed country such as the United States, academic libraries cannot be expected to be self-sufficient in purchasing all the materials required to meet the needs of their research and teaching program. Cooperation is an economic necessity. In the United States, considerable planning is being undertaken at the national level for coordinated collection development. This has been accomplished by the Research Libraries Group (RLG) Conspectus project. Through coordinated efforts, research libraries can be assured that unique or rare titles will be available to the nation's scholars. To this is added the availability of an online database from RLG. The objectives of the project were to identify national collection strengths, as well as to identify "endangered species," areas in which few member libraries were collecting sufficiently in strength. The Conspectus summarized existing collection strengths and current collecting intensities of RLG members. The project included approximately 5,000 subjects arranged by Library of Congress classification, indicating the strength of each library's current and retrospective collection. Standard codes for collection intensity and language coverage were indicated.

A more expansive national cooperative program is being undertaken, the North American Collection Inventory Project (NCIP). The NCIP is built on the work first developed by the RLG and Association for Research Libraries as a joint effort that eventually will involve research libraries throughout the United States and Canada. The eventual goal is to develop an online inventory of North American research library collections in which scholars can locate collections in specific subject areas to support their research.[6]

The concept of cooperative collection development may also be applied on a regional or statewide level. For example, in Albany, New York, the two largest research libraries, the New York State Library and the University Libraries of the State University of New York at Albany, are sharing their resources and coordinating the development of their collections. The cooperative agreement was a response to the mounting financial difficulties these libraries faced in keeping pace with publications and the information explosion. The two libraries recognized their strengths and weaknesses and cooperated in not purchasing in areas where the other was strong. The two institutions plan to have their online catalogs linked.[7] Hence, the benefits of coordinated and cooperative collection development encouraged each library to examine closely its own collection intensities and then turn outward to view a broader perspective of cooperation with other libraries.

For a nation the size of China, coordinated collection development at the local, regional, and national level would be appropriate. Especially in a developing country where foreign periodicals and books are expensive yet crucial for teaching and research, it is important to have some form of cooperative collection development. The most rational method would be to have each library aim for completeness in one or more fields and have the materials available to other libraries through interlibrary loan. (Interlibrary loan does exist in China but is not heavily utilized.) This would prevent unnecessary costly duplication, and the range of titles would be increased to provide wider subject coverage in the area.

China has not developed any organized collection development program, although several important articles have recently been written on the subject. A leading scholar in the field is Xiao Zili, vice-secretary-general of the National Steering Committee for University Libraries, Ministry of Education (now the State Educational Commission). In an important article, "Suggestions for Improving Our Country's Library Collection Development," Xiao showed that since 1947, the number of books in Chinese university libraries has grown rapidly:[8]

- 1947, 6.89 million volumes
- 1950, 7.94 million volumes
- 1956, 37.28 million volumes (at 212 universities and colleges)
- 1981, 200 million volumes (at 670 universities and colleges)

Between 1947 and 1950, book collections increased 15.2 percent; from 1950 to 1956, they increased 369.5 percent. During the twenty-five years from 1956 to

1981, the collections increased by 436.5 percent. Statistics show that by 1981, library collections at 670 universities and colleges had approached the 200 million mark, with many libraries possessing several hundreds of thousands or even millions of books, which play a major role in teaching and research. This growth has occurred despite the problems caused by the Cultural Revolution (1966–1976), which devastated the collection. Collection development had weak foundations, which were weakened even more by the ten-year catastrophe. During this time, scholarly publications ceased, and libraries were cut off from the West. Some collections were destroyed and acquisitions halted.

Other reasons contributed to the weak collection development, according to Xiao Zili. Although there was rapid growth, the quantity was still insufficient, and there was a low level of meeting the demands of the readers. He compared 1983 statistics of China's 700 universities and colleges with a total of 200 million plus volumes to the Soviet Union's 890 universities and colleges, which had 480 million volumes. Clearly the number of books in China could not meet the needs of the readers. For example, at the largest university library in China, Peking University Library, 40 percent of the foreign books and periodicals requested were not available to students and professors. The reason was that the books were either lost or checked out. Xiao related that a foreign professor once stated that the number of books required in his country to be consulted to write a dissertation was 200; in China at Nankai University, he could find only six of the books required. How could any collection development policy be constructed when resources were at such a low level? Xiao also attributed the low utilization rate to the improper use of the library's catalog, poor management, and the large number of obsolete and outdated books that flooded the libraries in China.

Xiao explained the low use rate should not be judged harshly, however, even when the cost of lending a book for one time is not cost-effective in terms of book expenses, salaries of workers, bookbinding fees, and office expenditures. Some materials if used only once may be of incalculable value economically, politically, and intellectually, just as "maintaining an army for a thousand days only to be used for an hour."

The fact that collection development has not yet caught a firm grasp he attributed to several factors. (1) Each unit in the library does things its own way, resulting in an irrational distribution of resources. There is a lack of unified planning and coordination. In addition, libraries are unable to buy more books because of limited budgets. Thus, more and more institutions are giving collection development serious thought, and some libraries have begun to do some coordination work. University libraries have put forth the suggestion of establishing core libraries and storage libraries, but all of these ideas remain at the discussion stage. (2) With the growth in book volumes, there is no formulation of policy regarding weeding of materials, with the result that there is an accumulation of outdated books and periodicals. The problem becomes one of space and low work efficiency. (3) Poor management has resulted in inaccurate statistics on the number of books acquired by the library. Some books acquired by the faculty for the departmental library have never even been recorded. (4) Collection development is simply a purchasing function, without any norms or guidelines, with a few assigned personnel and professional staff. Also the strained and unstable budgets have pointed to a need for establishing guidelines for the allocation of library materials budget.

Xiao offered five suggestions for collection development, citing Soviet and U.S. models where selectivity is thought to be important in building library collections.

1.   Exploration of rational collection quantity. Libraries in many countries have established different norms and methods for collection quantity control. Xiao pointed out that in Soviet libraries, the collection ratio is set at eight to twelve volumes for each reader (the minimum collection scale was obtained by multiplying the collection ratio by the total number of readers). Book circulation ratio could be another factor in controlling collection quantity. Certain books, whose circulation is fewer than two or three times a year should be reduced or weeded. American university libraries, in addition to the basic teaching collection, have also maintained quantity control according to the research fields of instructors and graduate students. It is important that the Chinese have a comprehensive understanding of these different theories and put forth their own collection quantity norms in combination with their own practical needs and experiences.

2.   Improve quality and increase information capacity of the collection. The latter is dependent on the high utilization rate of books being available for loan.

3.   Reorganize and improve the collection structure. Every library collects and arranges knowledge into different fields, different levels, different languages, and so on. In order to have the best collection system with distinguishing features, it is important to study collection structure.

4.   Formulate criteria to promote standardization of collection development. In the present situation—a vast number of new publications—buying indiscriminately is impossible. Therefore, libraries must have qualified librarians with proper guidelines to engage in book selection. In the United States, the American Library Association's *Guidelines for Collection Development* (1979) includes information for the formulation of guiding principles for collection development, evaluation of collection effectiveness, review of library collections, and allocation of library budgets as well as related materials. The Soviet Union has issued in the past twenty years more than ten rules on collection development. Based on the experiences and knowledge of advanced foreign countries, China must form and formulate its own guidelines for the standardization of collection development. This does not mean that each library will follow the same pattern. On the contrary, each library will be considered on its own merit, considering its history and present conditions.

5. Library collection is experiencing a history of development from institution collection, cooperative collection (more than two libraries), and regional collection to national and international collection.

What seems desirable is to have parallel coordination: nationwide coordination together with regional coordination. At present, there is no centralized organization to engage in unified planning and coordination; there are no regulations and rules on cooperation and coordination of libraries. China has to do research, analyze foreign experiences and lessons, and formulate a series of norms and regulations. Sharing of resources is a prerequisite for solving difficult problems in collection development, and methods of norms are necessary for national and regional collection development. China should combine theoretical research with practical knowledge. After studying other nations' achievements in collection development, it should seek to form its own collection theories and methods.

In another article, Xiao noted certain weaknesses in university libraries.[9] (1) Unlike foreign academic libraries where large number of microfiche materials have already been collected, China has few microform collections. (2) A large gap exists in many fields. For example, a Chinese survey that compared book titles and periodicals in sociology, law, computer science, and biology to a bibliography in the *International Encyclopedia of Higher Education* found that the holdings of foreign materials by the four major universities in Beijing were very low: the lowest was 17 percent and the highest 62 percent, for an average of 39 percent. Among the reasons for the shortage, foremost is the serious effects of the Cultural Revolution, when knowledge was deliberately repressed, there was little encouragement to train and upgrade librarians, and there was only a single unitary channel to import books, CNPIEC (China National Publications Import and Export Corporation). (3) Each library works independently. Based on its needs and limited budgets, it collects without thinking of others. (4) Budgets are low, especially the budget for importing foreign books. The lowest is several million dollars and the highest $30 million to $40 million, which is allocated to libraries and used in a decentralized way. With limited budgets, libraries cannot expect to attain an exhaustive collection in a particular subject. (5) Overall planning is absent. Chinese libraries and information institutions are separated into two organizational structures without any coordination. Difficulties emerge in overall development. The Chinese are at a discussion stage with regard to establishing a single entity (institution) to be in charge of organization, coordination, overall investigation, and general planning (including science and technology and social science, national and regional collection, and computer network).

Xiao continued by describing the experiences of other countries regarding collection development. For example, some coordinate in formulating collection guidelines by defining the range of subjects each library is responsible for collecting; others cooperate in purchasing valuable and costly materials or reproducing microfilms; others set up storage libraries. The sharing of resources involves not only books and periodicals but also equipment. Since World War II, several systems of resource sharing have been developed in the United States, including the Farmington Plan, Public Law 480, the National Program for Acquisitions and Cataloging of the Library of Congress based upon the provisions of the Higher Education Act of 1965, and the Center for Research Libraries. The establishment of networks extends not only to cooperation among several libraries but also to intraregional and multinational areas.

West Germany, Great Britain, France, Japan, and the Soviet Union have also adopted collection development plans, regional planning, and/or national coordinated networks. Smaller countries depend on international cooperation for their collections.

Xiao recommended that (1) collection development must have a well-defined policy and overall planning. (2) There should be an overall national institution in charge of planning, coordination, and supervision, as in West Germany, Great Britain, France, the Soviet Union, and the United States. (3) A stable budget must be provided to support the libraries participating in the coordinated collection. (4) The distribution center model could differ. Some could be totally centralized, some partially centralized according to type of subjects, and some distributed according to regions. Usually several models are used together.

Xiao presented some tentative ideas on China's collection development plans: (1) Be as comprehensive as possible in collecting valuable and important materials. (2) Collect two or three copies of important documents; for other rare materials, one copy is sufficient. (3) Assign certain institutions to national level collection development.

To achieve these objectives, Xiao suggested the development of a three-tier collection development system:

- Tier 1 would be special cities, provinces, and autonomous regions, which should form comprehensive libraries and information institutions (the latter refers to science and technology units affiliated with the Chinese Academy of Sciences) to fulfill 80 percent of the requirements in the regions concerned. These libraries could form their own computer networks.
- Tier 2 would be the specialized libraries, specialized information units, and core universities that could contribute to the national collection in their own way.
- Tier 3 would be the national library, which would collect valuable and rare materials for the nation. Tiers 2 and 3 would cooperate in forming the national network, which would be the backbone of the provincial collection network, combining centralization with regional collection development to meet Chinese needs.

According to Xiao, in 1983, 700 university libraries had a total collection of

200 million volumes, the annual budget for book purchase was 80 million yuan, and the library staff was 25,000, 44 percent of whom were university and college graduates. With this growth, university libraries should assume responsibilities in the regional and national library network development and the sharing of resources in collection development.

Xiao made the following suggestions for cooperative development plans for university libraries. (1) University libraries should have several complete and coherent collections in certain subjects. (2) A centralized distribution plan is desirable. Among the 700 universities and colleges, thirty to fifty libraries should be selected on the basis of their budgets and subject superiorities as professional collection centers. These universities would take on the tasks of specialized centers and coordinators in university collections in specialized fields. They might further develop into storage libraries for certain subjects. Ten of these libraries would be selected to be the core of the whole system and also part of the computer network. (3) Collection distribution should be divided into 200 or more subjects, with each university library assigned areas of collection responsibilities. (4) The National Steering Committee for University Libraries of the Ministry of Education could be the organizational and administrative body of the whole system. Its tasks would be to plan and coordinate the collection distribution of the entire system; to coordinate and allocate subsidized budgets to library centers; to explore materials resources, especially the import channels of foreign materials; and to supervise, examine, and evaluate the work of library centers. The Ministry of Education should provide the necessary personnel, budgets, and equipment for these library centers. China must provide foreign currency to import foreign materials of specialized subjects. (5) The National Steering Committee for University Libraries in the provinces, cities, and autonomous regions could organize and plan the collection distribution of local university and college libraries. If regional library coordination can be organized, the university libraries should take part and assume responsibilities.

At the April 21–26, 1983, meeting of the Conference of the National Steering Committee for University Libraries, Ministry of Education, held at Sichwan University, discussions were held on how to organize and implement research on collection development to improve this work in university libraries.[10] The symposium was attended by thirty-five delegates from thirty units of fifteen provinces and cities. Vice-Secretary General Xiao Zili of the National Steering Committee for University Libraries presided at the meetings and gave a report introducing the general state of university libraries in China and offered suggestions on how to strengthen studies of collection development. It was held that to improve collection development, one must combine theory with practice to solve actual problems. It was agreed that collection development is a basic function among university libraries and a weak link that urgently needs to be strengthened. Several research topics were listed for libraries and library staff to select and study in combination with their work and to report their research findings to the secretariat for coordination:

1. Overall requirements for collection development, including rational quantity, standards for meeting readers' demands, and utilization of the collection.
2. Standards and methods of collection evaluation.
3. Principles, criteria, and methods of collection weeding and storage.
4. Duplication formula.
5. Method of collection organization for different types of university libraries.
6. Organization of books for teaching.
7. Principles and methods of allocation of library budgets.
8. The mission and functions of university core libraries and storage libraries.
9. Sharing of resources and collection coordination.
10. Studies on selection theory and methods.
11. Effects of technology (for example, computers and microfiche) upon collection development.
12. After studying the theories and methods of collection development and recent achievements in foreign countries, formulation of a theory and method of collection development appropriate to China.
13. Special education of collection development staff.
14. Information service on collection development research.

It was planned that following the April 1983 meeting, a larger symposium would be held to discuss the ideas and plans set forth at the conference. It was hoped that eventually a handbook on collection development would be published and a textbook on collection development would evolve for college students.

Another article, this by Ma Hongxiang, acquisition librarian at Nanjing University, addressed some of the practices and problems with regard to collection development of university libraries in China.[11] Ma stated that no unified rules and guidelines concerning collection development have been developed by the Nanjing University Library. Moreover, many problems must be solved before such a program could be inaugurated. For instance, there is a tendency for each department to act independently from one another, without consulting with the main library and other departments related to its field. There is a strong sense of competition among departments in book purchasing and building up their own libraries. Some departmental libraries use research budgets to purchase large quantities of duplicates to satisfy the requirements of readers. These books are jealously guarded in professors' offices so that it is difficult or next to impossible to get a copy to use. The departmental libraries, which made additional purchases, did not send the books to be cataloged by the main library. Thus the catalogs of the main library do not give an accurate account of the books in the library system. There is a serious need for better management and a need to formulate weeding policy guidelines. Ma felt that the main library should be in charge of all collection development, in both the main and departmental librar- ies. Books and periodicals should be purchased and cataloged in a unified way. Ma also accepted the concept of sharing of resources. Finally, Ma felt that before the establishment of a national network center can be realized, there must first be a regional resource plan.

Both Xiao and Ma recognized the importance of collection development. Both also correctly realized a need for strong administrative leadership within each library system to establish clear-cut library policies for the main and departmen- tal libraries; there is far too much independence by the departmental libraries. This seems to be a major problem, for a successful collection development program requires the cooperation of librarians and faculty and the main and branch libraries. As soon as greater unity can be attained, guidelines can be formulated for rational collection development.

Xiao realized the importance of coordinated collection development. He also stressed the importance of having a national administrative agency to plan and coordinate the collection distribution of the entire system. Both Xiao and Ma recognized the need for good management planning.

Regarding sharing of resources in collection development, Xiao believed in having both a regional and a national library network, whereas Ma believed a regional resource plan should be developed before a national network.

CONCLUSION

From this study, it is evident there are certain basic needs that require attention before a collection development policy can be formulated and implemented in China.

The building of strong collections in academic libraries requires trained li- brarians. Professional librarians are needed for their knowledge and expertise in the library and subject fields—knowledge of the collection tools to be used in order to select the proper books, serials, and other important items. Granted that faculty members in China have played a part in book selection, it would be helpful for librarians to take a more active role as selectors or bibliographers and develop their acquisition skills not only in general fields but also in their respec- tive fields of interest. In this way, librarians and faculty could complement one another.

Another problem area is management. There is a need for better control and coordination between departmental or branch libraries and the main library. In each library system, a collection development officer or coordinator could man- age or see that library staff and faculty work cooperatively. Team effort and harmonious working relations are necessary for an effective collection develop- ment program.

For Chinese libraries, one advantage of having a collection development policy statement is that one would gain a better understanding of the nature of the academic programs and of the materials that should be acquired. Also, with the existence of specific guidelines, there would be more reason to justify the acquisition or exclusion of certain materials. And it would be helpful in evaluating the strengths and weaknesses of the collection, as well as establishing priorities among a variety of disciplines and programs.

A useful collection development policy—for example, of Western-language materials—could begin by examining the holdings of individual institutions. The policy might include a general statement of the library's mission and objectives, who is responsible for collection development, how selection is made, and how funds are allocated and materials acquired. Also indicated may be preferences or limitations on languages, emphasis or exclusion on geographical areas, chronological coverage of materials, types of materials included and excluded, lists of subject areas collected, and collecting levels. It would be helpful to have a written definition at each level. The main part of the collection development statement could be the individual selection policies by subject or by academic department; this part would require the cooperation of both the faculties and librarians who make the selection for the collection. It would be expected that some of these approaches could be adopted. It could be anticipated that there would be many variations and modifications in the collection development policy statement and the mode would be in accordance with Chinese needs and ways.

In China, as Xiao Zili agrees, regional coordination of collection development, together with national collection development, would be most appropriate. With the limited financial resources, high costs of Western-language books, and lack of space, it would be unrealistic to expect most Chinese academic libraries to build exhaustively or comprehensively in any one field or fields. It can be expected, however, that core libraries will have some comprehensive collections.

As an example of regional coordination, a provincial library could cooperate with adjacent provincial libraries. The libraries could build on existing strengths by agreeing on areas of strengths and weaknesses, thus complementing each other's collection. Regional libraries would be informed of strengths and would avoid duplications. It is hoped that local and regional libraries would be online, making interlibrary loan all the more easier. Users could first rely on local college libraries and other regional resources before going to the national core center libraries (core centers would include national and major academic research libraries in the country—for example, National Library of China, Peking University Library, Nanjing University Library, and Fudan University Library, similar to the Association of Research Libraries in the United States). It would seem reasonable to have these core libraries administered by the existing National Steering Committee for University Libraries, which is directed by the Ministry of Education. These core libraries would meet to determine which institutions are collecting which materials, how strong their collections are, and whether they plan to continue to collect at the same level of intensity. Discussions could center on the possible scholarly subjects to be collected or identified as collection strengths that libraries agree to support.

Eventually core libraries' collection would be online and thus available to users who could not obtain them regionally. Plans to have a national online system are already in the making; preparations are being made at the National Library of China for the development of a national bibliographic database and an automated retrieval center for books and periodicals. For Western materials, the National Library of China is using LC MARC tapes and ISDS (international Serials Data System).

As one can see from this study, many of the Chinese ideas and concepts of collection development are similar to those of the West. Collection development as part of the modernization of Chinese library development is gradually being realized. It is true that there are problems, but these obstacles can be overcome. By opening up to new ideas and through absorption, transformation, and creation, China will develop a collection development policy suited to its needs.

ACKNOWLEDGMENT

Research for this study was supported by a grant from the Council on Library Resrouces.

NOTES

1. Paul H. Mosher and Marcia Pankake, "A Guide to Coordinated and Collection Development," *Library Resources and Technical Services* 27 (4) (October–December 1983): 420.

2. Patricia Battin, "Research Libraries in the Network Environment: The Case for Cooperation," *Journal of Academic Librarianship* 6 (2) (May 1980): 70.

3. Rose Mary Magrill and Doralyn J. Hickey, *Acquisition Management and Collection Development in Libraries* (Chicago: American Library Association, 1984), pp. 3–4.

4. Philip Tompkins, ed., *Cooperative Collection Development in Multitype Library Networks: A Beginning—Goals and Methods: Proceedings of the 1980 Annual Conference of the Missouri Library Association* (Columbia: Missouri Library Association, 1981), p. 97.

5. *Two Reports on Research Libraries* (Washington, D.C.: Council on Library Resources, November 1983), p. 31.

6. "Conspectus Points Way to Cooperative Collection Development," *Research Libraries Group News*, no. 5 (September 1984): 12–14; Maxine K. Sitts, "Library Practices," *RTSD Newsletter* 10 (8) (1985): 96–97; Jutta Reed-Scott, *Manual for the North American Inventory of Research Library Collections* (Washington, D.C.: Association of Research Libraries, 1985), p. 4.

7. "SUNY-Albany and State Library Coordinate Collection Development," *Library Journal* 108 (2) (January 15, 1983): 84.

8. Zili Xiao, "Suggestions for Improving Our Country's Library Collection Development," *Daxue Tushuguan Tongxun* (Journal of University Libraries), no. 6 (June 20, 1983): 13–21.

9. Zili Xiao, "Our Country's Collection Development and the Mission of University Libraries," *Daxue Tushuguan Tongxun* (Journal of University Libraries), no. 6 (November 15, 1984); 3–14.

10. "Develop Research in Collection Development, Improve Collection Development Work," *Daxue Tushuguan Tongxun* (Journal of University Libraries), no. 6 (June 20, 1983): 8–9; "Brief Explanation of Research Topics in Collection Development," *Daxue Tushuguan Tongxun* (Journal of University Libraries), no. 6 (June 20, 1983): 11–12.

11. Hongxiang Ma, "Present Conditions and Reforms of the Collection System of University Libraries: On the Relationship between the Main Library and the Departmental Libraries" (Nanjing: Nanjing University Library, July 1984) (unpublished; in Chinese).

AN OVERVIEW OF THE STATE OF RESEARCH IN THE SCHOOL LIBRARY MEDIA FIELD, WITH A SELECTED ANNOTATED BIBLIOGRAPHY

P. Diane Snyder

INTRODUCTION

The United States probably leads the rest of the world in the provision of school library media centers. School library media specialists and their supporters stress the importance of the role of the school library media center in the educational program of the school and in the learning of children. Yet when budgets are cut, the school library media program is often the first to suffer; it is seen as a frill and

Advances in Library Administration and Organization,
Volume 7, pages 73–88.
Copyright © 1988 by JAI Press Inc.
All rights of reproduction in any form reserved.
ISBN: 0-89232-817-7

as expendable. Can we, as school library media specialists, prove our contribution to teaching and learning?

When school library media specialists turn to the literature for support, to demonstrate the validity and usefulness of their program, they find a noticeable lack of evidence, of critical research. In fact, most of the research they do find consists of quantitative standards for collection building, personnel, and facilities or "literature of exhortation, aspiration, and mutual support, where local practitioners describe to each other what they believe is succeeding, in what they hope they are doing, and where leading professional spokespeople urge their cohorts forward with eloquent statements of idealism." "They are rarely noted for either their theoretical thinking or the quality of their supporting evidence" (Beswick, 1983, pp. 3–4). Freeman (1985) concurs:

> Despite unprecedented growth in the numbers of librarians and resources, there are no scientific laws, few theories, and only a handful of useful models that one can point to for guidance. The field is not united by principles, but is rooted in common educational experience, a sharing of problems. . . (p. 29).

It is obvious that "the school library media field has a vast array of challenges to be resolved through research" (Chisholm, 1983, p. 147). In the past, much criticism has been directed at the research taking place in the library media field in general. Many critics feel that the field is not producing the quality or quantity of research that it should, and the results of the research that is being conducted are not generalizable (Stroud, 1982b).

More recently, however, interest in research in the library media field and, more specifically, the school library media field, has increased. More and more, practitioners are beginning to realize that data are needed to justify the existence of the school library media center, its programs, services, and staff: "As pressures mount to reduce staff and programs, school library media specialists seek evidence that they contribute to learning and teaching" (Grazier, 1982, p. 140). For far too long, school library media specialists have placed emphasis on reaching national guidelines without any attempt to determine if the existence of a good school library media program has any effect on student performance. Wilkinson (1982) concurs:

> Without evidence from such studies, it is difficult to counter claims that media programs can be severely reduced or eliminated without any loss in educational effectiveness. If funding is to be provided, there is a need for justification of the school media program that goes beyond the feeling that a school library is a "good thing" that should be available within the school. Media programs must be justified on the basis of the contribution that they make toward the goals and the mission of the school. . . As long as media programs are merely additive, being treated as supplementary to, or enrichment of, the instructional program, they will never be cost-effective. Without evidence of their contribution to learner outcomes, they can, with clear conscience, be treated as a disposable educational frill in times of economic hardship. When the resources of the media program are directly integrated into the instructional pro-

gram, the cost is high but the effectiveness of the program can be demonstrated directly on
learner outcomes and thus the program can be economically justified (pp. 37, 39, 42).

Media specialists are looking to research for ways to solve problems, to improve
practice, and to aid in their decision making: "There is a growing appreciation
among practitioners of the value of research" (Lynch, 1984, p. 381).

"Research is the systematic quest for facts related to some situation, concept,
or idea about which there is concern and about which there is insufficient understanding. Research is a way of approaching solutions to problems or answers to
questions" (Carter, 1981, p. 128). There are three basic types of research that
can be employed: basic research, applied research, and locally based research.
According to Kerlinger (1979), basic research is research done to test theory, to
study relations among phenomena in order to understand the phenomena, with
little or no thought of applications of the results of the research to practical
problems.

Applied research is research directed toward the solution of specified practical
problems from which improvement of some process or activity, or achievement
of practical goals, is expected (Kerlinger, 1979).

Locally based, or action, research, the third type of research, is gathering
momentum in the school library media field. According to Englert (1982), locally based research addresses real problems confronting decision makers; it is
situation specific; its purpose is to ameliorate a particular situation; and it is
systematic. School library media specialists, like other library media personnel,
are involved in the decision-making process on a daily basis, and many of these
decisions must be based on or relative to a given situation. A number of decisions
are made daily and with respect to the immediate situation as well as the future:
What type of media will be most effective for a student or group of students?
What format of media will fit best into the collection? What is the best way to
integrate the library media program and the curriculum? What is the role of the
school library media specialist? What services should the library media center
offer? How well is the school library media collection supporting the curriculum?
In the past, because of the lack of research, most of these decisions were made on
the basis of the school library media specialists' knowledge and experience.
More recently, however, school library media specialists are beginning to base
their decisions on research. They have begun to realize that they "can enhance
their decision-making by means of research" (Englert, 1982, p. 24). As a result,
school library media specialists are beginning to conduct their own research
"aimed at gathering data and drawing conclusions that are immediately applicable to the decisions being made" (Englert, 1982, p. 247). The aim of this locally
based research is

to provide a practitioner . . . [the school library media specialist] the information needed to
make a decision. . . . Locally based research is particularly useful because it addresses real

problems confronting the decision maker. This is so simply because locally based research is
situation specific and because the practitioner has control over the focus of the research
(Englert, 1982, p. 247).

School media specialists are interested in real-life, practical research that will
have a direct bearing on improving their present situation. Englert adds that
locally based research takes into account the uniqueness of the situation and
attempts to develop usable solutions. It is simply the "application of accepted
rules of scientific method to a concrete situation" (Englert, 1982, p. 248). The
steps involved in conducting locally based research are recognizing a problem;
exploring the problem; narrowing the range of possibilities; formulating specific
question hypotheses; designing a research plan; employing data collection instru-
ments; collecting the data; analyzing the data; and writing a report (Englert,
1982).

According to Englert (1982), locally based research supplies three benefits to
the media specialist who directly participates in locally based research:

1. Provide data relevant to practical problems in a concrete setting.
2. Contribute to the professional development of the school library media
   specialists who engage in it—research skills, creativity, critical thinking,
   and disciplined inquiry.
3. Contribute to the overall development of the school library media field.

Regardless of the type of research, there are several research methodologies
that are common to all. The research methodologies most often used in the
school library media field are the historical approach, the ex post facto approach,
and the survey approach, with the last used most often. Although the experimental approach is probably the most highly regarded method of research because it
has the ability to establish causal relationships, it is infrequently used in school
library media research. The difficulties and expense involved in the experimental
approach often lead researchers to utilize other methods. Also, the use of the
experimental approach in the school library media field would of necessity
involve people and actual school settings, and this poses obvious problems—
people are not easily manipulated and school settings are difficult to control
(Stroud, 1982b). However, Chisholm (1982), of the School of Librarianship,
University of Washington, expresses the view that "research in the school library media field cannot be considered adequate until we move dramatically in
the direction of pure or experimental research" (p. 147).

The historical approach, according to Carter (1981), attempts to assess the
meaning of and/or relationship among past events. This method uses, as much as
possible, documents from the period being studied.

Ex post facto (after the fact) research is popular in the school library media
field. It starts with dependent variables that already exist, and the researcher

merely observes the functional relationship between the independent and dependent variables after the fact. With this type of research, it is impossible to measure the cause-and-effect relationships so much needed by the school library media field (Chisholm, 1983).

It has been suggested that the survey approach has been used heavily in the school library media field because so much of the information needed in the field must be obtained from people, and the survey approach is well suited to this purpose (Stroud, 1982b). Stroud (1982b) examined doctoral dissertations in library science from 1976 to 1981 and found, for this five-year period, that approximately 56 percent employed the survey technique. According to Stroud,

> Survey research, attractive to librarians because it reflects current conditions or describes the status quo, has been roundly criticized because, while it can do a very good job of describing a situation as it exists, it does not have the capacity to explain why the situation is as it is (p. 127).

Ennis (1967) concurs, stating that the heavy use of the survey in library science research contributes to the research often being characterized as fragmentary and noncumulative since surveys are often carried out in isolation, the concerns are too parochial, and the results are not generalizable (Stroud, 1982b).

The most common types of survey research are the written questionnaire, the telephone survey, and the personal interview. Of the three, questionnaires are the principal means of the survey methodology. It is not difficult to understand the questionnaire's popularity. Bookstein (1985) states that probably the most important reason for the questionnaire's popularity is its simplicity and naturalness: "we are used to asking questions of others when we desire information, and the questionnaire is a straightforward formalization of this process" (p. 24). A second characteristic of the questionnaire that encourages its use is the form it imposes on the responses (Bookstein, 1985). According to Bookstein:

> Regardless of how the questionnaire was distributed, and the process by which each respondent came to an answer, the final result is a series of crisp, clean percentages, presented with error limits and encouraging statements about how much confidence we may place in our results (p. 124).

A third characteristic of the questionnaire that encourages its use is its "ability to collect great amounts of pertinent data from geographically spread individuals with great economy" (Swisher, 1980, p. 159).

Moran (1985) outlines the steps involved in the survey research:

- Know the problem.
- Gather as much information on the topic as possible.
- Identify the population to be surveyed and choose the sample.
- Construct a trial version of the questionnaire.

- Pretest the questionnaire.
- Design the actual survey instrument.
- Design a cover letter.
- Mail the survey.
- Keep track of the number of returns.
- Mail the first and then the second follow-up letters.
- Analyze the data.
- Report the results.

Most researchers believe that the survey approach will continue to be used heavily in librarianship.

Most research studies do not employ a single research methodology to the exclusion of all others but rather employ a combination of the above described research methodologies.

There are several major problems associated with research in the school library media field. One of these is "the lack of validation of research through replication in different situations" (Aaron, 1982a, pp. 73–74). According to Aaron,

> The emphasis in the school library media field is generally upon doing a different type of study rather than consciously building on what has been done. It is difficult to compare research studies and evaluate generalizability because investigations are so different (p. 74).

Stroud (1982b) concurs, stating that "throughout the relatively short research history in the library science field . . . the majority of the research is of the 'one-shot' variety; i.e., there has been little cumulative research or research built upon other research efforts" (p. 129).

A second major problem with research in the school library field is "the lack of an agreed upon research framework and research priorities" (Aaron, 1982a, p. 232). Aaron states that

> few attempts have been made to systematically delineate a unified framework into which each research study in the school media area can be placed. The establishment of a framework is a key to future progress since it will enable the profession to make more informed decisions about research priorities (p. 232).

She supports this position by stating that by providing a unified framework, major research areas, problems, gaps, and interrelationships will be specified in a logical way, people will know the status of research in the field, and as a result, decision makers will be starting with similar baseline data (p. 232). A further advantage of establishing research priorities would be the identification of top priority areas, which would encourage researchers to deal with major problems in the school library media field and would ideally build on what has already been done to create important new knowledge (Aaron, 1982b, p. 232).

A third major problem of research in the school library media field is the lack of a commitment of time and money to conduct research. Aaron (1982a) explains:

> We should have experienced researchers working full-time to solve the pressing problems that presently confront the field. Without this type of commitment, programs will continue to operate primarily on the basis of experience and tradition (p. 74).

A fourth problem of research in the school library media field is the fact that school library media researchers often tend to design complicated studies with too many independent interacting variables. Such large studies increase the possibility of design flaws and controls. What is needed are neat, simple studies that answer small questions. Such studies make better research designs and yield more reliable conclusions (Chisholm, 1983).

A fifth and final problem of research in the school library media field is how to disseminate the results of the research that is being done to practitioners in the field in a form that relates to their everyday problems: "The profession will continue to accord little value and recognition to research efforts until we find a way—whether by abstracting, use of professional journals, or some other means—to bridge the gap between research reports and the school library media specialist" (Aaron, 1983, p. 149). According to Carter (1981), "knowledge gained through research moves the profession toward more informed program planning, policymaking, and decision making" (p. 136). He adds that all research should be reported in written form, for the research report can serve to ignite interest in further research, and it can help other researchers avoid similar problems encountered in their research. "Journals are probably the most important vehicle in the overall process of dissemination and are the first place where findings are presented as a record to researchers" (Ali, 1985, p. 120). Abstracting and indexing services also play an important role in organizing and classifying information and assisting the individual researcher in looking for material relevant to a particular area of investigation (Ali, 1985).

One point not to be overlooked in discussing research is the importance of critically reading and evaluating the research that is being done. Study very carefully the methods employed in the conduct of the research, such as how the subjects were selected, how the data were collected, what data were collected, and how much control was provided by the research design. Analyze the data reported in terms of objectivity and bias and whether the data actually support the conclusions of the study. Two excellent articles address the problem of how to read and evaluate research in a critical manner: Margaret Hayes Grazier's article, "Critically Reading and Applying Research in School Library Media Centers," and M. Carl Drott's article, "How to Read Research: An Approach to the Literature for Practitioners."

Research in the school library media field has not had any lasting impact on the profession to this point. It is hoped that this situation will change as the pressure increases to justify school library media programs and their effects on teaching and learning. Priority areas need to be identified, problems in the field need to be examined in completely new ways, properly designed and executed research studies need to be conducted, and the results of research need to be disseminated. Research needs to be cumulative, less fragmentary, with more replication, fewer studies carried out in isolation, and the utilization of a wider range of research techniques. Research in the school library media field should be both theoretical and practical in order to build a set of data that can eventually provide objective answers to the important and difficult questions facing the profession. If the school library media profession is to build a strong knowledge base that will help create theories, clarify practices, and solve problems that confront all library media specialists, there must be a strong and coordinated program of research (Loertscher, 1982). Aaron (1982a) states that

> attention to the theory underlying the field is imperative. We concentrate on present problems (the what) to the exclusion of any investigation of the principles providing the foundation for practice. Until we develop a unified system of coherent principles, or at least examine the principles upon which we are operating, it is doubtful that the most effective practice of the profession will take place (p. 73).

Beswick (1983) suggests that "we need a case for the school library that is based on the harsh realities of schooling and of education: that is self-critical and invites critical discussion and experimentation: and that gives priority to the learning of the child" (p. 8). He adds that "we need a wealth of case studies of 'successful practice' carefully defined, critically examined and presented" (p. 9). Drott (1984) adds that "by affirming the importance of research we affirm the value of change, growth, and development within the profession." "Until we have information supporting our practices . . . school library media programs will remain largely an area governed by emotion rather than empirical data" (Mancall, 1983, p. 148).

SELECTED ANNOTATED BIBLIOGRAPHY

The following bibliography was constructed through a literature search of the following indexes: *Library Literature, ERIC, LISA,* and *CIJE* from 1980 to 1986. The majority of the articles relate to the school library media field directly; however, a few were selected on the basis of the information and insight they provide about research and librarianship in general.

Aaron, Shirley. (1982a). "Current Research." *School Library Media Quarterly* 10 (1): 73–74.

Dr. Aaron, outgoing editor of the "Current Research" column, shares her observations concerning research activities in the school library media field.

Aaron, Shirley. (1982b). "A Review of Selected Doctoral Dissertations about School Library Media Programs and Resources." *School Library Media Quarterly* 10 (3): 210–240, 245.

Provides a survey of doctoral dissertations concerning programs and resources in the field of school library media discovered through a computer search of *ERIC, LISA, Magazine Index,* and *Comprehensive Dissertation Abstracts* and a manual search of *Library Literature* and *Library Science Dissertations: 1925–1975.* It provides a short summary of each, discusses problems relating to research in school librarianship, and provides recommendations for future research studies.

Aaron, Shirley. (1983). "Current Research." *School Library Media Quarterly* 11 (2): 149–150.

Presentation made by Dr. Aaron at the American Association of School Librarians' second national conference in 1982. She addressed the reasons for the inadequate research base in the school library media field.

Ali, Nazim S. (1985). "Library and Information Science Literature: Research Results." *International Library Review* 17 (2): 117–128.

Provides a view of the growth of library and information science literature; briefly describes four major categories of research (academic research, action research, team research, and other); and describes the outlets available for the dissemination of research results, including journals, report literature, theses and dissertations, monographs, abstracting and indexing services, online databases, research registers, newsletters, and current awareness bulletins. Ali concludes by stating that although the expansion of library and information science literature has provided many more opportunities for the communication of research results, only a small percentage of journals report research regularly and are potentially useful to the profession as a whole.

Beswick, Norman. (1983). "The Controversial School Library: A Critical Reassessment and Proposed New Strategy." *Education Libraries Bulletin* 26 (2): 1–15.

During times of economic difficulty, the first program to be cut within the schools is the school library program. This article proports that school librarians and their supporters have not produced compelling evidence of their worth. *The School Library Media Program: Instructional Force for Excellence* by Ruth Ann Davies is critically examined, and strategies for the future are suggested.

Bookstein, Abraham. (1985). "Questionnaire Research in a Library Setting." *Journal of Academic Librarianship* 11 (1): 24–28.

The questionnaire, as an instrument for obtaining information, has some very serious faults. Yet it remains one of the principal means of gathering information in library research. The article discusses sources of error in using the questionnaire in library research with examples from two experiments.

Callison, Daniel. (1984). "Justification for Action in Future School Library Programs." *School Library Media Quarterly* 12 (3): 205–211.

Outlines some basic steps for the school library media specialist to follow in providing direction for his or her program, with emphasis on documentation and justification. It provides a list of four major reasons for documenting specific library media services and provides a step-by-step procedure for gathering the necessary data for program justification.

Carter, Jane Robbins, (1981). "Practical Research for Practicing Librarians." *Top of the News* 36 (2): 128–137.

Recommends the use of the scientific method of research to librarians. It discusses the seven steps involved in applying the scientific method of research: identifying the problem; developing a plan for designing and directing the research process; crystallizing the research problem; reducing the research problem into subproblems; developing hypotheses; collecting data and analyzing their meaning; and communicating the results of the research study. The author also briefly discusses the four principal research methodologies (the historical method, the descriptive-survey method, the analytical survey method, and the experimental method), several data collection techniques, as well as how data can be described.

Chisholm, Margaret. (1983). "Current Research: What Is an Adequate Research Base for the School Library Media Field?" *School Library Media Quarterly* 11 (2): 147–148.

Presentation made by Dr. Chisholm at the American Association of School Librarians' second national conference in 1982.

Didier, Elaine K. (1985). "An Overview of Research on the Impact of School Library Media Programs on Student Achievement." *School Library Media Quarterly* 14 (1): 33–36.

Presents a summary of the findings of a number of studies dealing with the impact of the library media program on student achievement, followed by a discussion of the implications of the studies for present practice and future research.

Drott, M. Carl. (1984). "How to Read Research: An Approach to the Literature for Practitioners." *School Library Media Quarterly* 12 (5): 445–449.

Discusses why librarians read research and why research is often difficult to read. Also identifies and describes the four basic sections found in any research report—literature review; methodology; analysis; and findings—and provides suggestions for the practioner reader in approaching research reports.

Englert, Richard M. (1982). "Locally Based Research and the School Library Media Specialist." *School Library Media Quarterly* 10 (3): 246–253.

Discusses the benefits and characteristics of locally based research, the two general phases, and the steps taken in carrying out locally based research. Concludes by describing the benefits of locally based research to those library media specialists who directly participate in it.

Ennis, Philip H. (1967). "Commitment of Research." *Wilson Library Bulletin* 41 (9): 899–901.

States that "library research is noncumulative, fragmentary, generally weak, and relentlessly oriented to immediate practice" and provides evidence to support this statement.

Freeman, Michael Stuart. (1985). "The Simplicity of His Pragmatism: Librarians and Research." *Library Journal* 110 (9): 27–29.

The field of librarianship has been plagued by inadequate research and the lack of development of underlying theories, principles, and models that can be applied in many different settings. Librarianship tends to rely on the sharing of problems and practical experience.

Gilliland, Mary J. (1986). "Can Libraries Make a Difference? Test Scores Say 'Yes!' A Program to Review Library Media Skills." *School Library Media Quarterly* 14 (2): 67–70.

Discusses the positive impact of library skills teaching and review on the California Assessment Program scores.

Grazier, Margaret Hayes. (1982). "Critically Reading and Applying Research in School Library Media Centers." *School Library Media Quarterly* 10 (2): 135–146.

Discusses library media specialists' purposes for reading research and provides guidelines for critically reading research and applying it at the local level.

Gwinn, Nancy E. (1980). "Funding Library Research." *College and Research Libraries* 41 (3): 207–209.

Describes good library research from a funding point of view, stating that good library research consists of "a good idea, well researched, with a pragmatic plan of action and reasonable budget, an idea that falls within the funder's areas of interest, and is to be carried out by a well-qualified person."

Hewitt, Joe A. (1983). "The Use of Research." *Library Resources and Technical Services* 27 (2): 123–131.
Emphasizes the use of and need for research in the area of technical services and discusses four major types of research: survey research, case study research, developmental research, and environmental status research.

Hodges. Gerald C. (1981). "The Instructional Role of the School Library Media Specialist: What the Research Says to Us Now." *School Library Media Quarterly* 9 (4): 281–285.
Reviews research findings concerning the instructional role of the school library media specialist and suggests the implications of these findings for library educators, professional associations, state and district library supervisors, and building-level library media specialists.

Hodges, Yvonne A.; Gray, Judy; and Reeves, William J. (1985). "High School Students' Attitudes towards the Library Media Program—What Makes the Difference?" *School Library Media Quarterly* 13 (3–4): 183–190.
Describes a research study conducted as part of the district-wide library media center program evaluation commissioned by the Calgary Board of Education.

Kerlinger, Fred N. (1979). *Behavioral Research: A Conceptual Approach.* New York, New York: Holt, Rinehart and Winston.
"The purpose of this book is to help people understand science and scientific research. Its central concern is the basic approach and principles of all science."

Loertscher, David. (1980). "A Future Edition of National Standards: Can Locally-based Research Help?" *School Library Media Quarterly* 9 (1): 54–56.
Emphasizes the need for a new edition of the national standards, one based on a solid foundation of research conducted by professional researchers and practicing library media specialists. Loertscher outlines six areas that need to be explored and stresses the importance of practitioners becoming involved in locally based research and communicating the results of such research. He feels that "it is time to have both formal and locally based researchers join hands in the school library media field to produce a more realistic view of program components."

Loertscher, David. (1982a). "School Library Media Centers: The Revolutionary Past." *Wilson Library Bulletin* 56 (6): 415–416.

Provides a look at the development of school library media centers, citing references to individuals who have played a part in its development. It concludes with a look at where we stand today after over thirty years of existence.

Loertscher, David. (1982b). "A School Library Media Research Program for Today and Tomorrow: What, Why, How." *School Library Media Quarterly* 10 (2): 109–123.

Discusses the three components of a research program in the school library media field: conducting research, synthesizing and evaluating research efforts, and disseminating research results. Proposals for each component are listed at the end of each section.

Loertscher, David. (1982c). "The Second Revolution: A Taxonomy for the 1980s." *Wilson Library Bulletin* 56 (6): 417–421.

Discusses the role of the library media specialist in instruction through the use of an eleven-step taxonomy of which the two essential components are a well-equipped, easily accessible, and easily utilized media center and a media staff that has a direct involvement in the educational process.

Lynch, Mary Jo. (1981). "Costing Small-scale Research." *Top of the News* 37 (2): 138–144.

Emphasizes the importance of knowing the true costs of a research project and examines the costs involved, step by step, in the conduct of research, including the planning stage, set-up, data collection, data reduction, analysis, and reporting.

Lynch, Mary Jo. (1984). "Research and Librarianship: An Uneasy Connection." *Library Trends* 32 (4): 367–383.

Defines four general categories of research—practical, bibliographical, scholarly, and scientific—and emphasizes the importance of scientific research, discussing its historical perspective, its uses, and the role of professional organizations and agencies in conducting research.

Magrill, Rose Mary. (1980). "Conducting Library Research." *College and Research Libraries* 41 (3): 200–206.

Magrill feels that the best place to find an idea for research is in studies that have already been completed. She discusses studies in four areas: the structure of information, user behavior, policy decisions, and performance measures. Magrill emphasizes the importance of research that replicates or builds on previous research.

Mancall, Jacqueline C. (1982). "Current Research: Measurement and Evaluation of the Collection." *School Library Media Quarterly* 10 (2): 185–189.

Provides a selected review of the literature on collection evaluation, describing the various methodologies employed, and emphasizing that little of the research on collection evaluation has actually taken place in school library media centers. Suggests that more studies need to be done in this area.

Mancall, Jacqueline C. (1985). "Evaluating Research: A Critical Consumer Approach." *Top of the News* 42 (1): 101–104.

Discusses the need for librarians to take a consumer approach to evaluating the utility of any given research study and outlines two authors' (Grazier and Drott) guidelines for reading and evaluating research.

Mancall, Jacqueline, ed. (1982). "Current Research." *School Library Media Quarterly* 10 (1): 73–74.

Presents remarks of Shirley Aaron, outgoing editor of the column, "Current Research." Dr. Aaron expresses optimism over the positive changes that have occurred in the field of school library media research but also concern over problems that still need to be addressed.

Mancall, Jacqueline, ed. (1983). "Current Research." *School Library Media Quarterly* 11 (2): 147–151.

Presents a summary of a program on research at the American Association of School Librarians' second national conference in Houston, Texas. Presentations were made by Dr. Margaret Chisholm, "What Is an Adequate Research Base for the School Library Media Field"; Dr. Jacqueline Mancall presented five reasons why we need to conduct research; Dr. Shirley Aaron addressed the reasons for the inadequate research base in the school library media field and what research is need; and Philip Baker, Dr. Mary Jo Lynch, and Dr. Blanche Woolls suggested strategies for developing a more adequate research base in the school library media field.

Mancall, Jacqueline; Fork, Don; and McIsaac, Marina Stock. (1982). "Avenues of Dissemination: Research to Practitioner." *School Library Media Quarterly* 10 (3): 254–262.

Discusses the major channels of communication in education that are used to improve the research dissemination process. It presents a brief summary of the various points of view regarding the dissemination process and points out representative examples of both formal and informal structures. A list of selected sources for disseminating research information in education is appended.

Marchant, Maurice P.; Broadway, Marsha D.; Robinson, Eileen; and Shields,

Dorothy M. (1984). "Research into Learning Resulting from Quality School Library Media Service." *School Library Journal* 30 (8): 20–22.

Contains an annotated bibliography of twenty research reports concerning the effects of library media services on learning.

Meyers, Judith K. (1978). "Research Responsibilities of the School Supervisor." *Drexel Library Quarterly* 14 (3): 113–127.

School media supervisors have a responsibility to encourage, utilize, and participate in research through collecting resources, assisting in information gathering, participating in pilot studies, utilizing research findings, conducting their own research, and disseminating research results.

Moran, Barbara A. (1985). "Survey Research for Librarians." *Southeastern Librarian* 35 (3): 78–81.

Describes the three types of survey research, along with the advantages and disadvantages of each. The survey research process is described step by step, from knowing the problem to data analysis. A discussion of sampling techniques and question writing, as well as cover letter writing, how to make the survey attractive, and the timing for mailing questionnaires, is included.

Patrick, Retta. (1982). "School Library Media Programs Today: The Taxonomy Applied." *Wilson Library Bulletin* 56 (6): 422–427.

This article expands on levels 6–11 of David Loertscher's library media center taxonomy—planned gathering (level 6); evangelistic outreach (level 7); scheduled planning (level 8); instruction design I (level 9); instructional design II (level 10); and curriculum development (level 11)—providing examples of each level from school library media centers in various parts of the United States.

Stroud, Janet. (1982a). "Library Media Center Taxonomy: Future Implications." *Wilson Library Bulletin* 56 (6): 428–433.

Discusses the role of the school library media specialist in the instructional design process and suggests reasons why school library media specialists are often reluctant to assume this role. The article also provides some suggestions as to how school library media specialists might increase their involvement in the instructional design process and in doing so increase the value of the school library media center to the educational program of the school.

Stroud, Janet. (1982b). "Research Methodology Used in School Library Dissertations." *School Library Media Quarterly* 10 (2): 124–134.

Assesses the level and type of research activity in school librarianship, including a discussion of the use of the experimental, historical, and descriptive approaches by researchers in the field. Emphasizes the importance of research that builds on prior research and offers some observations on research activity in the field.

Swisher, Robert. (1980). "Criteria for the Design of Mail Questionnaires." *Journal of Education for Librarianship* 21 (2): 159–165.

Presents a systematic approach to the development of a quality questionnaire instrument, one of the most frequently used data collection techniques in library research. It outlines the criteria required for a well-designed questionnaire: appearance, question writing, question organization, and cover letter. It also includes a summary checklist for questionnaire design.

Swisher, Robert. (1986). "Using Research." *Top of the News* 42 (2): 175–177.

Stresses the importance of practicing library media specialists' engaging in and assuming responsibility for action research.

White, Herbert. (1980). "The Shock That Hurts." *American Libraries* 11 (9): 534–535.

Discusses the chasm that exists between researchers and practitioners in librarianship and the importance of research to the field and answers the questions: what kind of research do we need; who should conduct research; where should it be done; and who should pay for it?

Wilkinson, Gene L. (1982). "Economics of School Library Media Programs." *Journal of Research and Development in Education* 16 (1): 37–43.

The importance of economically justifying the media program is addressed. This article stresses the importance of evaluating the cost-effectiveness of school library media programs in terms of their contribution to the educational program of the school and learner outcomes. Cost estimates for establishing and operating a program are given.

A COMPARISON OF CONTENT, PROMPTNESS, AND COVERAGE OF NEW FICTION TITLES REVIEWED IN *LIBRARY JOURNAL* and *BOOKLIST*, 1964–1984

Judith L. Palmer

INTRODUCTION

Statement of Problem

For librarians engaged in selection of materials for acquisition, book reviews provide the primary source of information concerning new titles. Just how

Advances in Library Administration and Organization,
Volume 7, pages 89–133.
Copyright © 1988 by JAI Press Inc.
All rights of reproduction in any form reserved.
ISBN: 0-89232-817-7

important reviews are to this process may be gauged by the number of articles and studies devoted to the subject in library literature over the years.

The publishing industry itself is well aware of librarians' need for quality book reviews. In the report of a joint study conducted by the Resources and Technical Services Division of the American Library Association and the Association of American Publishers, published in 1975, investigators found that libraries generated at least 40 percent of total sales for over one-half of the sixty-one publishers participating in the study.[1] The same study found that book reviews influence library book selection more than any other factor and that fewer than 10 percent of all books published in the United States are reviewed. The same groups have recently completed a second study.[2] In the current study, more than 40 percent of the eighty-one publishers who responded to the survey reported that over 70 percent of their sales are to libraries. Reviews are again reported to be the most important selection tool for libraries. It was again noted that large numbers of books published annually in the United States are not reviewed.

Certainly, the librarian who selects fiction has a need for reviews that contain the necessary content on which to make informed selections. These reviews must also be available as far in advance as possible. Under the best of circumstances, the librarian will be faced with demand from patrons who read popular reviews or hear a reviewer and/or author promoting a new title on radio or television on or about the publication date for the book in question.

In looking at fiction reviews, certain questions may be raised from the librarian's point of view. For those review sources primarily intended for librarians, how well covered by reviews are all new American fiction titles published annually? How early are reviews published? Do these reviews contain the necessary information for making decisions on acquisition? Does one journal consistently do a better job than another? It was to help answer these questions that this study was designed.

Studies on book reviewing in general have focused on a variety of review characteristics. Some have studied review favorability and unfavorability, length, timeliness, agreement of reviews for the same title between reviewing sources, and so on. Others have considered the reviewer's style and accuracy in predicting popularity or usefulness of a title. Another type of study has considered single sources or has compared two or more reviewing sources in an attempt to describe the usefulness of one or more sources as selection aids.

Review of Related Research

In planning this study, findings from earlier studies were used to determine which journals should be evaluated. In 1958, LeRoy Merritt, and others, published a book containing the results of their independent studies on book reviewing.[3] Merritt reported the results of his study, for 1948, for selected reviewing sources. He made a thorough study of review favorability, review length, timing of reviews in relation to book publication date, number of fiction reviews compared with nonfiction reviews, overlap of titles reviewed, and agreement between reviews utilizing six review sources: *Booklist, Library Journal, New York Times Book Review, Virginia Kirkus, New York Herald Tribune Weekly Book Review,* and *Saturday Review.* He found that of the three sources most used by librarians, *Kirkus* had the earliest reviews, followed by *Library Journal* and then *Booklist. Library Journal* contained more fiction reviews than either of the other two. All were strong in reviewing general fiction.

In 1968, Charles Busha reported studies done on book reviews for 1964 and 1965.[4] In studying book selection for public libraries, Busha evaluated four review sources: *Booklist, Library Journal, New York Times Book Review,* and *Saturday Review.* He found that *Library Journal* and *Booklist* best provided short, concise, and evaluative reviews. He also found that reviews appeared more promptly in *Library Journal* than in *Booklist.*

Busha's study was partly replicated in 1979 by Daniel Ream, who also evaluated four review sources: *Booklist, Library Journal, New York Times Book Review,* and *Choice.*[5] He found that where each category was weighted equally, *Library Journal* and *Booklist* ranked highest overall in the four categories studied: total number of adult books reviewed, total number of juvenile and young adult books reviewed, percentage of randomly selected American Library Association Notable Books for 1973, 1974, and 1975 that were reviewed, and the promptness of reviews in each of the four journals. He also found that reviews in *Library Journal* showed greater promptness than those in *Booklist.*

One other related study should be mentioned. This study addresses the question of which review sources are most used by librarians. As a minor consideration in his doctoral dissertation, published in 1966, John McCrossan asked twenty experienced, practicing librarians with selection responsibilities to name the two selection aids they found to be most useful.[6] As one of the two most useful, eight chose *Library Journal* and fourteen chose *Booklist.* Six chose both *Booklist* and *Library Journal* as the two most useful.

Because *Library Journal* and *Booklist* have, in previous studies, been shown to be the two best review sources overall for librarians, they were chosen for evaluation. Has each consistently performed well in reviewing fiction? How do they compare in terms of specific review content? How do they compare in coverage of new fiction titles published each year? Has this changed over time, and, if so, in what direction have changes occurred?

Statement of Hypotheses and Assumptions

There are several assumptions underlying this study. It is assumed that it is important for librarians to know if the two review sources most often rated highest have remained consistent, improved in content and promptness, or review a high percentage of new fiction titles. It is also assumed that timeliness and content of reviews are important to librarians who select fiction. It is further assumed that measuring review content by a set of standards is indeed one measure of the quality of a review.

One hypothesis was developed to shed more light on the actual number of fiction books reviewed in relation to the number published yearly. Two hypotheses were developed to determine the performance of each journal in regard to review content and promptness.

- Hypothesis #1:   Over time, the number of fiction titles reviewed in *Library Journal* and *Booklist* has not varied proportionally with the number of new fiction titles published annually in the United States.
- Hypothesis #2:   Content, or inclusion of specific information in reviews, has improved over time in *Library Journal* and *Booklist*.
- Hypothesis #3:   The promptness of reviews, relative to book publication, has improved over time in *Library Journal* and *Booklist*.

BACKGROUND

The Relationship of Fiction to Total Book Title Production

Over the past forty years, book publication in the United States has grown from 91,514 titles for the entire decade 1940–1949 to 53,380 titles for the single year 1983. In the decade 1940–1949, 16,196 fiction titles were published, representing a mean percentage of 18.03 of all titles published (Table 1). The mean percentage of fiction to total book publication continued to drop with succeeding decades, until by the end of the 1970–1979 decade, fiction accounted for only an 8.80 mean percent of the total.

Table 1.   Fiction Publication: 1940–1983

Interval	Total Book Publication	Total Fiction Title Output	Mean Percent Fiction Output
1940–1949	91,514	16,196	18.03
1950–1959	114,675	21,537	17.33
1960–1969	256,584	29,274	12.06
1970–1979[a]	402,861	35,356	8.80
1980–1983	191,485	40,286	10.02

Source: Bowker Annual.
[a]The totals are probably artificially low because of inaccurate reporting of mass market fiction paperback publication. A correction in counting method occurred in 1981, which was expected to result in greater accuracy.

Although fiction no longer accounts for as large a portion of total title production, the actual number of fiction titles produced has continued to grow. As may be seen in table 2, 28,451 titles were published in 1964. Of these, 3,271 were fiction. In 1983, of 53,380 titles published, 5,470 were fiction. The proportion of fiction titles published during the years under study has shown some fluctuation but overall has varied by less than 5 percent. If *Publishers Weekly* and *Weekly Record* compilers are correct in their belief that large numbers of mass market paperback fiction titles were undercounted prior to 1981, the percentage of

Table 2. Percentage of Fiction in Total
U.S. Title Output

Year	Total Output	Fiction Output	Percent Fiction of Total
1964	28,451	3,271	11.50
1965	28,595	3,241	11.33
1966	30,050	3,018	10.04
1967[a]	23,762	3,080	12.96
1968	30,387	2,811	9.25
1969	29,579	2,727	9.19
1970	36,071	3,137	8.70
1971	37,692	3,430	9.10
1972	38,053	3,260	8.57
1973	39,951	3,688	9.23
1974[b]	40,846	3,562	8.72
1975	39,372	3,805	9.67
1976[c]	41,698	3,836	9.20
1977	42,780	3,681	8.60
1978	41,216	3,693	8.96
1979	45,182	3,264	7.22
1980	42,377	2,835	6.69
1981[d]	48,793	5,655	11.59
1982	46,935	5,419	11.55
1983	53,380	5,470	10.25

Source: Bowker Annual.
Note: Total output figures exclude reissues, reprints, government publications, subscription books, and pamphlets of fewer than forty-nine pages.
[a]Change in counting multivolume sets. Now count each title if each volume has a different title and forms a complete unit.
[b]*Publishers Weekly* estimates as many as 1,500 paperback titles undercounted.
[c]*Weekly Record* now taking totals for eighteen months for more accuracy in counting. Also estimates possibly 2,500 paperback titles, fiction, undercounted for this year.
[d]*Weekly Record* now using *Paperbound Books in Print* for paperback totals. Year 1981 to become new base year for comparisons.

fiction to overall title output likely would be even more consistent over the twenty years of this study.

Review Coverage of Total U.S. Title Output

Since previous studies, notably the AAP/RTSD study cited earlier, have reported that fewer than 10 percent of all titles published annually are reviewed, the review coverage records for *Booklist* and *Library Journal* were examined. In order to evaluate how well each journal provided review coverage of titles published each year in the United States, the *Bowker Annual of Library and Book Trade Information* was consulted for the years 1965–1985. Figures for "Ameri-

Table 3.   Review Coverage of Total U.S. Title Output

		Booklist		Library Journal	
Year	Total U.S. Title Output	Total Book Reviews	Percent Coverage	Total Book Reviews	Percent Coverage
1964	28,451	3,418	12.01	6,391	22.46
1965	28,595	2,821	9.87	6,127	21.43
1966	30,050	2,816	9.37	6,987	23.25
1967[a]	23,762	3,172	13.35	7,738	32.56
1968	30,387	3,195	10.51	7,896	25.98
1969	29,579	3,700	12.51	7,032	23.77
1970[b]	36,071	3,658	10.14	8,826	24.47
1971	37,692	3,557	9.44	7,955	21.11
1972	38,053	3,228	8.48	7,767	20.41
1973	39,951	3,613	9.04	8,442	21.13
1974[c]	40,846	3,849	9.42	6,299	15.18
1975	39,372	4,218	10.71	6,147	15.61
1976[d]	41,698	4,719	11.32	5,819	13.96
1977	42,780	6,790	15.87	6,000	14.03
1978	41,216	5,490	13.32	5,800	14.07
1979[e]	45,182	5,812	12.86	6,014	13.31
1980	42,377	6,149	14.51	6,130	14.47
1981[f]	48,793	5,872	12.03	5,878	12.05
1982	46,935	6,584	14.03	5,100	10.87
1983	53,380	6,386	11.96	4,806	9.00

Source: Bowker Annual.

Note: Does not include reprints, reissues, government publications, subscription books, or pamphlets of fewer than forty-nine pages.

[a]Reflects a different counting method. Sets now count each title only if each volume has a different title and forms a complete unit.

[b]Increased output over 1969 may be due to better statistical methods and increased facsimile reprints.

[c]*Publishers Weekly* estimates as many as 1,500 paperback titles may not have been counted.

[d]*Weekly Record* now publishing final totals after eighteen months for greater accuracy.

[e]*Weekly Record* estimates as many as 2,500 mass market fiction paperbacks may not have been counted.

[f]*Weekly Record* now using *Paperbound Books in Print* for greater accuracy.

can Book Title Production,'' which has an individual listing for fiction, appear in each edition. Another feature in the *Bowker Annual* is the ''Book Review Media Statistics,'' which lists the total number of book reviews appearing annually in selected journals. Both *Library Journal* and *Booklist* were included for the twenty years studied. These figures were used to see what percentage of all reviews in each journal was devoted to fiction and in identifying publishing and review trends over time. These data have been set into tables to simplify comparison.

Table 3 shows total U.S. title output, total reviews provided by each journal, and the percentage of titles covered by reviews for each. The data show that the two journals have reversed themselves in the total number of reviews provided, with the final total for *Booklist*, in 1983, close to the first year, 1964 total, for *Library Journal*. However, in terms of percentage of total title output covered by reviews, *Library Journal* dropped below 10 percent only in the final year of the study. Percentage of coverage for *Library Journal* declined consistently over time, from a high of 32.56 in 1967 to a low of 9.00 percent in 1983. *Booklist* fell below 10 percent for six years of the twenty under study, all but one instance in the first decade. Percentages of review coverage in *Booklist* varied from a low of 8.48 in 1972 to a high of 15.87 in 1977.

Part of the decrease in *Library Journal* coverage may be attributed to the fact that all reviews of juvenile and young adult titles were removed when *School Library Journal* became a separate publication in 1974. In order to arrive at a true percentage of coverage of U.S. title output that could be expected of *Library Journal* from 1974 to 1984, totals for juvenile and young adult titles published were subtracted. Results are shown in Table 4.

When juvenile and young adult titles are subtracted from the total, *Library Journal* still shows a decline in percentage of review coverage. For the final two

Table 4.   Library Journal Review Coverage of Amended
U.S. Title Output, 1964–1984

Year	Total Adult U.S. Title Output	Library Journal	
		Total Reviews	Coverage (%)
1974	38,254	6,200	16.21
1975	37,080	6,147	16.58
1976	39,220	5,819	14.84
1977	39,862	6,000	15.05
1978	38,307	5,800	15.14
1979	42,130	6,014	14.27
1980	39,518	6,130	15.12
1981	45,691	5,878	12.86
1982	44,108	5,100	11.56
1983	50,183	4,806	9.58

Source: Bowker Annual.

years of the study, using figures or percentages from either table, *Booklist* took the lead in coverage of total output.

While *Library Journal* has declined in review coverage, *Booklist* has steadily increased in percentage of U.S. title output covered. For the first ten years of the study, *Library Journal* did a much better job than *Booklist,* often providing more than twice as many reviews. During the second decade, the journals were much closer, in both number of reviews and percentage of review coverage. If the observed trend continues, *Booklist* could be expected to provide greater total coverage of titles published yearly in the United States.

REVIEW COVERAGE OF NEW FICTION TITLES

- Hypothesis 1:   Over time, the number of fiction titles reviewed in *Library Journal* and *Booklist* has not varied proportionally to the number of new fiction titles published annually in the United States.

In order to test this hypothesis, figures for total U.S. fiction title output and new fiction title output were taken from the 1965–1985 editions of the *Bowker Annual*. Fiction reviews were counted for each year for each journal. Bibliographic essays were omitted, as were titles that received only a mention. Included were all reviews in the regular review column plus infrequently appearing columns, usually occurring at the end of the fiction review section. Most of these infrequent additions were separate listings for fiction genre: mystery, science fiction, western, and so on. Some of these were the work of only one reviewer; others were done by various reviewers. Also included were such sections as "Fiction in Brief," "For the Future, LJ Takes Notice of," and "Upfront."

Table 5 shows the relationship of new fiction title production to total fiction title output. The percentage of new titles among all fiction titles published rose from around 50 percent at the beginning of the study to 60–66 percent, with two years as high as 70 percent, through 1980. The years 1973–1979 saw the largest actual number of new fiction titles published, with not fewer than 2,300 each year. In the final four years of the study, 1980–1984, new fiction titles never regained their former high levels.

Over time, new fiction titles have outnumbered other fiction titles published. The exceptions were 1965, a year in which new and other fiction titles were almost evenly divided, and the final three years, in which other than new titles predominated.

Again it should be noted that compilers of publishing industry statistics believe that large numbers of paperback fiction titles were undercounted until 1981. If so, then the drop in new fiction titles published annually has actually been more dramatic than these figures show.

Table 5.   Comparison of New Fiction Titles with
Total U.S. Fiction Title Output

Year	Total Fiction Output	New Fiction Output	Other Fiction	% New of Total Fiction
1964	3,271	1,703	1,568	52.06
1965	3,241	1,615	1,626	49.83
1966	3,018	1,699	1,319	56.30
1967	3,080	1,981	1,099	64.32
1968	2,811	1,822	989	64.82
1969	2,717	1,816	901	66.84
1970	3,137	1,998	1,139	63.69
1971	3,430	2,066	1,364	60.23
1972	3,260	2,109	1,151	64.69
1973	3,688	2,591	1,097	70.25
1974[a]	3,562	2,382	1,180	66.87
1975	3,805	2,407	1,398	63.26
1976[b]	3,836	2,336	1,500	60.90
1977	3,681	2,317	1,364	62.94
1978	3,693	2,455	1,238	66.48
1979[c]	3,264	2,313	951	70.86
1980	2,835	1,918	917	67.65
1981[d]	5,655	1,906	3,749	33.70
1982	5,419	2,042	3,377	37.68
1983	5,470	2,258	3,212	41.28

Source: Bowker Annual.

[a]*Publishers Weekly* estimates as many as 1,500 titles, many "new light fiction," under-counted.

[b]*Weekly Record* now gives totals after eighteen months rather than twelve, as done previously.

[c]*Weekly Record* estimates possibly 2,500 mass market paperback titles undercounted.

[d]*Weekly Record* now uses *Paperbound Books in Print* for greater accuracy in paperback totals.

Review coverage of adult titles for each journal is shown in Table 6. The total number of adult titles reviewed in *Booklist* has increased over time, while the opposite has occurred for *Library Journal*. On the other hand, the percentage of adult reviews has decreased for *Booklist* and increased in *Library Journal*. A large part of the increase for *Library Journal* is accounted for by the fact that *School Library Journal* became a separate publication in 1974. However, though *Library Journal* should have experienced more available space for reviews, the actual number declined from a high of 6,200 in 1974 to a low of 4,806 in the final year under study, 1983.

Table 7 illustrates the relationship between the number of fiction reviews in *Booklist* and *Library Journal* and the number of new fiction titles published yearly. It may be seen that even if there was no overlapping of reviews of the

Table 6.   Review Coverage of Adult Titles

	Booklist			Library Journal		
Year	Total Reviews	Adult Reviews	% Reviews Adult Titles	Total Reviews	Adult Reviews	% Reviews Adult Titles
1964	3,418	2,547	74.52	6,391	4,221	66.04
1965	2,821	2,213	78.45	6,127	3,871	63.18
1966	2,816	2,072	73.58	6,987	4,709	67.40
1967	3,172	2,458	77.49	7,738	5,232	67.61
1968	3,195	2,144	67.10	7,896	5,471	69.29
1969	3,700	2,821	76.24	7,032	5,900	83.90
1970	3,658	2,729	74.60	8,826	6,003	68.01
1971	3,557	2,635	74.08	7,955	5,455	68.57
1972	3,228	2,440	75.59	7,767	5,705	73.45
1973	3,613	2,657	73.54	8,442	6,006	71.14
1974[a]	3,849	2,758	71.65	6,200	6,200	100.00
1975	4,218	2,718	64.44	6,147	6,147	100.00
1976	4,719	3,014	63.87	5,819	5,819	100.00
1977	6,790	4,635	68.26	6,000	6,000	100.00
1978	5,490	3,524	64.19	5,800	5,800	100.00
1979	5,812	2,900	49.90	6,014	6,014	100.00
1980	6,149	3,267	53.13	6,130	6,130	100.00
1981	5,872	3,022	51.46	5,878	5,878	100.00
1982	6,584	3,387	51.44	5,100	5,100	100.00
1983	6,386	3,427	53.66	4,806	4,806	100.00

Source: Bowker Annual.
[a]*School Library Journal* now published separately, taking all juvenile and young adult coverage.

same title in both journals, the totals added together would still fall short of the ideal.

Although the total number of fiction titles reviewed in *Booklist* has increased—in fact, doubled—over time, the percentage of total fiction titles reviewed decreased over the final three years studied. After remaining fairly consistent in the percentage of total fiction output reviewed, varying from about 10 percent to about 16 percent, coverage increased during the years 1977–1980. For the last three years, it declined to 13.90 in 1981, 15.39 in 1982, and 14.88 in 1983.

The percentage of coverage of new fiction titles in *Booklist* has increased over time. For three of the final four years studied, *Booklist* reviewed more than 40 percent of all new titles.

Total reviews of fiction titles for *Library Journal* have also increased over time. *Library Journal* has consistently reviewed more fiction titles than has *Booklist* throughout, with 800 or more provided for most of the years studied. The percentage of total fiction output reviewed has fluctuated somewhat but has

Table 7. Fiction Reviews Compared with fiction Titles Pulbished

Year	Total Fiction Published	New Fiction Published	Booklist			Library Journal		
			Total Reviews	% Total	% New	Total Reviews	% Total	% New
1964	3,271	1,703	404	12.35	23.72	651	19.90	38.23
1965	3,241	1,615	314	9.69	19.44	719	22.18	44.52
1966	3,018	1,699	335	11.10	19.72	854	28.30	50.26
1967	3,080	1,981	363	11.79	18.32	865	28.08	43.66
1968	2,811	1,822	393	13.98	21.57	838	29.81	45.99
1969	2,717	1,816	423	15.57	23.29	888	32.68	48.90
1970	3,137	1,998	478	15.24	23.92	922	29.39	46.15
1971	3,430	2,066	432	12.59	20.91	951	27.73	46.03
1972	3,260	2,109	540	16.56	25.60	930	28.53	44.10
1973	3,688	2,591	434	11.77	16.75	905	24.54	34.93
1974	3,562	2,382	454	12.75	19.06	932	26.17	39.13
1975	3,805	2,407	420	11.04	17.45	895	23.52	37.18
1976	3,836	2,336	624	16.27	26.71	811	21.14	34.72
1977	3,681	2,317	896	24.34	38.67	879	23.88	37.94
1978	3,693	2,455	874	23.67	35.60	927	25.10	37.76
1979	2,364	2,313	658	20.16	28.45	1,036	31.74	44.79
1980	2,835	1,918	779	27.48	40.62	1,196	42.19	62.36
1981	5,655	1,906	786	13.90	41.24	1,055	18.66	55.35
1982	5,419	2,042	834	15.39	40.84	1,087	20.06	53.23
1983	5,458	2,258	814	14.88	36.05	866	15.83	38.35

remained between 20 and 30 percent over time. The percentage of new fiction titles reviewed has remained above 40 percent for twelve of the years studied. Fifty percent or greater coverage was provided for four years. *Booklist* compares favorably with *Library Journal* in coverage of new fiction only in the final years of the twenty studied.

Trends may be seen more easily when figures for the twenty-year period are collapsed into five-year intervals. Table 8 represents the data in Table 7 divided into intervals for easier comparison. Total numbers of new and all fiction titles published are given for each five-year period. Figures for reviews are also the total number for each five-year interval. Percentages of review coverage of new and all fiction titles published were calculated for each interval.

Total fiction title output increased over the first three five-year intervals and then dropped back to slightly below the second (1969–1973) level. During the final five-year interval, more than twice as many fiction titles published were not new titles.

For *Booklist*, reviews of new fiction titles increased from 1,809 in the first five-year interval to 3,871 in the fourth. The percentage of all fiction titles reviewed varied from 11.87 in the 1964–1968 interval to a high of 17.59 in the

Table 8.   Total Fiction Reviews Compared with Total
New Fiction Title Output, in Five-Year Intervals

			Booklist			Library Journal		
Interval	Total Fiction Published	New Fiction Published	Total Reviews	% Total	% New	Total Reviews	% Total	% New
1964–1968	15,451	8,820	1,809	11.87	20.51	3,927	25.47	44.52
1969–1973	16,232	10,580	2,307	14.21	21.81	4,596	28.31	43.44
1974–1978	18,577	11,897	3,268	17.59	27.47	4,444	23.92	37.35
1979–1983	22,643	10,437	3,871	17.10	37.09	5,240	23.14	50.21

third (1974–1978) interval. The percentage of new titles reviewed rose consistently from 20.51 in the first period to 37.09 in the last.

For *Library Journal,* the total number of fiction reviews fluctuated somewhat: from 3,927 in the first five-year interval, to 4,596 in the second, dropping to 4,444 in the third, and increasing in the fourth to 5,240. The percentage of all fiction titles reviewed rose from 25.47 in the first interval to a high of 28.31 in the second and then decreased over each of the final two intervals, to a low of 23.14 in the fourth. *Library Journal* has lost ground in the percentage of total fiction titles reviewed. In percentage of new fiction titles reviewed, *Library Journal* has again fluctuated, dropping over the first three five-year intervals, from a percentage of 44.52 to a low of 37.35. In the fourth interval, however, *Library Journal* managed to review 50.21 percent of all new titles published.

Although *Booklist* has shown the greatest amount of growth in percentage of new titles reviewed, it has never equaled that of *Library Journal* in any of the four five-year intervals. Both, however, review considerably more new fiction than the 10 percent figure usually cited as the upper limit of titles reviewed annually.

Summary

Publishing industry statistics published in the *Bowker Annual* were used for total U.S. title output, total fiction output, total new fiction output, and overall number of reviews in each journal. Fiction reviews were counted for each journal.

Total U.S. title output almost doubled over the period studied—from 28,451 in 1964 to 53,350 in 1983. Fiction title production showed a steady increase in titles published—from over 3,000 to more than 5,400 a year. The percentage of fiction title output of total U.S. title output varied overall by less than 5 percent, averaging 9.62 percent over time.

New fiction title output showed a steady increase as well—from a low of

1,615 in 1965 to a high of 2,591 in 1973. The interval 1973–1979 saw the largest number of new titles published, with not fewer than 2,300 each year. Following 1979, publication of new titles declined over the remaining four years studied (1980–1984). If compilers of publishing industry statistics are correct that many mass market paperback fiction titles were undercounted prior to 1981, then the observed decline in titles published since then would be even more dramatic. Even so, new title publication dropped to below 2,000 for 1980 and 1981 and then began a slow upward climb to just over 2,000 in 1982 and more than 2,200 in 1983.

Review coverage of total U.S. title output has increased in *Booklist* from fewer than 3,500 to more than 6,000 over time. Over the same twenty-year period, reviews in *Library Journal* decreased from more than 6,000 to fewer than 5,000. Coverage in *Booklist* has varied from 8.5 percent to 15.87 percent of total U.S. title output, and that for *Library Journal* has varied from 9 percent to 32.56 percent. *Booklist* fell below 10 percent coverage of total output in six of the twenty years, while *Library Journal* reviewed less than 10 percent only in the final year studied.

Library Journal increased coverage of total adult title output from between 60–70 percent to 100 percent after *School Library Journal* became a separate publication in 1974. Review coverage of adult titles in *Booklist* decreased from about 75 percent to just over half.

When data are divided into five-year intervals for comparison, total fiction reviews in *Booklist* show a steady increase in each interval over time. The percentage of total fiction output reviewed increased from just under 12 percent to more than 17 percent. The percentage of new fiction titles reviewed in *Booklist* increased consistently in each of the four intervals, to a high of 37.09 percent in the fourth.

Total fiction title output reviewed in *Library Journal* also increased over time. The percentage of total output covered by reviews increased from the first to the second interval and then dropped slightly over the third and fourth. The percentage of new fiction reviewed decreased from the first to the third interval and then increased to a new high level of more than 50 percent in the fourth.

Although the percentage of fiction titles reviewed in *Library Journal* was somewhat erratic, it nevertheless outperformed *Booklist* in percentage of new fiction titles reviewed over the twenty-year period. In the first five-year interval, *Library Journal* reviewed 24.01 percent more than *Booklist*. In the second, it reviewed 21.63 percent more new fiction. In the third interval, at the point of lowest coverage, *Library Journal* still reviewed 9.88 percent more new fiction titles. In the final interval, *Library Journal* reviewed 13.12 percent more fiction.

For the first interval, new fiction titles published accounted for 6.24 percent of all titles published. For the second interval, 8.95 percent of all titles were new fiction titles, and in the third interval, 5.78 percent of all new titles were fiction.

In the final interval, 4.41 percent of all titles were new fiction. The portion of new fiction titles reviewed in both journals varies, but neither varies in proportion to the number of new titles published. Therefore, the null hypothesis—that over time, the number of fiction reviews in *Library Journal* and *Booklist* has not varied proportionally to the number of new fiction titles published—is accepted.

Although neither journal has been able to review as many new fiction titles as librarians want and need, both have exceeded the 10 percent usually reported for maximum overall coverage of all titles. Indeed, as percentages for data in five-year intervals show, 11.87 percent coverage of new fiction titles for the first interval in *Booklist* is the lowest coverage provided. Across the four intervals, *Booklist*'s coverage has increased by 16.58 percent to a high of 37.09 percent. The record for *Library Journal* has been even better. The lowest amount of coverage of new fiction was in the third interval, with 37.35 percent reviewed. In the final interval, *Library Journal* reviewed 50.21 percent of all new fiction titles.

Trends identified over time indicate that *Booklist* has increased in comprehensive coverage of U.S. title output, fiction and nonfiction. This is particularly evident during the second decade studied. *Library Journal,* on the other hand, has become less general in its coverage, dropping juvenile and young adult reviews altogether with the departure of *School Library Journal* in 1974.

Clearly *Library Journal* emphasizes fiction reviews to a greater extent than does *Booklist.* This is borne out by the fact that although the total number of reviews in *Library Journal* has decreased over time, the total number of reviews of new fiction has increased. Dependent on the quality and timeliness of reviews, *Library Journal* would seem to be the more important of the two in selection of new fiction titles for acquisition; however, *Booklist* has steadily increased the percentage of new fiction reviewed and may in future years reach parity with *Library Journal,* or even exceed it, if the trend identified here continues. It has closed the gap in coverage considerably over the twenty years studied and must also be considered an important source for reviews of new titles.

REVIEW CONTENT

- Hypothesis #2:   Content, or inclusion of specific information in reviews, has improved over time in *Library Journal* and *Booklist.*

For this study, *content of a review* was operationally defined as the degree to which a review included the following seven items of information, or criteria, that should be present in a fiction book review. These were based on a syntehsis of review criteria given in two standard works on collection development, Bonk and Magrill, *Building Library Collections,*[7] and Katz, *Collection Development: The Selection of Materials for Libraries:*[8]

1. Bibliographic data (author, title, publisher, month or date of publication, and cost).
2. Comment on the flow of the narrative (easy to follow, holds reader's attention, and so on).
3. Summary of plot.
4. Comparison (either with books of the same type or with the author's previous works).
5. Comment on strengths and weaknesses.
6. Recommendation (to buy or not to buy).
7. Credentials of reviewer (signature and job title). In the case of *Booklist*, reviews are unsigned, but the reputation of the journal will allow acceptance of reviewers as qualified.

It will be noted that the International Standard Book Number (ISBN) is omitted from the first criterion, bibliographic data. Although its use is now widespread and it is often used in ordering, the ISBN was not adopted for use in the United States until the late 1960s. It was not until the mid-1970s that ISBNs became a common feature of bibliographic data given in reviews, based on the samples collected for this study.

Content analysis was chosen as an appropriate method for studying review content. In an effort to make the study as objective as possible, the content analyzed was restricted to items that could be counted, thus avoiding a subjective evaluation of the quality of the reviews.

The population for each journal was identified as consisting of all fiction reviews appearing in the regular review section of each issue for the period of time studied (1964–1984). Reviews contained in articles, infrequently appearing columns, columns written by one reviewer, and bibliographic essays were omitted. Also excluded was the "Upfront" column begun in *Booklist* in 1980, since this was physically separated from the regular fiction review section.

All fiction reviews in the regular book review section were counted for each journal for each year. It was decided to draw from each population a sample of twenty-five reviews per year. A stratified systematic sample was drawn for each year. A sampling fraction was obtained by dividing the total number of reviews per year by twenty-five. A table of random numbers was then used to obtain the first review chosen from the first issue of each volume. Reviews of short story collections were omitted. The distance between chosen reviews was determined by the sampling fraction and varied according to the size of each yearly population. Content data were collected on a specially designed 3 x 5 form. (See the Appendix for all forms used.) After each sample had been scored for content, results were recorded on the "Analysis of Review Characteristics" form, which tabulated the presence of criteria successfully met by each review in each yearly sample. Using this form, it was easy to see patterns, strengths, and weaknesses of reviews for each journal. On this form, too, mean content scores were calculated. Each review was measured against the seven criteria and given a score. Scores could theoretically range from 0–7. A perfect score of 7 indicated inclusion of all items. While only one review in *Library Journal* received a score of 0, a score of 7 was obtained in eight cases (of 1,000): three in *Library Journal,* in 1965 and 1966, and five in *Booklist,* in 1977, 1978, 1982, and 1983.

Validity for this study was based on authority. Reliability for review content scoring was established by having two or more coders evaluate a single sample using the same method in order to be reasonably certain that results obtained would be the same. For reliability in content analysis, a correlation coefficient that is in the high range ($r = .9-1.00$) should be obtained, according to Berelson.[9]

In achieving reliability for this study, the procedure was refined several times. On the first try, the coder and the researcher achieved moderate success, but careful scrutiny revealed that whole the coders may have given a review the same overall score, several individual reviews were scored differently in regard to inclusion of criteria. The two items that gave no difficulty from the outset were the two most objective: "full bibliographic data," and "credentials of reviewer." The others were more subjective, and reliability required that they be made increasingly arbitrary. For instance, it became necessary to insist that in order to credit the review with a comparison, a specific title must have been named with which the present book was compared. The final version of instructions to coders was formulated in order to give directions to a class of collection development students who each evaluated two reviews. A copy of these instructions appears in the Appendix.

Since it was possible for coders to give the same score to a review for which different items were credited, it was decided that scores for each of the individual items would be used for reliability testing rather than just overall scores. The researcher and two other librarian-coders each coded the same sample using the instructions formulated for the students. Scattergrams showed close correlations in both cases. Pearson product-moment correlations were calculated. Coder 1 and the researcher achieved a high correlation ($r = .962$.) Coder 2 and the researcher also had a high correlation ($r = .970$.) It was concluded that the method developed for determining review content scores was reliable since both proved to be significant at $p = .05$.

Analysis of Data

Table 9 presents a summary of review content scores where all seven criteria are considered. Over the twenty-year period, *Booklist* performed better on inclusion of all criteria considered necessary for fiction reviews. Except for the initial three years of the study, *Booklist* consistently obtained higher review scores.

A review in *Booklist* is assumed to be recommended,and reviewers are assumed to be qualified. These assumptions are based on the book review policy of

Table 9. Rating 1: Review
Content Mean Scores Where
All Seven Variables Are
Considered

Year	Booklist $\bar{X}$	Library Journal $\bar{X}$
1964	4.20	4.64
1965	4.16	4.36
1966	4.28	4.84
1967	3.76	3.16
1968	3.72	3.24
1969	3.52	3.20
1970	3.80	2.60
1971	3.88	2.84
1972	3.92	2.56
1973	3.88	3.08
1974	4.36	3.04
1975	4.48	3.72
1976	4.32	3.52
1977	4.80	3.40
1978	4.72	3.32
1979	4.28	3.76
1980	4.60	3.96
1981	4.24	3.72
1982	5.40	3.80
1983	5.12	3.80

Note: Overall mean rating for each yearly
sample on a scale of 0–7, where 5
indicated inclusion of all criteria and
0 indicated none of criteria met.

the journal, which has appeared as a formal statement in the journal at various times over the years. The statement that all books appearing in the regular review columns are recommended appears in each issue. The same is not true of *Library Journal*. Although some articles have reported that reviewers for *Library Journal* are librarians, teaching faculty members, and occasionally professionals in other fields, no statement to that effect was found in issues of the journal used in this study.[10] Therefore the assumptions made for *Booklist* were not made for *Library Journal*, and the review received credit for this criterion only where the signed review indicated the job title or a master's degree in library science for the reviewer.

Since titles reviewed in *Booklist* are automatically recommended and reviewers are considered to be qualified, it was decided to compare the review scores omitting first the reviewer credentials (Rating 2) and then omitting both reviewer credentials and recommendations (Rating 3). Results are shown in Tables 10 and 11, respectively.

Mean content scores for Rating 2, which omits reviewer credentials, are somewhat mixed. Scores for both are close in some cases, and although *Library Journal* most often has the higher score, in seven years *Booklist* had higher scores.

In results of comparison of mean scores where both reviewer credentials and recommendation are omitted, Rating 3, clearer differences exist. *Library Journal* takes a definite lead, with only one year in which *Booklist* achieved a higher score.

In order to determine if the differences found between the two journals were statistically significant, t-tests were performed. The ABC statistical package was

Table 10. Rating 2:
Review Content Mean
Scores Where Reviewer
Credentials Variable Is
Omitted

Year	Booklist $\bar{X}$	Library Journal $\bar{X}$
1964	3.20	3.68
1965	3.16	3.40
1966	3.28	3.92
1967	2.76	3.16
1968	2.72	3.16
1969	2.52	3.16
1970	2.80	2.60
1971	2.88	2.76
1972	2.92	2.56
1973	2.88	3.08
1974	3.36	3.00
1975	3.48	3.60
1976	3.32	3.48
1977	3.80	3.40
1978	3.72	3.28
1979	3.28	3.76
1980	3.60	3.88
1981	3.32	3.68
1982	3.40	3.76
1983	4.12	3.76

Note: Mean rating for each yearly sample on a scale of 0–6.

Table 11. Rating 3:
Review Content Mean
Scores Where Both
Reviewer Credentials and
Recommendation Variables
Are Omitted

Year	Booklist $\bar{X}$	Library Journal $\bar{X}$
1964	2.20	3.08
1965	2.16	2.96
1966	2.28	3.44
1967	1.76	2.56
1968	1.72	2.56
1969	1.52	2.68
1970	1.80	2.12
1971	1.88	2.36
1972	1.92	2.40
1973	1.88	2.96
1974	2.36	2.84
1975	2.48	3.40
1976	2.32	3.44
1977	2.80	3.24
1978	2.72	3.16
1979	2.28	3.24
1980	2.60	3.52
1981	2.24	3.32
1982	3.40	3.32
1983	3.12	3.28

Note: Mean rating for each yearly sample
on a scale of 0–5.

used in performing two-tailed tests for significance. Results of t-tests for all three ratings are shown in Table 12.

Results of t-tests on Rating 1, where all seven items are included, indicate that differences are indeed significant at $p = .05$ in fifteen of twenty-five cases. These findings support *Booklist* as consistently superior over time to *Library Journal* in providing all seven items of information required of fiction reviews.

For Rating 2, where the reviewer credentials criterion was omitted, results were mixed. No statistically significant difference was found between the two journals at $p = .05$.

When both reviewer credentials and recommendations variables were omitted from consideration, it was possible to examine the record of each journal over

Table 12.   Book Review Content: t-Tests
for Significance Using Three Ratings

Year	Rating 1	Rating 2	Rating 3
1964	1.555	1.791	3.110*
1965	.645	.317	2.388*
1966	1.886	2.388*	4.099*
1967	−2.239*	1.581	3.162*
1968	−1.791	1.642	2.968*
1969	−1.077	2.155*	3.742*
1970	−3.582*	− .707	1.265
1971	−3.104*	− .404	1.791
1972	−4.223*	−1.423	1.897
1973	−2.694*	.746	3.816*
1974	−4.444*	−1.423	2.025*
1975	−2.836*	.474	3.433*
1976	−2.581*	.565	3.478*
1977	−4.516*	−1.688	1.739
1978	−3.694*	−1.313	1.366
1979	−2.055*	1.897	3.392*
1980	−2.065*	.989	3.251*
1981	−2.055*	1.857	3.816*
1982	−6.400*	−2.286	−2.666*
1983	−4.258*	−1.423	.632

Critical value of t at p = .05 with 48 df = ±2.021

Note: A negative t-value indicates that *Booklist* scored higher.
A positive t-value indicates that *Library Journal* scored
higher. Rating 1 is based on scores when all variables are
considered; Rating 2 is based on scores when "reviewer
credentials" variable is omitted; Rating 3 is based on
scores when both "reviewer credentials" and "recommendation" variables are omitted.
*Indicates t-values found to be statistically significant.

time with respect to the five remaining criteria: (1) provision of full bibliographic data, (2) flow of the narrative, (3) plot summary, (4) statement of comparison, and (5) strengths or weaknesses.

Clear differences were observed in mean content scores where only these five criteria are considered in Rating 3 (Table 11). Results of t-tests performed on Rating 3 are reported in Table 12. Differences were found to be statistically significant at p = .05. When only these five variables are considered, *Library Journal* now consistently scores higher than *Booklist* over the twenty-year period. It may be concluded that *Booklist* owes its higher overall score, where all variables are considered, to the two automatic assumptions that titles are recommended and that reviewers are qualified.

To compare further the two journals, it was useful to look at how consistently each journal included the five remaining variables when each was isolated for consideration.

Inclusion of Full Bibliographic Data

Content scores for inclusion of full bibliographic data are shown in Table 13. Over time, *Library Journal* more consistently provided complete bibliographic data. *Library Journal* averaged 50.4 percent inclusion of this information, whereas *Booklist* averaged 15.8 percent. Neither journal fulfilled this obligation for all twenty-five reviews in the sample for any year. There were two years for which *Library Journal* did not provide complete information for any of the sample reviews. There were five years for which *Booklist* failed to provide complete bibliographic information for any year's sample reviews. It should be noted, however, that *Booklist* did show improvement in the final two years studied.

Comment on the Flow of the Narrative

This variable refers to comments on whether the book is slow or easy to read, holds reader's attention, is interesting, dull, exciting, boring, and so on. Scores for inclusion of this information are recorded in Table 14. The two journals were fairly close in scores, although *Library Journal* did maintain a lead, with an average inclusion of 65 percent compared with 52.4 percent for *Booklist* over time. It may be concluded, therefore, that *Library Journal* did a somewhat better job of reporting on the flow of the narrative than did *Booklist*. During the first decade studied, *Booklist* did less well than *Library Journal* and less well than it

Table 13. Content Scores: Inclusion of Full Bibliographic Data

Year	Booklist	Library Journal	Year	Booklist	Library Journal
1964	4	10	1974	1	14
1965	1	15	1975	2	13
1966	3	24	1976	7	15
1967	1	0	1977	8	13
1968	1	0	1978	9	14
1969	1	4	1979	2	15
1970	0	6	1980	0	18
1971	0	6	1981	0	18
1972	0	8	1982	21	20
1973	1	17	1983	17	22

Average inclusion over time: *Booklist* = 15.8%, *Library Journal* = 50.4%
Total possible score for each journal/year = 25

Table 14.   Content Scores: Comment on Flow of the Narrative

Year	Booklist	Library Journal	Year	Booklist	Library Journal
1964	14	16	1974	14	13
1965	15	17	1975	11	23
1966	14	18	1976	11	22
1967	8	15	1977	16	16
1968	11	18	1978	14	18
1969	10	19	1979	12	14
1970	9	11	1980	18	19
1971	10	15	1981	16	14
1972	11	12	1982	22	16
1973	9	16	1983	17	13

Average inclusion over time: *Booklist* = 52.4%, *Library Journal* = 65%
Total possible score for each journal/year = 25

did in the second decade studied. While scores for *Library Journal* did not vary widely over time, *Booklist* showed improvement in the second decade. During the final three years, *Booklist* outscored *Library Journal*. If the trend continues, *Booklist* may soon overtake *Library Journal*.

Statement of Comparison

Both journals obtained consistently low scores for reporting comparison between the novel being reviewed and any other (Table 15). This probably reflects the necessity of including only those that named a specific title with which the

Table 15.   Content Scores: Statement of Comparison

Year	Booklist	Library Journal	Year	Booklist	Library Journal
1964	2	7	1974	5	3
1965	3	4	1975	10	2
1966	8	5	1976	6	1
1967	5	9	1977	6	4
1968	3	8	1978	6	2
1969	3	4	1979	5	6
1970	3	3	1980	4	4
1971	1	2	1981	0	4
1972	1	3	1982	1	5
1973	2	2	1983	5	6

Average inclusion over time: *Booklist* = 15.8%, *Library Journal* = 16.8%
Total possible score for each journal/year = 25

reviewed book was being compared. This strict application was necessary to achieve acceptable reliability between coders as previously discussed.

Summary of the Plot

In reporting plot summaries, *Booklist* led *Library Journal* with 85.6 percent inclusion over time, compared with 77.4 percent for *Library Journal* (Table 16). For seven years, *Booklist* reported this criterion in more than 90 percent of reviews. *Library Journal* reported plot summaries in more than 90 percent of reviews in only one year; however, both journals reported this information for at least 64 percent of all reviews in all years studied. In one year, 1980, both journals reported plot summaries in all sample reviews, and one other year, 1981, in which *Booklist* again reported this information for all reviews in the sample. Both journals show improvement when each decade is considered separately. For fifteen of twenty years, *Booklist* reported plot summaries in as many as twenty of twenty-five reviews. *Library Journal* reported as many as twenty of twenty-five possible plot summaries in only nine years, though all but one were in the second decade.

Comment on Strengths and Weaknesses

This variable refers to how well or how poorly done was the writing. Statements that qualified as satisfying this criterion were such comments as characterization that was solid or wooden, confusing or well written, and so on. *Library Journal* consistently outperformed *Booklist* in providing this information, with 89.8 percent average inclusion against 57.6 percent for *Booklist* (Table 17). In only one year did *Library Journal* fail to report strengths or weaknesses in fewer

Table 16.   Content Scores: Summary of the Plot

Year	Booklist	Library Journal	Year	Booklist	Library Journal
1964	21	21	1974	22	18
1965	16	16	1975	23	23
1966	23	16	1976	21	24
1967	17	18	1977	22	24
1968	18	17	1978	21	21
1969	18	17	1979	23	22
1970	20	14	1980	25	25
1971	23	14	1981	25	23
1972	23	17	1982	24	19
1973	21	18	1983	22	20

Average inclusion over time: *Booklist* = 85.6%, *Library Journal* = 77.4%
Total possible score for each journal/year = 25

Table 17.   Content Scores: Comment on
Strengths or Weaknesses

Year	Booklist	Library Journal	Year	Booklist	Library Journal
1964	14	23	1974	15	23
1965	19	21	1975	16	24
1966	9	23	1976	13	24
1967	13	22	1977	17	24
1968	10	21	1978	18	23
1969	8	23	1979	16	25
1970	13	19	1980	18	22
1971	13	22	1981	15	24
1972	13	20	1982	17	23
1973	14	21	1983	17	22

Average inclusion over time: *Booklist* = 57.6%, *Library Journal* = 89.8%
Total possible score for each journal/year = 25

than twenty of twenty-five reviews. Reviews in *Booklist* included this information in fewer than twenty of twenty-five reviews for all years. Indeed, in only 1965 did *Booklist* give strengths or weaknesses in as many as nineteen reviews out of twenty-five.

Analysis of the Three Most Important Criteria for Selection Decisions

A summary of the plot is one of the most important items for the librarian dependent on reviews for selection of fiction. Both journals have improved over time in provision of these, although *Booklist* has done a slightly better job overall.

In addition to plot summary, the provision of strengths and/or weaknesses and comments on the flow of the narrative are important to selection decisions. Although *Library Journal* has done a better job in providing these other items over time, both journals have improved.

It was thought that it would be useful to know which journal reports most frequently all three variables in individual reviews or at least two of the three. Table 18 provides this comparison for each journal for each year. Scores given are actual raw scores. For ease of comparison, Table 19 collapses the same data into five-year intervals and lists average percentage of inclusion for these combinations of variables.

As indicated in Table 19, provision of all three variables in the same review has improved for *Booklist* from 16.8 percent in the first interval to 38.4 percent in the four interval. At the same time, *Booklist* has steadily improved in provision of plot summaries—from 76 percent in 1964–1968 to 95.2 percent in the

Table 18.   Reviews Containing Plot Summaries, Strengths/Weaknesses, and Flow of Narrative

	Booklist			Library Journal		
Year	Plot Summary	All Three	Two of Three	Plot Summary	All Three	Two of Three
1964	21	6	13	21	12	8
1965	16	8	3	16	10	5
1966	23	4	11	16	8	1
1967	17	1	11	18	8	3
1968	18	2	9	17	9	7
1969	18	3	7	17	14	3
1970	20	5	8	14	4	6
1971	23	3	14	14	8	6
1972	23	7	8	17	5	11
1973	21	3	12	18	10	4
1974	22	5	12	18	8	8
1975	23	8	10	23	20	3
1976	21	4	6	24	21	2
1977	22	8	13	24	14	10
1978	21	10	7	21	16	5
1979	23	5	15	22	13	9
1980	25	14	8	25	16	8
1981	25	7	17	23	13	9
1982	24	14	5	19	13	4
1983	22	8	12	20	8	11

Table 19.   Content Scores for Reviews Containing Plot Summaries, Strengths/Weaknesses, and Flow of Narrative, and Two of the Three Variables, in Five-Year Intervals

	Booklist			Library Journal		
Interval	Plot Summary (%)	All Three (%)	Two of Three (%)	Plot Summary (%)	All Three (%)	Two of Three (%)
1964–1968	76.0	16.8	37.6	70.4	37.6	19.2
1969–1973	84.0	16.8	39.2	64.0	32.8	24.0
1974–1978	87.2	28.0	38.4	88.0	63.2	22.4
1979–1983	95.2	38.4	45.6	87.2	50.4	32.8

fourth interval. Where *Booklist* has not provided all three in the same review, it has improved in inclusion of two of the three—from 37.6 percent to 45.6 percent in the final interval.

Library Journal has improved also in provision of all three items of information. The percentage of *Library Journal* reviews providing all three has improved from 37.6 in the first interval, to 50.4 in the fourth, after having attained 63.2 in the third. While *Booklist* may have provided more plot summaries, *Library Journal* has more consistently provided all three criteria in the same review based on the data in Table 19.

Summary and Conclusions

Review content was operationally defined as a review that included seven items of information, or criteria, that should be present in a fiction book review. Content analysis was chosen as an appropriate method of studying review content.

The population was confined to fiction book reviews appearing in the regular review section of each journal. These were counted for each journal for each year of the study, 1964–1984. A stratified systematic sample of twenty-five reviews per year was drawn. A random start for each volume was used.

Each review chosen was measured against the seven criteria and scored on a scale of 0–7, indicating the number of criteria met by the review. A score of 7 indicated a perfect score.

Validity was based on the authority of two standard collection development texts. These were used to determine which criteria to study. Reliability was obtained by having coders evaluate the same sample. The process was refined over several tests. Finally acceptably high Pearson product-moment correlations were obtained.

Where inclusion of all seven criteria was considered, *Booklist* performed better over time than did *Library Journal*. Differences were found to be statistically significant using two-tailed tests for significance.

Since recommendation of all titles reviewed and qualifications of reviewers were assumed for *Booklist* but not for *Library Journal*, two additional ratings were conducted. Where only the reviewer credentials varible was omitted, results were mixed and not statistically significant. However, when both the reviewer credentials and recommendation variables were omitted, *Library Journal* outperformed *Booklist* in providing the remaining five variables. These differences were found to be statistically significant.

The other five criteria were studied separately. Over time, *Library Journal* more consistently provided complete bibliographic data. Scores for the two journals reporting on the flow of the narrative were close, though *Library Journal* led by a small margin. Both journals obtained low scores for inclusion of statements of comparison, probably because of the narrow definition that had to be adopted in order to obtain reliability. *Booklist* outscored *Library Journal* on provision of plot summaries over time, though both journals showed improvement. *Library Journal* consistently outperformed *Booklist* in providing comments on strengths and/or weaknesses, though here again both journals showed improvement in the second decade studied.

An analysis of three important criteria for fiction selection was undertaken: plot summary, flow of the narrative, and comments on strengths or weaknesses. Data were collapsed into five-year intervals, and mean scores were calculated. Although *Booklist* has provided plot summaries better, *Library Journal* has provided the combination of the three criteria felt to be important to selection decisions better.

The hypothesis that review content has improved over time for both journals was accepted based on the findings in this study. Although both journals have improved over time, *Library Journal* was found to be somewhat better overall. It must be remembered, however, that no attempt was made to judge the quality of reviews in either journal except for items that should be included. What reviewers had to say about specific titles or their accuracy in reviewing played no part in this study.

REVIEW PROMPTNESS

- Hypothesis #3:   The promptness of reviews, relative to book publication date, in *Library Journal* and *Booklist* has improved over time.

In this study, *promptness of a review* was operationally defined as the publication date of the review in a journal relative to the publication date of the book reviewed. The appearance of a review in a journal was considered to be the review publication date. The appearance of a book title in an issue of the *Weekly Record* was taken to be the book publication date. The use of the *Weekly Record* to verify book publication date follows the method used by Busha.[11] Although it is a secondary source, it was felt to be the best for determining actual book publication to the nearest week.

The "Yearly Individual Review Score Sheet" (see Appendix) was used to record book title, review publication date, and book publication date. The purpose of this form was to provide a comparison of review and book publication dates in order to determine promptness. The "Analysis of Review Promptness," form (see Appendix) was used to record dates of book reviews and expected publication dates where this information was given in the review. It also allowed for coding of review promptness in days before or after the appearance of the title in an issue of the *Weekly Record*. Promptness data could result in positive scores denoting that the review was published prior to book publication, expressed in number of days. Negative scores would indicate that the book was published before the review appeared in the journal.

The use of the *Weekly Record* to verify book publication dates proved less than satisfactory before this portion of the study was complete. There were two particular problems associated with its use. The more difficult one concerned the lack of availability of complete holdings of back issues.

The resources of five libraries were used in attempting to locate publication dates for all titles: the libraries of North Texas State University, Texas Woman's University, and the University of Dallas and two public libraries, the Irving Public Library and the Fort Worth Public Library. The Dallas Public Library did not have back issues. All five libraries maintained back issues of *Publishers Weekly,* so as long as the *Weekly Record* was part of that publication, there was no problem. However, when the *Weekly Record* became a separate publication in September 1974, complete holdings became more difficult to locate.

During the course of data gathering, both the University of Dallas and North Texas State University withdrew all but recent issues. Since the Irving Public Library had no holdings of this publication and Texas Woman's University had only the first few bound volumes, it was a great loss when the two academic libraries withdrew their back issues. In addition to its unavailability in paper copy, this publication is also unavailable in microform.

Unfortunately, holdings at the Fort Worth Public Library were not complete. Those holdings that were available were not bound; issues and even large parts of several years had been lost. Therefore it was not possible to find enough book publication dates to make valid comparisons during the last half of the time period covered by the study.

When as many as nineteen of twenty-five book publication dates could be found, these years were included in the analysis. Mean review promptness scores, in number of days before or after the appearance of the book review, were calculated for 1964 through 1974, 1976, and 1982. Results are shown in Tables 20 and 21.

Wide variation was found in both journals in regard to review promptness. As shown in mean scores, *Library Journal* more consistently provided reviews prior to book publication in all but two years. The opposite was true for *Booklist*, which had positive mean scores in only two years. Most of the reviews in *Library Journal* appeared at least one month before the book was published. Most *Booklist* reviews appeared about two weeks after book publication.

The second difficulty encountered in trying to verify book publication dates relates directly to the first, the problem of access. Since there was frequently great disparity between review and book publication dates, it was difficult to be certain that the title, when found in the *Weekly Record,* was indeed the first edition, not a reissue or a new edition. In those cases where publication date varied widely, an attempt was made to verify the earliest publication date using OCLC database. A study reported in 1981 by Elizabeth Groot found the OCLC database to be quite effective as a verification tool after the year the book was

Table 20. *Booklist* Review Promptness in Days from Book Publication

Year	Publication Dates Found	Maximum Days before Book Publication	Maximum Days after Book Publication	Mean	Standard Deviation
1964	25	57	−153	−29.3	42.8
1965	23	238	−112	−13.7	69.6
1966	22	220	− 79	−16.3	61.6
1967	24	47	− 93	−40.7	32.9
1968	24	263	−109	− 9.7	86.6
1969	24	440	−144	−13.3	108.4
1970	23	269	−119	−12.9	78.9
1971	22	118	−122	−28.1	46.4
1972	22	208	−192	−20.9	76.4
1973	23	57	−153	−21.5	49.1
1974	24	244	− 82	9.1	72.6
1976	23	247	−142	− 9.5	76.5
1982	20	181	−160	12.5	79.9

imprinted.[12] It proved to be helpful in this study as well. It was at least possible to check some of the promptness scores, which at first seemed too far before or too far after the review appeared.

Although both journals had higher scores for the last year considered, 1982, the absence of data for other years in the latter part of the study made it impossible to determine improvement overall in review promptness for either journal.

Table 21. *Library Journal* Review Promptness in Days from Book Publication

Year	Publication Dates Found	Maximum Days before Book Publication	Maximum Days after Book Publication	Mean	Standard Deviation
1964	24	52	−113	− 3.6	39.6
1965	22	70	− 63	− 2.2	28.6
1966	24	227	− 17	47.3	55.5
1967	21	110	− 18	40.4	35.9
1968	24	203	− 63	47.3	56.5
1969	21	191	−218	43.4	91.9
1970	21	185	− 27	47.8	52.9
1971	20	154	− 21	46.8	41.5
1972	19	254	− 61	73.9	78.2
1973	21	253	− 59	62.5	80.1
1974	22	182	− 85	33.4	70.6
1976	22	209	− 76	19.5	64.8
1982	19	237	− 51	61.9	87.1

Therefore it was not possible to accept or reject the hypothesis that improvement has occurred.

An attempt was made to analyze the usefulness of expected book publication dates as reported in book reviews. *Library Journal* reported expected book publication dates for a much larger number of reviews than did *Booklist* over time. However, these proved not to be accurate predictors of actual book publication dates. These data are given in Tables 22 and 23.

For *Library Journal,* in all but two years, there were more expected publication dates that proved to be either late or early when compared to actual book publication dates. For *Booklist* also, most expected publication dates proved to be wrong.

The problems associated with setting and keeping expected book publication dates were addressed in a 1981 article in *Publishers Weekly* by Robert Dahlin.[13] Dahlin observed that not only are publication dates changed because of publishing problems but may also be changed to accommodate desires of authors, when the publicity department believes that an earlier or later date would be more beneficial, when a book is chosen by a book club, and for other reasons as well.

Table 22. Analysis of Accuracy of Expected Book Publication Dates Given in *Booklist*

Year	Publication in Expected Month	Books Published Early	Books Published Late	Reviews Giving Publication Date	Titles Not Found
1964	3	0	1	4	0
1965	1	0	0	1	0
1966	1	0	2	3	0
1967	1	0	0	1	0
1968	0	0	0	1	1
1969	0	0	0	0	0
1970	0	0	0	0	0
1971	0	0	0	0	0
1972	0	0	0	0	0
1973	0	0	0	1	1
1974	0	0	1	1	0
1975	0	0	1	2	1
1976	2	3	2	7	0
1977	4	2	1	8	1
1978	3	0	1	9	5
1979	1	1	0	2	0
1980	0	0	0	0	0
1981	0	0	0	0	0
1982	4	3	9	21	5
1983	3	3	6	16	4

Table 23.   Analysis of Accuracy of Expected Book
Publication Dates Given in *Library Journal*

Year	Publication in Expected Month	Books Published Early	Books Published Late	Reviews Giving Publication Date	Titles Not Found
1964	7	0	3	10	0
1965	6	0	7	15	2
1966	10	0	13	24	1
1967	0	0	0	0	0
1968	0	0	0	0	0
1969	0	0	3	4	1
1970	2	0	2	6	1
1971	1	1	2	6	2
1972	0	0	5	8	3
1973	1	2	9	16	4
1974	1	2	10	14	1
1975	5	5	3	13	0
1976	6	2	4	14	2
1977	3	4	5	13	1
1978	3	1	9	15	2
1979	4	1	4	16	7
1980	6	4	4	18	4
1981	5	1	10	18	2
1982	7	3	6	20	4
1983	6	4	9	22	3

It must be concluded that confidence may not be placed firmly in a stated book publication date. It may serve as a guide only. Results obtained with the limited data available make it impossible to identify trends over time accurately. From the limited data available, however, it appears that although expected publication dates are often inaccurate, more books come out when expected, or later, than those that are published earlier. This should be a positive finding from the librarian's point of view since it provides a better chance of acquiring needed titles before demand is high.

Summary and Conclusions

In this portion of the study, an attempt was made to determine the timeliness, or promptness, of journal reviews relative to book publication dates. The appearance of a review in a journal was defined as the review publication date. The appearance of the title in an issue of the *Weekly Record* was defined as the book publication date. When a title was found, it was given a promptness score based on the number of days between review date and book publication date.

The use of the *Weekly Record* as the source for book publication dates proved to be unsatisfactory in the long run. Data collection moved along smoothly for the first decade of the study, from 1964 until 1974, as long as the *Weekly Record* was contained in *Publishers Weekly*. When it became a separate publication in September 1974, many libraries apparently made the decision not to keep and bind issues since it is cumulated monthly in the *American Book Publishing Record*. Several academic and public libraries were found to have some of the back issues, and these were used for data collection. During the data collection phase, however, two academic libraries withdrew all back issues, leaving only one library in the area with holdings. Unfortunately, these had been kept as loose copies, and holdings were not complete, since some had apparently been lost over the years. This publication is unavailable in microform as well.

Because of the difficulties in gathering needed data, it was not possible to determine trends in review promptness beyond the first decade of the study. Therefore it was not possible to accept or reject the hypothesis that review promptness has improved over time. However, for data that were available, it was noted that mean promptness scores for *Library Journal* were usually positive, indicating that reviews appeared before the book was published, and scores for *Booklist* were usually negative.

Data that were obtained tend to confirm Merritt's (1948) findings and those of Busha (1964–1965) and Ream (1979). All three found *Library Journal* had timelier reviews.[14] It would appear, then, that little has changed in terms of review promptness since Merritt's 1948 study.

An attempt was made to analyze the usefulness of expected book publication dates as given in reviews. Based on available data, these proved to be unreliable predictors of actual book publication dates. However, it was also noted that books more often came out on time, or late, than early. This should tend to work in the librarian's favor, allowing acquisition opportunity before the books are in demand, subject to ordering cycles and other acquisition procedures of individual libraries.

DISCUSSION, SUMMARY, AND CONCLUSION

Summary

It is well documented and generally agreed that book reviews are the primary selection tool of librarians. Fiction librarians, charged with meeting the recreational reading needs of their patrons, must have reviews of new titles as early as possible if they are to have desired titles on hand as soon as they are wanted.

Previous book review studies have found that *Library Journal* and *Booklist* are the two best and most used review sources overall. Therefore it was decided to evaluate these journals, over time, in regard to review coverage of new fiction titles, content, and promptness of reviews. Three hypotheses were formulated to reflect these objectives.

It was hypothesized that, over time, the number of reviews in *Library Journal* and *Booklist* would not vary proportionally with the number of new fiction titles published yearly. In order to test this hypothesis, publishing industry statistics appearing in the *Bowker Annual, 1965–1985*, were used for yearly total U.S. title output, total fiction output, total new fiction output, and the overall number of reviews appearing in each journal. Fiction reviews for each were counted.

Total U.S. title output almost doubled over the twenty years studied, from 28,451 in 1964 to 53,350 in 1983. Fiction title production steadily increased from over 3,000 to more than 5,400 per year. The percentage of fiction title output averaged 9.62 percent over time and varied overall by less than 5 percent.

New fiction title output increased as well, from a low of 1,615 in 1965 to a high of 2,591 in 1973. The 1973–1979 interval saw the largest number of new titles published, with not fewer than 2,300 each year. Following 1979, publication of new fiction titles declined over the final four years studied.

Review coverage of total U.S. title output increased in *Booklist* from fewer than 3,500 to more than 6,000 over time. The number of reviews in *Library Journal* decreased from more than 6,000 to fewer than 5,000.

Library Journal increased its coverage of adult titles from between 60 and 70 percent to 100 percent after *School Library Journal* became a separate publication in 1974. *Booklist* decreased its coverage of adult titles from about 75 percent to less than 54 percent. The percentages of fiction and new fiction titles reviewed increased for both journals.

Library Journal consistently exceeded the 10 percent often reported for maximum overall review coverage of titles published each year. The only exception to this came in the final year of the study, when only 9 percent of total U.S. title output was reviewed. *Booklist* exceeded 10 percent coverage in fourteen of twenty years and did not fall below 10 percent in any of the final nine years. Both have consistently reviewed more than 10 percent of all new fiction titles published. *Library Journal* has consistently reviewed more new titles than *Booklist* over time.

Although totals for publication of new fiction titles and for reviews of these have changed in the same direction (both increased), the number of reviews in each journal did not vary in proportion to the number of new fiction titles published. Therefore the null hypothesis was accepted.

Review trends identified over time indicate that *Booklist* has increased in comprehensive coverage of all U.S. title output. *Library Journal* has become less general in its converage. It now reviews only adult titles and emphasizes fiction to a greater extent than does *Booklist*. The latter is evident by the fact that although the total number of reviews in *Library Journal* has decreased over time, the total number of fiction reviews has increased. In addition, *Library Journal* has consistently reviewed more fiction titles than has *Booklist*.

Library Journal would seem to be the more important of the two to the librarian who selects fiction. It should be noted, though, that *Booklist* has steadily increased the percentage of new fiction reviewed and appears to be closing the gap between the journals. If the trend continues, *Booklist* may well reach parity with *Library Journal* in the near future.

The content of reviews was also considered important to librarians who select fiction. Seven items of information, or criteria, were synthesized from two standard works on collection development. These seven items should be present in every fiction review: (1) full bibliographic data, (2) a comment on the flow of the narrative, (3) plot summary, (4) a statement of comparison, (5) a comment on strengths and/or weaknesses, (6) recommendation to buy or not to buy, and (7) reviewer credentials. The hypothesis was made that content of reviews in *Library Journal* and *Booklist* has improved over time. It was decided to evaluate reviews by comparing them with the seven criteria.

Content analysis was chosen as an appropriate method for testing the hypothesis. There was no attempt to evaluate the quality or accuracy of reviews or reviewers, except in the provision of information required to satisfy the seven criteria.

The population was confined to reviews appearing in the regular fiction review section in each issue of each journal. These were counted to obtain the size of the population. A stratified systematic sample of twenty-five reviews per year was drawn. A random start for each volume was used.

Each review was measured against the seven criteria. Each was given a score of 0–7 based on the number of criteria met by the review.

Validity for the study was based on authority. Reliability was established through a process of refining instructions to coders and then testing for reliability using Pearson product-moment correlations.

Where inclusion of all seven criteria was considered, *Booklist* maintained higher scores over time than did *Library Journal*. The ABC statistical package was used in the evaluation. Differences were found to be statistically significant using two-tailed tests for significance.

Based on published policy statements, all titles appearing in the regular review sections of *Booklist* were automatically assumed to be recommended and all reviewers qualified. These assumptions were not made for *Library Journal* since no published policy was found. Therefore the decision was made to compare the journals on the remaining criteria. Two additional ratings were performed.

When the reviewer credentials variable was omitted, results were mixed. Differences between the journals were found not to be statistically significant. With the omission of the reviewer credentials and recommendation variables, clear differences existed that were found to be significant. In this case, *Library Journal* outscored *Booklist* on the remaining five variables as a whole.

To evaluate the journals further, inclusion of each of the other five variables was considered separately. Over time, *Library Journal* more consistently provided complete bibliographic data, comments on the flow of the narrative, and comments on strengths and weaknesses. *Booklist* outscored *Library Journal* on provision of plot summaries. Scores for both journals were low for provision of statements of comparison, probably because of the narrow definition adopted to achieve reliability.

Further analysis was undertaken to see how well each journal supplied three criteria important to selection decisions, in combination, in each review: provision of plot summaries, comments on flow of narrative, and comments on strenghts and weaknesses. Data were collapsed into five-year intervals, and percentages of inclusion were calculated. Although *Booklist* better provided plot summaries, *Library Journal* better provided the combination of criteria.

Based on the findings in this study, the hypothesis that review content has improved over time was accepted. Although each has shown improvement, *Library Journal* was found to be somewhat better overall.

The third element of this study was review promptness relative to book publication date. It was hypothesized that promptness of reviews in *Library Journal* and *Booklist* has improved over time. The appearance of a review in a journal was defined as the review publication date. The appearance of the title in an issue of the *Weekly Record* was defined as the book publication date.

Review promptness was scored in days before or after book publication date. Promptness data resulted in positive scores indicating that the review was published prior to book publication or negative scores having the opposite meaning.

Use of the *Weekly Record* to define book publication date became a considerable problem after it became a separate publication in 1974. Because of difficulties in obtaining needed data, it was not possible to identify trends over the twenty-year period. Neither was it possible to accept or reject the hypothesis that promptness had improved over time.

For those data that were available, it was noted that mean promptness scores for *Library Journal* were usually positive, indicating that reviews appeared before book publication, while those for *Booklist* were usually negative. This tends to confirm findings of Merritt (1948), Busha (1964–1965), and Ream (1979). All found that *Library Journal* reviews appeared more promptly than those in *Booklist*.

One additional feature was studied. An attempt was made to analyze the usefulness of expected book publication dates as given in reviews. Based on available data, these proved to be unreliable predictors of actual book publication dates. It was also noted, however, that books came out more often late or on time than early. This offers an advantage to the librarian. Subject to order cycles and other acquisition procedures, the librarian has a better chance of acquiring titles before they are in demand.

Limitations of the Study

An obvious limitation to this study is the reliance on secondary sources such as the *Bowker Annual* or the *Weekly Record* for publishing data. Each could contain errors.

The use of the *Weekly Record* to supply book publication date became another limitation when later holdings proved to be unavailable. This, in turn, led to insufficient data to complete the third part of the study adequately. Any findings derived from incomplete data must be cautiously examined.

Reviews used to determine the population of fiction reviews to be sampled were limited by the operational definition. This excluded a number of reviews that did not appear in the regular review section on a regular basis.

Review content evaluated was limited to the presence or absence of certain criteria. No attempt was made to assess any other type of quality in the reviews. It is not possible to state that reviews in one journal are more accurate than the other.

The entire study is limited to observing and reporting trends over time. The structure of the study does not permit prediction beyond the confines of the years studied. Though strong observed strends may point to future developments, there is no basis on which to predict this accurately. Such a case is the one in which *Booklist* has steadily increased the number and percentage of new fiction titles reviewed. It may be surmised that if the trend continues, *Booklist* will catch up with or overtake *Library Journal*, but there is no other basis for prediction.

Conclusions and Recommendations

While total U.S. title output nearly doubled between 1964 and 1984, fiction averaged 9.62 percent and varied by less than 5 percent. New fiction title output increased in number over time, peaking between 1973 and 1980. Since that time, new fiction title production has remained at lower levels, although overall fiction title production has continued to grow. From 1980 through 1983, new editions and reprints accounted for a much greater share of fiction title production than at any other time during the period studied.

Priorities in review coverage have changed over time for both journals. Fiction reviewing, however, has received increasingly greater emphasis by both.

Booklist has increased coverage of total title output, indicating a move toward more comprehensive coverage. While decreasing the volume of coverage of all adults titles, it has nevertheless increased its fiction coverage. *Booklist* presented a strong challenge to *Library Journal* in this area but at the end of the twenty years had not yet reached parity.

In contrast, overall review coverage in *Library Journal* has decreased steadily over the entire period, it now devotes much less space to reviews. The allocation of available remaining space has changed as well. Its coverage of adult title reviewing moved upward consistently until, after *School Library Journal* became a separate publication in 1974, it has reviewed adult titles exclusively. While *Library Journal* has appeared to downplay its function as a review journal, it has increased the volume of fiction titles reviewed.

Reviews of new fiction titles did increase in each journal, but the number of titles reviewed did not vary in proportion to the number of new fiction titles published yearly. Therefore the null hypothesis that stated that they would not vary in proportion was accepted.

The study of review content revealed that *Booklist* owed its higher scores when all criteria were considered to the two automatic assumptions that reviewers were qualified and that all titles in the review section were recommended. Otherwise, *Library Journal* obtained the superior scores. *Library Journal* reviewed not only more titles but also provided more of the information needed for selection decisions.

Both journals did improve in provision of the seven types of information required of fiction reviews over the twenty years studied. Therefore the hypothesis that this would be the case was accepted.

Although data for review promptness were incomplete, from those that were available, thirteen of twenty years, *Library Journal* appeared to do a better job of providing early reviews. This tends to confirm findings of earlier studies. It was not possible to accept or reject the hypothesis that both journals had improved in promptness since data were incomplete.

Based on the evidence of this study, it is concluded that *Library Journal* has done a better overall job of reviewing new fiction. However, *Booklist* has also improved and now does a better job than it did in the 1960s. It may be that *Booklist* has been hampered over time in matching the quantity of reviews that *Library Journal* has provided because it has been dependent on a staff of professional reviewers that is a smaller group than the volunteers who review for *Library Journal*.

It is difficult to understand why *Library Journal*'s volunteers better provided the information necessary to satisfy the criteria needed for fiction reviews. It would seem that professional reviewers should provide this as well as, or better than, volunteers. Possibly these reviewers have tended to make some assumptions of their own. Some may have assumed that because the reviewed titles were recommended, their audience would assume that the flow of the narrative and any weaknesses would be within acceptable limits as well. If reviews were indeed looked at in this light, reviewers might feel little need to comment except in unusual cases. If *Booklist*'s reviewers have made these assumptions, it would be unfortunate, since readers might not always make the same assumptions.

There is still much that we do not know about the type and quality of coverage of new titles. Short-term studies using the methodology of this study would provide a basis for comparison between the two journals studied here and other commonly used review media. It is precisely because we are so dependent on reviews that we should constantly monitor the providers of these. We must insist on high-quality reviews.

The perennial problem of amount of coverage still exists. As Busha stated in his 1968 article, "Something must be done quickly to greatly increase review coverage."[15] The need is still with us.

Although title overlap studied have been done in various contexts, it would be useful to know how much overlap in coverage there is in reviews. While it *is* helpful to have a title reviewed in several sources, each occurrence may limit the number of titles reviewed. If we had a clearer understanding of the impact of multiple reviews for the same title, we could begin to assess more accurately the magnitude of the problem of unreviewed books.

We need to know which subject areas receive most and least coverage. As this study of fiction reviews has shown, many more titles in this category are reviewed than the 10 percent usually estimated as maximum review coverage of all yearly title output. *Booklist* and *Library Journal* emphasize fiction reviewing. What other reviewing strengths does each have? What do other review media emphasize? What factors influence review media to give greater emphasis to one subject area than another? Do the perceptions of these media accurately represent the needs of librarians?

It would also be useful to know the degree of domination of review columns by large publishers. What percentage of titles published by small and university presses is given review space? How are these decisions made? Even fiction is published by some of these presses. How many get reviewed? By whom?

NOTES

1.   Sandra K. Paul and Carol A. Neymeyer, "Book Marketing and Selection: Selected Findings from the Current AAP/ALA Study," *Publishers Weekly* 207 (June 16, 1975): 42–43.

2.   Hendrik Edelman and Karen Muller, "A New Look at the Library Market," *Publishers Weekly* 231 (May 29, 1987): 30, 32.

3.   LeRoy C. Merritt, Martha Boaz, and Kenneth S. Tisdell, *Reviews in Library Book Selection* (Detroit: Wayne State University Press, 1958), p. 33.

4.   Charles H. Busha, "Book Selection in Public Libraries: An Evaluation of Four Commonly-Used Review Media," *Southeastern Librarian* (Summer 1968): 97.

5.   Daniel Ream, "An Evaluation of Four Book Review Journals," *RQ* 19 (Winter 1979): 152.

6.   John Anthony McCrossan, "Library Science Education and Its Relationship to Competence in Adult Book Selection in Public Libraries" (Ph.D. diss., University of Illinois, 1966), p. 72.

7.   Wallace John Bonk and Rose Mary Magrill, *Building Library Collections*, 5th ed. (Metuchen, N.J.: Scarecrow, 1979), pp. 87–90, 105–106.

8.   William A. Katz, *Collection Development: The Selection of Materials for Libraries* (New York: Holt, Rinehart and Winston, 1980), pp. 127–128.

9.   Bernard Berelson, *Content Analysis in Communication Research* (Glencoe, Ill.: Free Press, 1952), p. 172.

10.   Beth Macleod, "*Library Journal* and *Choice*: A Review of Reviews," *Journal of Academic Librarianship* 7 (March 1981): 24.

11.   Busha, "Book Selection," p. 93.

12.   Elizabeth H. Groot, "A Comparison of Library Tools for Monograph Verification," *Library Resources and Technical Services* 25 (April–June 1981): 160.

13. Robert Dahlin, "Do Pub Dates Mean *Anything* Any More?" *Publishers Weekly* 220 (September 25, 1981): 24–28.

14. Merritt, Boaz, and Tisdell, *Reviews,* p. 33; Busha, "Book Selection," pp. 95–96; Ream, "An Evaluation," p. 150.

15. Busha, "Book Selection," p. 100.

APPENDIX: FORMS USED IN DATA COLLECTION

Instructions to Coder

A fiction book review should provide information in the seven categories listed below. Read the description of content for each category, then evaluate each review. If you feel that the reviewer has provided you with the necessary information as described for a category, place a check in the "YES" column beside that category. If not, or if you are not sure, mark the "NO" column. To give the review a score, total the checks in the "YES" column.

1. *BIBLIOGRAPHIC DATA:*
   To check "yes" the review must have Author, Title, Publisher, Month of Publication, and Cost of the Book.
2. *COMMENT ON FLOW OF THE NARRATIVE:*
   The reviewer should tell you if the story is interesting, dull, exciting, boring, etc.
3. *SUMMARY OF THE PLOT:*
   Has the reviewer told you what happens in the story?
4. *COMPARISON WITH OTHER BOOKS:*
   Is the title of another book mentioned? If so, does the reviewer compare the two?
5. *COMMENT ON STRENGTHS OR WEAKNESSES:*
   How well or how poorly done was the writing? Such comments might be "solid characterization," "wooden characters," "well written," "confusing," etc.
6. *RECOMMENDATION:*
   To check "yes" the reviewer must say "recommended," "for" any type of library or group of people, "not for" libraries, "buy" or "don't buy."
7. *CREDENTIALS OF REVIEWER:*
   Reviewer must give name and job title. It is not enough to mention the place where he/she works.

Form to be used for the
collection of content
review data.

YEAR	REVIEW CONTENT SCORE CARD Journal: _____Month & Day			
Rev. No.	ITEM:		Present	
			Yes	No
	1	Bibliographic Data		
Score	2	Comment on Flow of Narrative		
	3	Summary of Plot		
	4	Comparison		
	5	Comment on Strengths/Weakness		
	6	Recommendation		
	7	Credentials of Reviewer		
		Total Review Score		

YEAR:

JOURNAL:

Analysis of Review Promptness

Rev. No.	Early Review Before Bk. Pub.	Review in Month Expected Bk. Pub.	Review After Expected Bk. Pub.	Issue in Which Review Appears	Actual Book Publicat. Reported	Review Promptness in Days
1						
2						
3						
4						
5						
6						
7						
8						

(*continued*)

Appendix 2 (*Continued*)

Rev. No.	Early Review Before Bk. Pub.	Review in Month Expected Bk. Pub.	Review After Expected Bk. Pub.	Issue in Which Review Appears	Actual Book Publicat. Reported	Review Promptness in Days
9						
10						
11						
12						
13						
14						
15						
16						
17						
18						
19						
20						
21						
22						
23						
24						
25						

YEAR:
JOURNAL:

Analysis of Review Characteristics

Rev. No.	Full Bibliograph. Data	Flow of Narrative	Plot Summary	Comparison	Strengths/ Weaknesses	Recommendation	Reviewer Credentials	Total
1								
2								
3								
4								
5								
6								
7								
8								
9								
10								
11								
12								
13								
14								
15								
16								
17								
18								
19								
20								

(*continued*)

Rev. No.	Full Bibliograph. Data	Flow of Narrative	Plot Summary	Comparison	Strengths/ Weaknesses	Recommendation	Reviewer Credentials	Total
21								
22								
23								
24								
25								

Items checked indicate criteria met by review.

YEAR:
JOURNAL:

Yearly Individual Review Score Sheet

Rev. No.	Review Publication	Book Publication	Title of Book	Review Scores	
				Content	Promptness
1					
2					
3					
4					
5					
6					
7					
8					

(continued)

Appendix 4 (*Continued*)

Rev. No.	Review Publica-tion	Book Publica-tion	Title of Book	Review Scores	
				Content	Prompt-ness
9					
10					
11					
12					
13					
14					
15					
16					
17					
18					
19					
20					
21					
22					
23					
24					
25					

SELECTED BIBLIOGRAPHY

Sources Used for Technical Background

Berelson, Bernard. *Content Analysis in Communication Research*. Glencoe, Ill.: Free Press, 1952.
Bonk, Wallace John, and Rose Mary Magrill. *Building Library Collections*. 5th ed. Metuchen, N.J.: Scarecrow, 1979.

Bowker Annual of Library and Book Trade Information, 1965–1985. New York: R. R. Bowker.

Budd, Richard W., Robert K. Thorp, and Lewis Donohew. *Content Analysis of Communications.* New York: Macmillan, 1967.

Busha, Charles H., and Stephen P. Harter. *Research Methods in Librarianship: Techniques and Interpretation.* New York: Academic Press, 1980.

Elzey, Freeman F. *A Programmed Introduction to Statistics.* 2d ed. Belmont, Calif.: Brooks/Cole, 1971.

Goldhor, Herbert. *An Introduction to Scientific Research in Librarianship.* Urbana, Ill.: Graduate School of Library Science, University of Illinois, 1972.

Groot, Elizabeth H. "A Comparison of Library Tools for Monograph Verification." *Library Resources and Technical Services* 25 (April–June 1981): 149–161.

Katz, William A. *Collection Development: The Selection of Materials for Libraries.* New York: Holt, Rinehart, and Winston, 1980.

"The Weekly Record," *Publishers Weekly,* 1963–1974. *Weekly Record,* 1974–1983.

Related Articles and Studies on Book Reviewing

Busha, Charles H. "Book Selection in Public Libraries: An Evaluation of Four Commonly-Used Review Media." *Southeastern Librarian* (Summer 1968): 92–100.

Dahlin, Robert. "Do Pub Dates Mean *Anything* Any More?" *Publishers Weekly* 220 (September 25, 1981): 24–28.

Duree, Barbara J. "Serving Your Needs: A Summary Report." *Booklist* 76 (June 1980): 1471–1472.

Edelman, Hendrik, and Karen Muller. "A New Look at the Library Market." *Publishers Weekly* 231 (May 29, 1987): 30–35.

Goodrich, Chris. "Book Reviews as Book Promotion." *Publishers Weekly* 226 (May 29, 1984): 30–32.

Hargrave, Victoria E. "A Comparison of Reviews of Books in the Social Sciences in General and in Scholarly Periodicals." *Library Quarterly* 18 (July 1948): 206–217.

Macleod, Beth. "*Library Journal* and *Choice:* A Review of Reviews." *Journal of Academic Librarianship* 7 (March 1981): 23–28.

McCrossan, John Anthony. "Library Science Education and Its Relationship to Competence in Adult Book Selection in Public Libraries." (Ph.D. dissertation, University of Illinois, 1966.

Merritt, LeRoy C., Martha Boaz. and Kenneth S. Tisdell. *Reviews in Library Book Selection.* Detroit: Wayne State University Press, 1958.

Noble, D. H., and C. M. Noble. "A Survey of Book Reviews." *Library Association Record* 76 (May 1974): 90, 92.

Norman, Ronald V. "A Method of Book Selection for a Small Public Library." *RQ* 17 (Winter 1977): 143–145.

Paul, Sandra K., and Carol A. Neymeyer. "Book Marketing and Selection: Selected Findings from the Current AAP/ALA Study." *Publishers Weekly* 207 (June 16, 1975): 42–45.

Ream, Daniel. "An Evaluation of Four Book Review Journals." *RQ* 19 (Winter 1979): 149–153.

Ross, Ann K. "A Comparison of Fiction Reviews in the *Library Journal* and the *Virginia Kirkus Service* in 1965."Master's thesis, Catholic University of America, 1967.

Schmitt, John P., and Stewart Saunders. "Research Notes: An Assessment of *Choice* as a Tool for Selection." *College and Research Libraries* 44 (September 1983): 375–380.

Simpson, Jerome D. "The Dependable Ones: Book Reviewing Media." *RQ* 8 (Fall 1968): 35–36.

"What Makes a Good Review? Ten Experts Speak." *Top of the News* 35 (Winter 1979): 146–152.

Wyatt, Robert. "Book Page Editor Blues." *Publishers Weekly* 226 (September 21, 1984): 28–30.

LIBRARIANS AS TEACHERS:
A STUDY OF COMPENSATION AND STATUS ISSUES

Barbara I. Dewey and J. Louise Malcomb

INTRODUCTION

Librarians teach library science courses at most of the sixty ALA-accredited library schools. They also teach in numerous other academic disciplines and for-credit bibliographic instruction courses. Many have done research and written about librarians' status and tenure concerns and on general aspects of library instruction and library education, but there is almost no current research on the role of librarians as teachers in terms of compensation, impact on the subject taught, faculty status and rank, tenure considerations and attitudes of librarians, library school administrators, and library administrators. The goal of the study reported here was to identify the situation for librarians who are teachers and to

Advances in Library Administration and Organization,
Volume 7, pages 135-148.
Copyright © 1988 by JAI Press Inc.
All rights of reproduction in any form reserved.
ISBN: 0-89232-817-7

define and explore compensation and status issues concerning the librarian-teacher role from three points of view; the librarian-teacher, the library administrator, and the library school director or dean.

BACKGROUND

The literature search for this paper comprised an examination of the literature of the library, medical, and legal professions. The medical and legal professions were examined in particular because both have significant practitioner teaching activity.

The library literature appears to treat the teaching role of librarians in two ways: a philosophical treatise on the practical versus theoretical curriculum in library education and general faculty status issues as they pertain to librarians. Rayward points out the necessity of library schools to hire "adjunct or part-time staff to teach specialized courses lying outside the expertise of the regular teaching." He writes about the different orientations of librarians and library educators toward the body of knowledge within the field and the manner in which this knowledge is developed.[1] Very little is found concerning librarians' role in teaching library science in general however.

Other writings concentrate on some aspects of defining librarians as teachers or the inclusion of a teaching role within the librarian's job. In a much cited article, Wilson discusses her views on what she terms the mythology of using the word *teacher* to define, in part, the role of librarian. Wilson uses the example of academic librarians teaching library instruction classes and calling themselves professors when in fact they do not gain additional status or recognition for this work. She goes so far as to say that such a definition "deters the development of a consistent professional self-image among librarians."[2]

David Peele, in a related article, agreed with Wilson that the definition of librarians as teachers is a myth perpetuated by the faculty status model recently embraced by librarians. He made the point that institutions with different academic structures (professor, assistant professor versus librarian, assistant librarian) also have different pay schedules and benefits, with librarians having lower levels of both. He also recognized that in some institutions, librarians who teach and those who do not receive the same salary and benefits. Peele makes the point that courses on bibliographic instruction are not comparable to other courses on campus because they are usually only one or two lectures in length.[3] In response to Peele's article, John Budd makes the point that Peele and others define teaching too narrowly.[4]

Another set of articles on the librarian-teacher role describes organizational structures. Mary Huston discusses the Evergreen State College model where librarians hold joint appointments with the faculty and the library. Not only do the librarians teach regular courses, but the faculty take turns working in the library. Librarians may choose this model or another where they do not teach. Most librarians have chosen to teach.[5]

Joanne C. Callard discusses the appointment of University of Oklahoma medical librarians to the College of Pharmacy to teach library instruction to pharmacy students. Callard indicates that these activities are "extracurricular," which probably means no additional reimbursement for the librarians who teach.[6]

The concept of librarians' teaching a course for credit is described in an article by Elizabeth Burns. She notes that librarians teaching library instruction courses for credit have "more visibility in the educational process." She notes that library instruction courses that are offered for credit are much more successful than other patterns of library instruction tried by colleges and universities but that librarians often hesitate pursuing this avenue because of "lack of definition specification as to their teaching role."[7]

Most of the literature, then, seems to be a description of or debate about the overall teaching role of librarians and libraries. Very little of it covers the personnel issues surrounding the librarian who teaches a course for credit. Gary Wiggins addresses the question of academic rank and salary for librarians who teach over and above their other duties. This situation is common among librarians who teach courses as adjunct faculty for library schools. He notes that at Indiana University, librarians who teach outside their full-time duties should consider the following: (1) the limits of teaching responsibilities and their impact on promotion and/or tenure; (2) the amount of the overload salary to be paid as compared to institutional limitations on overload salaries (at Indiana University, twelve-month-salary librarians are limited to receiving no more than 20 percent of that salary in a fiscal year—a potential problem if the librarian teaches more than one class during the year); and (3) the policy or lack of policy on determining what rank should be offered to a librarian teaching a departmental course. Wiggins notes, for example, that librarians teaching at the Indiana University School of Library and Information Science in 1983–1984 had seven different ranks. Wiggins suggests a strengthening of policies in the area of librarians who teach.[8]

Two studies partially address these issues. In 1968 a survey questionnaire was sent to ARL directors and all other state university libraries to collect information about the activities and opportunities of librarians in academia. Teaching was included on the questionnaire. This activity was found to be the least popular among the directors, although two-thirds of librarians were given time from their regular work to teach. Eighty-nine percent of the directors reported that their librarians taught some type of course, with Library science and bibliography courses taught slightly more than courses in other subjects. Also it was found that university policy rather than library policy determined arrangements to be made for accommodating teaching. The researchers noted that "librarians apparently follow prevailing campus patterns whether that be allowed time, extra compensation, or divided appointments." The actual volume of teaching by librarians was reported to be low on each campus.[9]

A 1978 study by Christine Brock and Gayle Edelman examines teaching practices of law librarians. This survey was designed to explore any correlation between administrative load, status, and teaching loads and salaries and whether teaching was being done by law library directors. Results did not show any correlation between salaries and rank or between salaries and teaching.[10]

OTHER PROFESSIONALS WHO TEACH

Since we found only a limited amount of information about the particulars of librarians who teach, we decided to look at literature from the health sciences profession because many practicing physicians and nurses teach. Interestingly, these two groups are concerned not about compensation and other policies regarding their teaching function but about their participation in clinical practice, which is either optional or required of students. An article in *Nursing Outlook* concluded that if nursing faculty are to maintain clinical expertise, there must be substantial rewards for participation in professional practice. The current trend is to require nursing educators to be involved in clinical practice (almost the opposite problem librarians have) without additional compensation,[11] while physicians are concerned because of limits in the compensation they can take home from clinical practice.[12] Neither of these professions has solved the dilemma, but they indicate that clear institutional policies are a possible solution.

METHODOLOGY

A questionnaire survey methodology survey was chosen for this study. The target population consisted of three groups: library school directors and deans, library administrators, and librarians who teach. We asked the first two groups, easily identifiable through the *American Library Directory,* to identify librarians who teach courses for credit. This could include any type of course. Our intention for the target group of librarians who teach was to limit it to academic librarians. Thus, we asked the two groups of administrators to identify the librarians and then asked the librarians themselves to answer only one questionnaire, reducing the possibility of duplication.

We selected academic institutions by limiting the study to American Library Association–accredited library schools and the college and university library systems at these schools, excluding our home institution, Indiana University. Three separate questionnaires were then sent to the groups at these institutions. Because we did not know the total number of librarians who teach and could not specifically identify them, we had to depend on the library and library school directors to identify the librarian-teacher pool.

We sent questionnaires to fifty-two library administrators and fifty-two library school directors or deans. The response rate was 65.4 percent for the administrators and 53.8 percent for the directors-deans. Forty-two questionnaires were returned from librarian-teachers out of a possible pool indicated by library administrators of seventy-five, for an approximate return rate (since this total cannot be verified as totally accurate) of 56 percent.

RESULTS

Librarian-Teacher Responses

The most common area of specialization noted by librarians who teach was bibliographic instruction, followed by information science; however, most respondents who checked the "miscellaneous" section indicated they taught in a variety of areas (Table 1). Since librarians could check more than one box, it may be that they indicated areas in which they feel they have expertise, as well as areas in which they actually teach. Ninety-seven percent of the respondents had

Table 1. Area of Expertise in Library and Information Science

Other[a]	65.81%
Bibliographic instruction	22.22
Reference	5.98
Government documents	3.42
Technical services	1.71
Management	.86
Total	100.00

[a]Other library science courses listed included: business information sources, automation, database searching, bibliography of science and technology, music information resources, legal bibliography, serials librarianship, special libraries, Slavic bibliography, rare books librarianship, archives administration, public librarianship, African bibliography, records management, bibliography of engineering, bibliography of the humanities, resources in health sciences, children's literature, video-based information systems, introduction to instructional technology, multimedia materials, and practicums. Courses in other disciplines listed were pharmacy, music, history, biochemistry, African studies, women's studies, composition, art, law, communication, engineering, freshman seminar, and honors program.

four or more years of library experience, and 53 percent had taught more than four years (Tables 2 and 3).

Most taught courses in their own institution (Table 4). Eighty-one percent taught courses in the library school, 15 percent taught in other departments, and only 4 percent taught credit courses sponsored by the library (Table 5). Other departments where librarians teach included departments in the sciences, social sciences, and humanities. As might be expected, 60 percent of the responding librarians listed one course (Table 6). Forty-seven respondents listed two or more courses, and two listed five courses. Courses listed varied, but reference and bibliographic instruction predominated those listed.

The respondents indicated that most of their employers (the library administrators) supported their role as teachers, although 22 percent noted that their administrations did not support this function (Table 7). Most respondents also indicated that their role as teacher had some influence on promotion and tenure considerations (Table 10). About half of the respondents indicated that they have faculty status (Table 8). Fewer than half noted that they did not hold a separate rank in their teaching function, such as lecturer or assistant professor (Table 9).

Table 2. Years of Professional Library Experience

4 or more	97.41%
1–3	2.59
Total	100.00

Table 3. Years Engaged in Teaching

1–3	52.99%
4 or more	29.92
Less than 1	17.09
Total	100.00

Table 4. Location of Teaching Assignment

Same institution as full-time position	82.76%
Different institution	17.24
Total	100.00

Table 5. Department Offering Course

Library school	81.13%
Library	3.77
Other	15.10
Total	100.00

Table 6. Number of Courses Taught

1	59.83%
2	24.79
3	13.67
4	0
5	1.71
	100.00

Table 7. Library Administration Encourages Teaching

Yes	78.22%
No	21.78
Total	100.00

Table 8. Librarians Hold Faculty Rank

Yes	49.56%	
No	46.96	
Other	3.58	(does not pertain to their institution)
Total	100.00	

Table 9. Librarians Hold Separate Rank for Teaching Assignments

Yes	44.25%
No	55.75
Total	100.00

Table 10.   Teaching
Is Considered for
Promotion-Tenure
Decisions

Yes	64.49%
No	35.51
Total	100.00

The most common form of compensation was by stipend (39 percent), followed by miscellaneous methods (34 percent), no compensation (20 percent), and compensatory time off (7 percent) (Table 11). The miscellaneous forms of compensation included provision of graduate assistants and combinations of the other methods.

Comments by librarians were numerous and lengthy. Many noted that they received personal satisfaction and growth from teaching despite the lack of compensation, support, or recognition from their administration. Benefits of teaching included bringing back new knowledge to the regular position, an opportunity to reflect on the philosophies and foundations of librarianship (no time to do this on the job), and learning from students. Others indicated that teaching provided a greater understanding of student-faculty concerns, experience in curriculum development, and an opportunity to synthesize ideas for future research projects. Librarians also noted that it allowed a refreshing change in routine. Most librarians indicated that the greatest benefit for the librarian-teacher situation was that librarians bring to the classroom valuable practical experience. A number of respondents indicated concern that library school faculty were not as current as they should be in technological areas and that librarians could bring the latest applications to the classroom.

Negative comments toward the role of librarian-teacher included frustration that teaching was not encouraged more by the library and/or university administration. Librarians felt that teaching was rewarding but were frustrated with the

Table 11.   Methods of
Compensation for Teaching

Monetary stipend	39.31%
Other	34.19
No compensation	19.66
Compensatory time	6.84
Total	100.00

time pressures it brought on top of their regular position. Some responded that their teaching responsibilities had not been beneficial in obtaining promotions, although the experience "looks good" on the resume.

Library Administrators

Almost 80 percent of the library administrators indicated that librarians in their institutions teach, and 62 percent said that they encourage this teaching role. Most of the libraries responding to this study do not have any formal agreements with the library schools at their institutions nor did they have specific guidelines regarding compensation or rank for librarians who teach (yet library schools indicate that they do have such policies). Thirty-five percent indicated that their librarians received some type of overload compensation, usually in the form of a stipend. Thirteen percent indicated that these courses were taught on a volunteer basis, and 19 percent viewed these teaching responsibilities as part of the librarian's regular position (Table 13).

Table 12. Librarians Teaching Credit Courses

Librarians do teach credit courses	79.41%
Librarians do not teach	17.65
Other	2.94
Total	100.00

Table 13. How Librarians Are Compensated for Teaching

Monetary stipend (overload)	35.48%
Considered part of their regular responsibilities	19.35
Done on a volunteer basis	12.90
Other (some combination)	32.27
Total	100.00

Table 14. Written Guidelines for Teacher Compensation

No written guidelines	67.74%
Guidelines are available	32.26
Total	100.00

Table 15. Working
Agreements with
Library Schools

No	78.79%
Yes	21.21
Total	100.00

Table 16. Library Administration
Encouragement of Teaching: Library
Administrators' View

Teaching is encouraged	61.77%
Teaching is not encouraged	32.35
Neither encouraged nor discouraged	5.88
Total	100.00

Library administrators indicated in their comments that funding has limited the library itself in offering for-credit courses because there are not enough librarians to teach. In addition, administrators are concerned that librarians who work full time should limit their teaching activities. Administrators also voiced the frustration that while librarians go into the library school environment to teach, library school faculty rarely reciprocate, similar to the clinical issue raised by the medical profession. However, it was pointed out that the librarian-teacher helps to facilitate communication between library educators and libraries.

Library School Administrators

A majority of the library schools responding indicated that they use librarians to teach their courses from time to time (Table 17). Most library school respondents use librarians to fill in for regular faculty for certain courses and to teach courses in specialized areas (Table 18). Approximately 70 percent have specific requirements for librarians who teach for them (Table 19). Sixty-two and one-half percent indicated that they have agreements with the library administration concerning librarians who teach, although most library administrators did not acknowledge such agreements (Table 15).

Approximately half the library schools have specific practices and guidelines for assigning ranks to librarians who teach, (Table 21), and the majority use a stipend for compensation (Table 22). All of the library school respondents indicated that they had success with librarians' teaching their courses, both from the students' and their own point of view (Tables 23 and 24). Ninety-six percent of

Talbe 17. Librarians
Are Used to Teach by
Library School

Yes	86%
No	14
Total	100

Table 18. Primary Reasons for Using Librarians to
Teach

Offer courses in areas not covered by school's faculty	91.67%
Fill in while teaching positions are vacant	62.5
Enhance dual degree programs	4.1
Other	20.8
(more than one response checked)	

Table 19. Library School
Requirements for Librarians
Who Teach

Have specific requirements	69.57%
No specific requirements	30.43
Total	100.00

Table 20. Agreement
with Library
Administration

Yes	62.50%
No	37.50
Total	100.00

Table 21. Ranks
Assigned to Librarians
Who Teach

Yes	50%
No	50
Total	100

Table 22.   Compensation

Monetary stipend	60.87%
Compensatory time off	4.35
No compensation	13.04
Other	21.74
Total	100.00

Table 23.   Success of
Librarians Who Teach

Successful	86.96%
Satisfactory	13.04
Total	100.00

Table 24.   Students'
Impressions of
Librarians Who Teach

Successful	86.96%
Satisfactory	13.04
Total	100.00

Table 25.   Evaluation of
Librarians Who Teach

Yes, they are evaluated	95.83%
No, not evaluated	4.17

the library schools evaluate the librarians who teach in some way (Table 25). Comments from library school administrators indicated that they were most interested in using librarians to teach specialized courses rather than general courses. Several respondents indicated concern that librarians were less successful in teaching general courses because their approach was too "local" or because they tend to "train" rather than "educate." An equal number of respondents indicated the benefits of librarians who bring practical knowledge and background into the classroom. Some library schools noted that most librarians who teach do not have the earned doctorate and were less likely to know about research in the field. This problem also limits some library schools from using librarians because of policies within their graduate schools that do not allow faculty without doctorates to teach graduate courses. One respondent noted the importance of librarians who teach to be active in professional organizations and to publish. In fact, this library school requires librarians to have published at least one article between appointments.

GENERAL CONCLUSIONS

The results of the questionnaire indicate that, for the most part, the librarian-teacher model is necessary and successful. The librarians and library school administrators were more confident of this than library administrators, however. Library administrators want to see more practice put into library education, but they may not want or be able to support librarians in this role.

Librarians tend to teach more often in specialty rather than in general areas of librarianship for library schools. They do not teach often in other disciplines, but when they do, it is usually in specific subject areas. Almost all of the library-sponsored for-credit courses taught by librarians were bibliographic instruction courses.

The status and compensation for librarians who teach is in a state of flux. Some institutions pay; others do not. This state of affairs seems to be due to either institutional policy, where a university prohibits full-time librarians from accepting overload pay, or philosophical considerations of the library admin-istrator, which considers teaching part of the job. Rank and status are usually nonexistent; no separate title is given to librarians who teach that is different from their regular title.

Librarians who teach are uncertain as to the level and intensity of support of their library administration. They are unsure that the rewards outweigh the lack of time, compensation, and recognition for their teaching function. They feel, however, that it provides intrinsic benefits for them and larger educational bene-fits for librarianship as a whole. Therefore, they appear ready to continue to teach at various levels.

NOTES

1. W. Boyd Rayward, "Conflict, Interdependence, Mediocrity: Librarians and Library Edu-cators," *Library Journal* 108 (13) (July 1983): 1313–1317.

2. Pauline Wilson, "Librarians as Teachers: The Study of an Organizational Fiction," *Library Quarterly* 49 (2) (April 1979): 146–162.

3. David Peele, "Librarians as Teachers: Some Reality, Mostly Myth," *Journal of Academic Librarianship* 10 (5) (November 1984): 267–271.

4. John Budd, "Another View of Reality: A Response to David Peele," *The Journal of Academ-ic Librarianship* 10 (5) (November 1984): 271.

5. Mary Huston, "Research in a Rotating Librarian/Faculty Program," *C&RL News* 46 (1) (January 1985): 13.

6.   Joanne C. Callard, "The Medical Librarian's Role as Adjunct Faculty Member of a College within a Health Sciences Center," *Bulletin of the Med. Libr. Assoc.* 67 (October 1979): 399–400.

7.   Elizabeth S. Burns, "The Library Course for Credit: Problems and Opportunities," in *Essays from the New England Academic Librarians Writing Seminar,* ed. Norman D. Stevens (Metuchen, N.J.: Scarecrow Press, 1980); pp. 83–104.

8. Gary Wiggins. "Librarians Who Teach: Overloading with Pay or without," *Inula Innuendo* 1 (3) (August 1984): 1–5.

9. W. Porter Kellam and Dale L. Barker, "Activities and Opportunities of University Librarians for Full Participation in the Educational Enterprise," *College and Research Libraries* 29 (3) (May 1968): 195–199.

10. Christine Brock and Gayle Edelman, "Teaching Practices of Academic Law Librarians," *Law Library Journal* 71 (1978): 96–117.

11. Gloria R. Smith, "Compensating Faculty for their Clinical Practice" *Nursing Outlook* 28 (November 1980): 673–676.

12. "Welcome to the Faculty of the Franchise," *Pediatrics* 73 (June 1984).

ACADEMIC LIBRARY BUILDINGS:
THEIR EVOLUTION AND PROSPECTS

David Kaser

INTRODUCTION

The first free-standing university library building in the United States was constructed at the University of South Carolina almost a century and a half ago. Since that time, American academic libraries have gone through four distinct building styles, each requiring thirty-five years to run its course. This paper will first look briefly at these four styles and the causes of their popularity and decline and then review where they seem to be going today.

THEIR EVOLUTION

The academic library building style first utilized in the United States and typified by the building at the University of South Carolina was based on its sole require-

Advances in Library Administration and Organization,
Volume 7, pages 149–160.
Copyright © **1988 by JAI Press Inc.**
All rights of reproduction in any form reserved.
ISBN: 0-89232-817-7

ment to house books. Until the time of the Civil War, American academic libraries were open only one or two hours weekly, they had only one part-time staff member, and they offered little, if any, service. They could thus best meet this unidimensional purpose of book storage in a single rectangular room with shelves extending to the exterior walls from two rows of columns ranging the length of the hall. Examples of such early libraries include, from the South where they were uniformly wrapped in classic revival dress, South Carolina's 1840 building, which is still used as a library, and North Carolina's 1851 building, which serves today as the Playmakers' Theater. In the North where the romantic era was in vogue, most early libraries took on Gothic exteriors. Examples include Harvard's Gore Hall, built in 1841 and razed in 1913 to make room for Widener, Yale's library built in 1846 and converted in 1931 to Dwight Chapel, and Wesleyan's 1868 Rich Hall, which serves today as the institution's '92 Theater.

This simple style sufficed for exactly thirty-five years. By 1875, such single-purpose buildings could no longer meet the needs of university life. Scholarship was now gravitating to universities, and libraries were having to provide study facilities for readers through many hours each day, as well as work stations for the many staff members now required. Library buildings thus now had to be multipartitioned into separate spaces that could be assigned to these various new functions. Princeton's Chancellor Green building, built as a library in 1873, Lehigh's present Linderman Library begun in 1876, Michigan's 1883 library (since torn down), Pennsylvania's Furness library erected in 1890 and now its School of Architecture, and Cornell's 1891 library, today the Uris Undergraduate Library, were all representative of this period. These and others of the era, however, while dedicating separate spaces for their varied functions, never managed to articulate them into efficient and integrated wholes, and none was regarded as fully successful. Many, such as those built at Syracuse in 1889, Indiana in 1890, Ohio State in 1893, Kansas in 1894, and Illinois in 1897, were so unsuccessful that they were abandoned as libraries within three decades of their construction in favor of more responsive designs. All of these structures are still standing, however, and serve their institutions today, albeit not well, for other academic purposes.

It took librarians and architects exactly thirty-five years of experimentation with these multifunction buildings, trying to arrange their many activities into efficient proximities, before it was first successfully accomplished at the University of California following the San Francisco earthquake. Beginning in 1910 patrons of California's new library building entered at its center-front and climbed one flight of stairs to the catalog, delivery desk, and a huge main reading room that extended the entire width of the building. A multitier structural steel closed stack, two levels of which articulated with each floor of the building, extended to the rear of the structure, with other services, offices, and functions wrapped around it. This felicitous configuration was immediately stereotyped

University of North Carolina Library, 1851. Alcoved book room.

University of Kansas Library, 1894. Multipartitioned structure.

UCLA Library, 1926. Reading rooms and multi-tiered structural stack.

into all buildings constructed thereafter, including the one at Texas in 1912, at Michigan in 1919, at Minnesota in 1924, at Washington, Illinois, and UCLA in 1926, at Oklahoma and North Carolina in 1930, and at Columbia in 1933.

Again it took exactly thirty-five years for this pattern to outlive its usefulness. Always uneasy about the inflexibility of its structural stack that discouraged patron access to the book shelves, librarians by the time of World War II were seeking new solutions to their space problems. A new solution was first incorporated into the new library at Hardin-Simmons, which was opened in 1947, improved upon in the Firestone Library at Princeton in 1948 and at North Dakota State in 1949, and perfected at Iowa in 1951. This innovation, known as modular, was a rectangular structure of regularly spaced and uniform columns, slabs, and curtain walls, containing as few fixed-function elements as possible. Floors everywhere in the building were designed to carry the weight of free-standing stacks, allowing total flexibility in the deployment throughout the building of books, reader stations, and library services.

The desirable qualities of modular design were so compelling that virtually all of the hundreds of academic library buildings erected since World War II have utilized it. This is not to say that poor buildings have not been built during that time. Many, many bad buildings have been built, especially since the early 1960s, when the original virginal simplicity of modular design began to give way to ill-advised efforts to sophisticate it, and decadence set in. Their deficiencies, however, have seldom resulted from their modularity but from compromises of it. Unusual shapes, inadequate lighting, open wells and atria, inappropriate use of fenestration, and obtrusive fixed-function elements have all impaired the effectiveness of recently built academic libraries. All of these are weaknesses born of ignorance or arrogance rather than anything inherent in the modular concept itself.

This current pattern came into use not thirty-five but forty years ago, so we are already living beyond our traditional cycle. There does not, however, appear to be any radical departure from present-day academic library building style in the immediate offing. Should that trouble us? Should we be more assiduous or daring in our search for structural or architectural improvements that will enhance library services above and beyond what has been and remains possible in modular structures? Let us examine this question in the light of recent and anticipated changes in the nature of academic library activities, services, and use patterns, which, if Louis Sullivan was right when he said that form must follow function, should determine library design.

Let us first review the causes of the three periods of major change that have occurred in past library building design. The shift that took place in the 1870s resulted from a quantum change in pedagogical style that required more students to go to the library more frequently and remain there through more hours in the day. The design changes that occurred in the 1910s, on the other hand, resulted from architectural innovations that enabled libraries to perform the same ac-

North Dakota State University Library, 1949. Early modular design.

tivities but with greater efficiency. And the changes of the 1940s resulted from a combination of two factors: a desire on the part of the library profession to facilitate use of their materials by patrons and new structural techniques in the tool kits of architects.

PROSPECTS FOR CHANGE

Are any such changes occurring in the environment today that presage alterations in library building design? First, few appear willing to suggest that there are any major revisions in higher education pedagogy either underway or on the horizon. Rather, it seems likely that university-level instruction will continue for some time into the future in much the same mode as it has over recent decades. Second, however, librarians are bringing about massive changes in the way they make their services available to patrons. And, third, some architectural innovation is taking place that can facilitate accommodation of these changes.

Let us look first at how evolving library technology is already modifying information delivery capabilities. In some disciplines, patrons no longer need to go to a library building to develop bibliographies on an assigned topic. They can do it at home on their own terminals instead. In some disciplines, they can also winnow this bibliography to a few choice items by consulting abstracts, again on their own terminals at home. In some institutions, they can dial up the library's catalog on their terminals at home and learn which, if any, of their desiderata the library owns. In some, they can dial into the library's circulation system and determine the status of a needed item. In some institutions, they can then call the library and request that the material be sent to them or be interlibrary borrowed without even leaving their dorm room. Perhaps most important, they can do this work not just during the hours that the library is open but in accord with their own, sometimes inscrutable, circadian rhythms.

Now why, given such capabilities, should a student or faculty member trek to a library at all? It is difficult to think of any good *library* reason for one to do so, although a number of nonlibrary reasons come to mind. This scenario, as it evolves, will obviously have a marked impact on library building planning. For the past fifty years, for example, academic librarians have known that they must provide at any given moment seats for 25 percent of their full-time enrollment, and this figure is now wrapped into library building standards. One must now ask, however, if this standard is any longer justified. Perhaps in some libraries, it is already adequate to seat only 22 or 23, instead of 25, percent of the student body, and this figure can probably be expected to drift slowly downward as more and more information seekers learn these more efficient techniques of bibliographical reconnaissance. A 3 percent reduction in seating may not sound like much of a shift, but in a large university library, it can account for building cost savings mounting easily into seven figures.

University of California, San Diego, Library, 1970. Lacking "virginal simplicity . . ."

What about space needed for housing library collections? Throughout the past century, this has usually been determined by projecting current acquisition rates over a particular time frame and adding the resulting number to existing holdings. Will that method continue to serve in a time when alternate forms of information are coming so increasingly into use? More sophisticated interinstitutional programs of materials sharing are available today than were to be had as short a time ago as five years. Greater compaction and microreduction techniques are at hand, and electronic transmission of full text will eventually come into library use. Sooner or later the profession must establish a system for archiving last copies of seldom-used materials at joint expense so that research libraries can begin to weed vigorously and with impunity.

In programming new library space for collections, it may be time for institutions to consider a situation wherein the accession of physical volumes will decline in number, where indeed they might eventually attain a steady state, or may someday even, *mirabile dictu,* experience negative growth. Not only does such a view extrapolate smaller buildings in the first place, but it also affects the amount of campus space that needs to be reserved for their later expansion. Most important perhaps, it also dictates that library buildings planned today be more flexible than they have had to be in the past, because it just may be desirable in the year 2040 to give some of their floor space back to the parent institution for nonlibrary purposes entirely.

These considerations also speak to such matters as siting libraries throughout a campus. After all, if a person need not go to a library at all, then it matters little just where the library is located. If *Chemical Abstracts* is used only online, as is the case in increasing numbers of institutions, the bound volumes hardly need be shelved in the chemistry library or indeed on campus at all. Universities may wish soon to discontinue calling such departmental facilities ''libraries'' at all and call them ''information centers'' instead. In many peoples' minds, the word *library* elicits a specific image of books and journals, an image that may well be an impediment to their full modernization in the years just ahead. A more appropriate designation as ''biology information center'' is less fraught with traditional images, and the contents and equipment in a space so designated will thus be easier to modify as information delivery capabilities continue to evolve and improve.

What about architectural developments? Are there innovations in construction capabilities that can hasten improvements in university library buildings? There appear to be some, although most are minor. Recent experience has demonstrated, for example, that options for expanding library buildings have increased by 50 percent. Whereas in the past expansion has been possible in only four directions—north, east, south, and west—we now know that we can also expand down and up. Successful below-grade libraries have been built recently at Illinois, Harvard, Michigan, and elsewhere. Although few, if any, high-rise library buildings have been successful, we now know that we can build in air space above rivers, highways, or even above other buildings, and this opens up new possibilities for difficult sites.

There has also come into being recently a body of architectural literature on what are being called "smart buildings," or buildings that can facilitate relocation or modification of their electronic capacity. In recent years, many library builders have attempted to accomplish these ends by simply embedding empty conduit grids in their floor slabs and bus ducts in their perimeter walls, but the waste and cost of doing so have been very large. Indeed a whole new industry, called "wire management," has pervaded the worlds of building construction and office furnishings, and libraries are among its early customers and beneficiaries. Meanwhile, the simple expedient of laying down flat cable on top of floor slabs and covering it with carpet tile is satisfactorily providing many libraries with a high level of flexibility in deploying their power, telecommunication, and electronic capabilities.

Advances in structure-related technology are also coming to aid research libraries in meeting their responsibilities of preserving unique, rare, or valuable records and documents. The exclusion of ultraviolet rays from both artificial and natural illumination, so deleterious to paper, can be much more effectively accomplished today than it could even five years ago. Air-handling systems conducive to longer life expectancy in paper are also more readily available, and dry processes for fighting fires in libraries and archives have become more sophisticated.

One additional way in which libraries and architects can work together to improve the quality of library buildings is in making them simpler to use. Much is said these days about developing user-friendly computer systems, but perhaps too little attention is being given to developing user-friendly library buildings. This is not a reference to more sybaritic book palaces, of which the world already has vastly too many, but rather libraries that are just plain easy to use. This effort must begin with librarians because in most cases they are responsible for many of the complications in the first place. More books than are actually needed in reference are often kept shelved there. Separate departments are often developed for government publications instead of simply entering documents into union catalogs and classifying them onto the shelves with other materials on the same subject. Current periodicals are sometimes arranged not in a single alphabet by title, where any numbskull can find them, but rather grouped first in some subject categorization that is fully comprehensible only to the arranger. Books are sometimes kept on reserve longer than necessary, resulting in their inaccessibility to browsers. Most libraries will recognize dozens of similar complications in their own operations.

Architects, moreover, sometimes seem to assume that book shelves can be put into any kind of space, regardless of its size, shape, or relationship to the rest of the building, and as a result, the location capability of the classification scheme is abrogated or compromised. To be truly effective, a stack should be laid out before a building is massed rather than just retrofitted into a space because the space is there. This course is seldom followed in building planning, however, and as a result the effectiveness of most stack installations is impaired by cul-de-sacs of shelving that do not articulate clearly with the rest of the stack, small pockets of ranges that are secreted behind stairwells or restrooms where they are difficult to find, or other similar aberrations.

Profit-sector agencies learned long ago the importance of simplicity if their products and services were to succeed. Libraries probably have a similar potential for simplicity, but lacking an inexorable dollar incentive, we too often unnecessarily complicate them and then have to give courses of bibliographical instruction so that people can understand our self-introduced complications. We teach library skills, but we can also deskill the library, and at the present time the potential of the latter for improvement may be even greater than the former. Librarians and architects can effect much improvement in library user efficiency by working more closely than they have in the past in designing and renovating library buildings.

Thus, no radical departures in architectural style appear on the horizon that are likely to aid in library building enhancement over the next couple of decades, except, it is hoped, some kind of return to classical simplicity. The rapid continuing advance in the use by libraries of telecommunication and computer technology, however, will modify considerably internal library operation, and architectural and structural techniques will facilitate the advent of these modifications. Many of these same modifications, however, will reduce the frequency and length of library patrons' visits to library buildings, and these factors seem likely also to retard rates of collection growth. Both of these factors will mean that the need for additional academic library floor space will grow less rapidly in the years ahead than it has since World War II. If librarians and architects can work together to configure library space and services that are easier to use than most are today, they will brighten the lives and earn the affection of information seekers everywhere.

ACCREDITATION AND THE PROCESS OF CHANGE IN ACADEMIC LIBRARIES

Delmus E. Williams

INTRODUCTION

Every ten years, colleges and universities and their libraries expend much energy on studies to support regional accreditation. Self-studies are completed covering the activities of each of the major functions of the school, and teams are brought to campus to evaluate programs. But questions remain as to what effect all of this has on the capacity of the university and its library to adapt to changing situations. There are those who have found evidence of a correlation between accreditation and change in libraries. William E. Troutt (1978) noted that the standards of all of the regional associations reflect an appreciation of the need for a good library. All of the regional associations devote a standard to the library,

Advances in Library Administration and Organization,
Volume 7, pages 161–207.
Copyright © **1988 by JAI Press Inc.**
All rights of reproduction in any form reserved.
ISBN: 0-89232-817-7

and, as a result, much attention is given to library collections and programs during the process.

And it appears that this attention often pays off for the library program. Herbert V. Ferster (1971) found in a content analysis of accreditation reports that the library was one of the six areas most often cited in recommendations of visiting teams. But the relationship between the energy invested in the process and the results achieved is vague enough that it is not always apparent that the payoff is worth the effort. This paper will attempt to clarify this relationship. It will begin with a discussion of the philosophy behind the process and then follow with a design for an effective accreditation evaluation. It will then focus on two cases in which accreditation visits were followed by substantial changes in the library and conclude with an examination of how well the model reflects what happened in those organizations.

THE PHILOSOPHY OF ACCREDITATION

Voluntary accreditation is a process that was developed at the end of the nineteenth century to ensure that quality was maintained in emerging institutions of higher education. According to Kenneth Young (1979), it is based on the premises that:

1. As a general rule, self-regulation of institutions is preferable and in the long run more effective than external regulation.
2. Any system of external regulation can be effective only to the extent that it recognizes and builds upon a community's willingness to engage in self-regulation.
3.   A substantial number of individuals and institutions will regulate themselves if they know what behavior is expected and why.
4. An overwhelming majority of individuals and institutions will regulate themselves if they believe they might otherwise be identified by their peers as doing something wrong.
5. Only a small number of individuals or institutions deliberately engage in behavior that they know is not in the public interest.

Leaders in higher education generally see the process as fulfilling two functions. First, it identifies for public purposes educational programs that meet nationally recognized standards. In so doing, it protects both the public and the educational community from inferior institutions. Second, accreditation serves to stimulate improvement in institutions by forcing institutions to examine themselves on a regular basis against a set of accepted norms (Miller, 1972). In this way, it is expected that the process will encourage institutions to develop a continuing process of self-examination and self-improvement.

There are essentially two kinds of accreditation. Specialized accrediting agencies evaluate programs in subject disciplines like business, chemistry, and nursing, and they tend to have very specific criteria to ensure that the areas on which they focus are well served. Regional accreditation is a broader process that looks at the whole institution. This kind of evaluation is conducted under the auspices of one of six groups: the North Central Association of Colleges and Secondary Schools, the New England Association of Colleges and Secondary Schools, the Middle States Association of Colleges and Secondary Schools, the Northwest Association of Secondary and Higher Schools, the Southern Association of Colleges and Schools, and the Western Association of Schools and Colleges. This paper will focus on the efforts of the College Delegate Assembly of the Southern Association (SACS), which can be viewed as representative of the process of regional accreditation. The Southern Association uses a process that is more rigorous than some of the accrediting bodies. The process used in the South provides a more definite trail than that of some other groups, allowing for the tracking of the recommendations that are generated in accreditation while being close enough to the process of other associations to allow for some generalization.

THE ACCREDITATION PROCESS

Accreditation uses a two-step process combining institutional self-assessment with an external evaluation by representatives from peer institutions. Dudley V. Yates (1976) found that most librarians serving on visiting teams believe that the self-study is by far the more important part of the process. The study is conducted by a group of faculty, administrators, staff members, and students of the institution under the guidance of a steering committee. Generally, committees are set up to examine each of the components of the campus and the university's program, and extensive data gathering over a period of six months to two years results in a report that reflects the conditions of the campus and its plans for the following decade.

Once this document is completed, a schedule is set for an evaluation by people working in similar institutions. The composition of the visiting team varies from association to association. In the North Central Association, the team is limited to five members, while in the Southern Association, one member is selected for the team for each major area of emphasis of the university, meaning that the team can be quite large. In the South, every team includes at least one librarian.

The visiting team is expected to validate the self-study during a three-day visit to the campus. The short duration of the visit puts added emphasis on the quality of the self-study, and the agenda for the visit tends to follow closely those issues identified in the document prepared by the institution. As a result of the visit and conversations with the library administration, other staff members, faculty, and students, a set of conclusions is developed and presented to the Commission on Colleges.

After the report of the visiting team is filed with the Southern Association, the institution is given a chance to respond to the recommendations and suggestions contained in it, to include comments about the institution's efforts to overcome weaknesses identified in the process and differences that the institution might have with conclusions reached by the visiting team. When this is completed, the institution stands for membership before representatives of all of the other members of the association in the College Delegate Assembly.

THE EFFECTIVENESS OF ACCREDITATION

Although the description above is a simplistic view of the process used in accreditation, it should be obvious to readers that institutions invest large amounts of time and energy in this kind of evaluation. Over the years, much discussion has taken place as to how justified this investment has been. These arguments center on questions about the capacity of the process to serve its quality assurance function and its capacity to influence change in the library.

Quality Assurance and Accreditation

The standards used in the process are general enough to allow the associations to evaluate everything from the smallest colleges to the largest universities and, in some cases, even specialized training institutions are included under this umbrella. While these standards are frequently supplemented by other kinds of standards (such as the College Library Standards of the Association of College and Research Libraries), there is continuing discussion as to whether the standards are specific enough to justify the effort.

There is also another question that troubles critics relating to the two primary missions of accreditation. If Miller (1972) is right, institutions expect accreditation to certify their quality while finding enough information through a critical evaluation of their programs to bring about meaningful change. The cost of losing accreditation has intangible penalties like a loss of prestige, and that is regrettable. But as Kenneth Ashworth (1979) noted, the tangible costs are much higher. The loss of federal governmental and foundation support that can result can mean the end of the institution. Can institutions be expected to look at themselves critically when so much is at stake?

A third question about accreditation arises as a result of the general nature of the process. Accreditation is designed both to ensure quality in education and to allow for diversity among institutions. The regional associations use the same standards for Millsaps College, East Carolina University, and Duke University. Institutions are expected to establish a set of goals, and once it has been agreed that these fit within the general parameters of what constitutes good higher education, those goals become the standard against which the institution is judged. While accreditation might serves as a threat to smaller, less stable institutions, it is unlikely that Duke University has any fear of losing its accreditation. As a result, Ashworth (1979) feels that there is a growing feeling in the community of higher education that institutions of this sort will see little need to continue to cooperate with the accrediting agencies and withdraw the kind of leadership that only they can provide to the association.

There is also some feeling that librarians and other evaluators on the visiting teams may not be properly prepared for the work that is being asked of them. The premise upon which evaluators are selected, as Alan Pfinster (1973) noted, is that "any person from any reasonably good institution can evaluate any other program." Gerald Baysore (1971) felt that examiners selected have already been identified as experts in their specialty area and that it can be assumed that their professional experience qualifies them for the task at hand. But Dudley Yates's (1976) study of library evaluators on visiting teams in SACS found that little training is given to potential evaluators. He concluded that the "fluctuation in quality in evaluation which is caused by the individual evaluator's inability to translate a nebulous, ill-defined standard into specific needs and recommendations was the major cause for continuing calls for consumer protection in higher education" (p. 12).

However, with all of accreditation's shortcomings or potential shortcomings, it appears that there is a fair level of satisfaction with the results of the process. George Calvin Grant (1982) found that most library directors in institutions accredited by the Middle States Association were not dissatisfied with either the processes or the criteria used for the evaluation of libraries.

Accreditation and Change

Accreditation is also expected to help libraries and their parent institutions make needed changes so that they might improve their programs. As Cyril Houle (1972) explained, this expectation is based on the premise that "anyone who asks and keeps on asking 'how well are we doing?' . . . is likely to arouse an uneasiness among his colleagues which leads eventually to a broader awareness for the need for fundamental change in the program." Most of the regional associations see this as the most important function of the accreditation process. In fact, Paul Dressel (1971) maintains that "self-study is wasted effort unless it serves as an agent of change" (p. 288).

But the capacity of accreditation to influence change has been the subject of some debate. In a 1977 study of small midwestern colleges, college president Brent Poppenhagen found that accreditation was perceived to influence positively the capacity of institutions to adapt in virtually all areas with the exception of encouraging the development of new criteria for evaluation. It should be noted that the group studied here felt that libraries were improved as a result of the process in areas like the budget that is available for instructional materials, the rate of library acquisitions, and the distribution of materials across disciplinary lines. But while Morris Gelfand (1960) found that librarians viewed accreditation as a stimulus to change, Marilyn List (1969) could find no relationship between evaluation of this sort and positive changes in organizations. A more careful examination of how organizations change is required to understand these contradictory findings.

The Change Process

Within any organization, there are two different types of organizational structure. The first (the *formal* organization) follows the basic lines of authority established by management and is represented by the organization chart. The second (the *informal* organization) is based on the personal relationships of workers in the organization. While it is possible to change an organization using the power that is vested in the formal organization, it is the position of this paper that, to be effective, change must be accepted by the informal organizational network and that accreditation and other evaluative techniques are critical to gaining that acceptance. To understand this, one must first understand how decisions are made in academic libraries.

The model used here is referred to in the organizational literature as the *conflict model* of change. It holds that an understanding of tangible characteristics of an organization (such as the organizational structure) is less important than an examination of the values that operate within it in understanding how to make the organization more flexible. This model is based on the premise that the informal organization is made up of a number of individuals or groups of individuals, each of whom brings his or her own set of values to that organization. In this view, the change agent is expected to identify the interest groups operating in the organization, to determine what their values are, and to determine how each of them influences the decision-making process. In this way, change can be approached in ways that make them more acceptable to the various constituencies of the organization (Baldridge, 1971; House, 1974; Lindquist, 1968).

Accreditation and the Change Model

If one views organization in this light, it is far easier to understand how the principle of organizational develoment (OD) that is used as the basis of accreditation can be effective in changing organizations like libraries when it is incorporated into a general evaluation program. The Southern Association's *Manual for the Institutional Self-study Program* (1972) and other guides published by the association reflect this model and provide assistance for institutions. It also provides a reason for periodic evaluation as prescribed by Havelock (1972) and others. The broad participation envisioned in these documents is designed to build a constituency behind changes that are proposed and to co-opt people into supporting the recommendations that emerge. There are also clear indications that the values operating in the organization are to be considered in the evaluation and that the marketing of the changes once accreditation is completed is considered in the design of the process.

OTHER KINDS OF EVALUATION USED IN THE UNIVERSITY

While it is important to consider the guides of the Southern Association in describing how accreditation works, there is very little beyond that in the literature of accreditation that describes how well the process fulfills its mission. Therefore it is necessary to look at other kinds of evaluations that are used in the context of the university to find characteristics of successful evaluations. Most often, evaluation in the academy takes the form of a self-study. This form of evaluation seems particularly suited to the kind of collegial governance that is prevalent in universities, and it is not confined to use in support of accreditation. In fact, the most prevalent use seems to be in institutional development programs. While there is evidence that these are perceived to be effective in some quarters, Dwight Ladd (1970) concluded in a study commissioned by the Carnegie Commission that, in studies not related to accreditation, it is unlikely that change will result from the process unless a significant portion of the faculty has accepted the need for change prior to the beginning of the study or unless significant pressure for change is exerted from outside the institution. He contends that the main function of the self-study is to package innovations that have wide support on campus in a way that will make them acceptable to those in authority.

Kells and the Self-study Process

H. R. Kells (1980) has produced what is perhaps the best single guide available to the self-study in his *Self-study Processes: A Guide for Post-Secondary Institutions*. He believes that the success of this kind of program depends on the support given to the process by the senior administrators and the degree to which the institution focuses on its goals in implementing the process. It is his expectation that the main impact of the process comes from the work of the committee that is making the evaluation. Kells contends that the document that is eventually produced for outsiders tends to be a formality in the best self-studies and that, therefore, the process of developing it is a fine opportunity to build consensus in the community around proposed changes. The process used in the self-study should ensure the widest possible discussion of the issues treated prior to publication. Kells feels that the individual self-study process chosen for the study is critical to its success, as is the readiness of the organization to accept change. A good evaluation is intellectually and emotionally draining, and it is difficult to get the level of commitment from participants if they are not mentally prepared for it.

Self-evaluation and the Library

Management Review and Analysis Program

In academic libraries, the most widely used forms of self-study in recent years have been the Management Review and Analysis Project (MRAP) for large libraries and the Academic Library Development Project (ALDP) for smaller ones. These were developed by the Office of Management Studies of the Association of Research Libraries. They follow a process that consciously draws on OD to help libraries through a highly structured evaluation. Grady Morein (1979) says that self-study was selected for the process because it was assumed that the library staff is in the best position to understand what the organization needs and that the inclusion of the staff will encourage participation in group decision-making process in the library. Duane Webster (1974) contends that if change is to occur as a result of an MRAP study, the staff must be ready to change, administrative support for it must be available, and staff must be involved in planning the course of the change.

MRAP has gotten mixed reviews as to its effectiveness. Edward Johnson, Stuart Mann, and Carol Whiting (1977) found in their evaluation of the program that although 60 percent of the recommendations made in MRAP studies were implemented, the rate of implementation varied from institution to institution, from a low of 10 percent to a high of 90 percent. They also found that staff satisfaction with the process ranged widely among institutions and even within individual institutions. They emphasized the need for increased preparation for evaluation, and they stressed the central role that administrators must play in the self-study process. In general, the study supported the contentions of Duane Webster cited earlier, but the inconsistency of its findings indicates that evaluations are highly individualistic in nature and that general studies of them may not be helpful. In the final analysis, it appears that the limited success of the MRAP relates directly to failures to build support within the library for the process as prescribed by Kells (1980).

Evaluation in Human Service Delivery

Before ending the discussion of evaluation processes, it seems useful to expand into evaluation procedures used in social service organizations. There is an extensive literature on the evaluation of human service delivery programs, relating particularly to the development of procedures that can gauge the effectiveness of not-for-profit enterprises, and some of these bear close resemblance to library activities. But even there, impact studies are scarce, and the bulk of the studies present evidence in the form of case studies. However, Howard R. Davis and Susan E. Salasin (1975) did conclude that those evaluations that are most often effective are those that take into account the political realities of the organization. Going further, Peter Rossi, Howard Freeman, and Sonia Wright (1978) contend that the primary use of evaluation is as a political lever that plays the role of the expert witness to the effectiveness of the program. The researchers concluded that evaluation is particularly effective when there is a clearly demonstrated need for change and when the recommendations conform to the goals and values of the audience to whom they are addressed. They contend that the issues most successfully addressed are those where technical advice provides solutions to clearly defined problems or those for which a better alternative is offered to replace something that has clearly failed.

There is also a following among social service evaluators for the idea that organizations vary in terms of their capacity to absorb the results of evaluation. Howard Davis and Susan Salasin (1975), Joseph Wholey (1981), and others contend that it is important to assess the "evaluability" of programs and to prepare them for evaluation through careful planning as one considers implementing a full-scale evaluation program.

DECISION-MAKING IN THE UNIVERSITY LIBRARY

To gauge the impact of evaluation, we must, in addition to knowing about the subject, understand how decisions are made in the organization. Decision making in academic libraries is generally based on a political model that combines the kinds of quantitative information used in economic policymaking with more qualitative data about the values operating within the library organization. While libraries are basically bureaucracies (Lynch, 1978), there is a strong tradition of collegiality in the larger academic community that spills into its organization. As a result, many libraries have moved from a "rational" decision-making model with centralized control to a more democratic one.

The degree to which collegiality comes into play varies from campus to campus, but in every case, the demand by librarians for more participation brings library faculty from outside the hierarchy into decision making. In addition, users of the library have a strong interest in its services and are likely to be drawn into the decision-making process. They may come into the process as librarians and others in the library reach out to find support in the larger university community for their particular positions. Or they might make their voices heard through various groups with responsibility for overseeing the activities of the library. In either case, it can be expected that teaching faculty and other users will influence decisions made in the university about the library program.

As more people involve themselves in making decisions for the library, new goals are introduced into the process. Some of these will reinforce the stated mission of the library, but others will relate to the specific needs of those who advocate them. Goals from the internal staff might include objectives related to job satisfaction or professional achievement. User goals relate to matters of personal privilege or to specific service needs. In any case, the new goals introduced informally will compete for resources with the formal goals of the organization. Coalitions of librarians, teaching faculty, students, and other library staff members form around certain issues and weight decisions to favor one position or another. Decision making becomes a bargaining process in which the manager develops coalitions to support various policies that are felt to contribute to the fulfillment of stated library goals by balancing the interests of the groups operating in the organization against each other (Baldridge, 1971).

Political decision making is not irrational, however. It merely forces its users to examine the premises upon which data for decision making are being gathered. It assumes that people working within an organization will form groups to support their own interests as policy is developed. While most library staff members will generally support the aims of the library, decisions made for it have to take into account the human dynamics within the informal structure of the organization and the needs of its members for personal and professional fulfillment. Information relating to these values must be combined with less subjective data to determine the course of action to be taken.

A number of assumptions underlie the political decision-making process, including the following:

1. *There is never only one way to solve a problem.* There are a number of reasonable solutions, each of which can meet the programatic needs of the library. The one chosen should be tailored so that it fits the specific needs of the organization at the point that it is applied.

2. *One cannot assume that there is a universal system of values shared by the staff and faculty of the library and its users.* While the goals and objectives of the library may be clearly stated and the values used to justify positions may be accepted by all, the goals toward which different individuals and groups in the organization are actually working may be quite different. These personal goals and the values that they reflect may lead to differing interpretations of organizational goals and will lead to conflict within the library.

3. *It is often difficult to weigh the conflicting value systems against each other.* They find expression in absolute terms (professionalism, ideals of service, human dignity, etc.) and reflect situations in which the manager cannot afford to discount the importance of any of them. As a result, the actual ranking of program priorities must be made pragmatically to reflect the situation at a given time, and that ranking is likely to be very temporary.

4. *It is not reasonable to assume that library decision makers act solely on the basis of the stated goals of the library.* These people have personal needs and objectives within the program, and they tend to try to maximize the personal rewards that the program can produce for them.
5. *The more political decision making becomes, the more conservative it is likely to be.* Existing policies and programs always have their constituencies, while change requires efforts to decrease the allegiance of the organization to existing policies and to develop support for new ones. As a result, a library organization using more democratic processes can reasonably be expected to tolerate change only so long as it does not impinge on existing values. It is likely to encourage innovation (Raffel, 1974: Baldridge, 1971).

The Environment, the Library, and Organization Politics

While political decision making must carefully consider internal factors like collections, staff size and capabilities, and financial resources, the environment is also a primary factor in decision making. Rational or economic decision structures might use statistical data to determine the cost-effectiveness of a service, but political decision making requires that this be combined with an analysis of who is providing the service, who might be using it, what their interests in it are, and how much influence those people have on decision makers in the university. As a requisite good, the library must understand the nature of its clientele and how it approaches the library so that it can develop the kind of support that is required to retain its funding support and to limit interference in its internal operations. Quantitative data are still an important element in this effort since arguments that can be supported statistically are perceived to be more persuasive. However, the presentation of data takes on a new importance as more attention is given to the need to respond to demands placed on the library by its clientele and the need to get their support for the library program (Raffel, 1974).

Evaluation and Political Decision Making

The role of evaluation in political decision making is to provide a reasonable assessment of how the organization operates in a specific context and to develop a capacity within the organization to provide the kind of information needed to improve its operations. Evaluation's primary functions are to generate information about the general health of the library organization and to present those data in a way that is useful to the people who initiated the process. While this is likely to include some quantitative data, it should also provide an assessment of the values on which decisions in the library are based.

Context is all important in choosing tools for evaluation. It determines the areas of the general library program that are of interest for the study and the goals of the evaluation, and those, in turn, limit the choice of techniques. For instance,

MRAP and library surveys are designed to give the library organization and its administrators a better idea of how well the library works and what can be done to improve it. As a result, these tools emphasize internal concerns. Professional accreditation is concerned primarily with the capacity of the library to support the broader programs of the university and views the library operations and collections accordingly. In general, evaluation can be a constructive element in the life of the library in that it forces library decision makers to reexamine the formal goals of the organization and to look at the library program within the framework of the goals of those who use the library. This can help develop a capacity to plan by developing the skills needed to examine the organization critically. It can also provide channels for communication inside the organization and between the library and its clientele.

ACCREDITATION AS AN EVALUATION PROCESS

Accreditation as performed by the Southern Association is a specific kind of self-evaluation designed to view all parts of an educational institution. It assumes the "right and responsibility of assuring that the total program of a complex institution is coordinated, administered, and held in proper balance" (SACS, 1977, p. 1). The self-study process used and the work of the visiting team examine all of the components of the university program as a single unit. The assessment of the strength of the library is an important part of this evaluation. Standard 6 of the Southern Association's *Standards of the College Delegate Assembly* (1977) states that the evaluator is expected to ensure that "the library is a vital instrument of instruction" (p. 14). In particular, the standard specifies that the library should have an adequate collection, budget enough to support the educational program, reasonable facilities, proper staffing in terms of training and numbers, reasonable levels of service, and mechanisms for communicating with its clientele. Throughout the standard, the focus is on the points at which there is direct involvement by the library in the broader programs of the university.

The model accreditation process outlined by the Southern Association combines an interest in values and political bargaining (Baldridge, 1971) with an open process and strong human relations skills reminiscent of the OD literature (Havelock, 1972; Kells, 1980). This model contains four basic elements. First, accreditation should begin with an effort to assess the readiness the organization has to accept evaluation and identify those elements within the library and the university community that can either help or hinder the capacity of the process to influence change. Second, a good self-evaluation process will address the specific needs of the library and its clientele. Third, the visiting team must be used to best advantage. And, fourth, the ideas treated in the evaluation and its reports should be selected on the basis of their importance to the larger community and dealt with in terms that will hold the attention of decision makers in the university. An amplification of these points follows.

Planning for Accreditation

Prior to the initiation of the accreditation process, it is necessary to consider the environment in which the process will operate. In any situation in which evolution is expected to influence internal decision making, certain conditions must exist. First, the library must be viewed as part of the larger university. It is not a separate organization but an integral part of the institution. Second, the central administration of the university must make it clear that it considers the process to be an important tool for internal use and that it is willing to provide the planning, resources, and access to information required to ensure that the evaluation is done well. This attitude must also be reflected in the attitude of both the university and the library administration at all levels. Third, the institution must assume at the outset that it will retain its accreditation. This ensures that the potential threat of the process is minimized and that the teams charged with making the self-study can develop a program to meet the needs of the university (Kells, 1980). While Ashworth (1979) feels that the lack of a threat handicaps the process, Kells and Kirkwood (1978) contend that since the most effective kind of evaluation is one that assumes that it is for internal consumption, the absence of a threat may actually improve the capacity of accreditation to influence change. They feel that it is unlikely that the process will be carried out in a way that can be helpful unless the university assumes that it can fully meet the standards of the accrediting body. This latter position is far more convincing.

Beyond these general conditions, the literature suggests that the success of accreditation in influencing change depends on a number of factors in the organization itself. In other kinds of evaluations, the presence or absence of these characteristics might dicate the timing of a self-study. However, since the timing of regional accreditation studies is based on a specific schedule determined by the broader needs of the university and the requirements of the Southern Association, the library may have to accept organizational factors as given. Still, an understanding of those conditions in the library that will help the organization adapt and those that must be overcome if change is to take place is essential to the development of a politically sensitive evaluation. Some of these factors can be summarized as follows:

1. *The seniority of the library director has a direct impact on the willingness of the library organization to accept recommendations for change.* A more junior director has less invested in the status quo and is more likely to accept the notion of change according to this way of thinking.
2. *The capacity to change is enhanced when the library administration is secure within the university.* When those in the library hierarchy enjoy the

confidence of those to whom they report and are respected by those they serve, the idea of change is less threatening.

3.   *A library that has the support of the campus and that is well funded is more likely to accept change easily than one that has done less well in this area.* Change requires both tolerance from those who use the library and money that can be spent for things other than the basic library program. Unless these are available, administrators tend to be more conservative and less willing to accept recommendations for change.

4.   *A library that has a tradition of openness in its decision making is more likely to produce an effective self-study document than one that is less open.* A reputation for openness gives the impression that the evaluation has a purpose, and the willingness of administrators to entertain new ideas and to encourage those who might generate them lends credence to the process.

5.   *There is a direct relationship between the willingness of an organization to look at itself critically and the amount of energy it can and will give the process.* A library in which there is a major conflict or that is emerging from a long period of conflict tends to be more conservative and more cynical than those that have had a less difficult time.

6.   *On the other hand, libraries that have become used to orderly change are more likely to accept change.* An organization that accepts one change and is pleased with the result is more likely to entertain new proposals for change. The willingness of the university to change and the importance placed on generating ideas for improvements by its senior administrators are also critical to the process. This relates directly to the need noted earlier for the administration to make it clear at every level that it views the accreditation process as important and that it expects to use the results (Kells, 1980; Wholey, 1981; Studer, 1980; Davis and Salasin, 1975).

These preconditions are presumed to influence both the capacity of the library to change and the willingness of those who makes decisions for the library to accept the kind of criticism that can lead to change. The methods used to make library evaluators understand the degree to which these elements might have an influence will vary. But it is critical that those in charge of the self-study understand early in the process the effect that these factors might have so that they can design a politically effective evaluation.

In the light of these preconditions, an effective accreditation process will tailor the self-study to meet the specific needs and goals of the organization. The next step in model building will be to describe the kind of self-study that will most effectively promote change.

The Self-Study

The way in which the self-study process is conducted has a direct relationship to the degree to which the results of that study will be used. If it is clear that the self-study and the accreditation visit that follows are expected to bring about change and that if wide participation is to be encouraged throughout the process, it is easier to build enthusiasm for the work that must be done (Kells, 1980; Wholey, 1981). This understanding also helps to tailor the evaluation so that it can influence the thinking of those who make decisions about the library program. Some of the characteristics of the process that are expected to enhance the capacity of accreditation to influence change in the library can be summarized as follows:

1. *Self-study is most effective when the library director, the university administration, and the self-study committee agree that it will be used to bring about change.* Administrative support for the self-study and a clear understanding that the administration views accreditation as something that is important to the life of the library are critical for its success.

2. *Self-study is most effective when the chair of the self-study committee and the library and university administration respect each other.* If the administration begins with the assumption that the criticisms that emerge from the study will be objective and realistic in terms of the programs of the library and the university, the report is more likely to be read and used.

3. *The best self-study is one that has clearly identified its audience and that develops its study and frames its recommendations for that audience.* In general, accreditation self-studies are aimed more at the central administration and the larger university community than at the library staff. The efforts of the self-study committee and the report that results from those efforts should reflect this bias. Time may be given to internal library issues as part of the process, but the focus of the evaluation should be elsewhere.

4. *The self-study committee and its chair must understand the values of the library and the university as it conducts its study if it is to effect change.* This is necessary to put specific problems into perspective and to send them forward in a way that is meaningful.

5. *In order to be effective, the self-study should make the best possible use of existing data.* Evaluation is expensive, and it can try the patience of those contributing to it if they are repeatedly asked the same questions.

6. *Information gathering for the self-study should be as open as possible.* One should assume that the process will build support for change as it identifies the need for it and requires input from all segments of the library's clientele. If the study is perceived to have listened to a variety of opinions, it can be expected that people who have contributed to the study will have more of a stake in ensuring that its recommendations are used.

7. *To be effective, the evaluation must include a clear plan for co-opting the library director into the study while maintaining the objectivity of the self-study committee.* A good evaluation must establish its objectivity, but the library director must feel that the results of the study are reasonable and

that they accurately reflect conditions in the library. As a result, efforts should be made to make the general findings of the committee available to the director as they emerge in the course of the study and to solicit that person's comments.

8. *Accreditation self-studies should be part of an ongoing planning process in the library.* They should take into account other planning documents that relate to the library program and contribute to the ongoing processes by which the library adapts its organization and programs to meet the changing needs of its community.

The actual process used in the self-study will vary from campus to campus. Whether the university chooses a traditional self-study or one that focuses on specific parts of the university program, the evaluators should view themselves as change agents who are expected to develop a set of recommendations for change that can be implemented and to build a constituency to support their findings. When the report of the self-study is produced, it should be considered a working document developed as part of an ongoing planning process for the library, which also happens to meet the requirements of the Southern Association.

The Visiting Team

The self-study is only half of the evaluation process used for accreditation. At the point that the self-study is completed, a visiting team is appointed by the Southern Association to visit the campus and evaluate its programs. This team fulfills two roles. The first is to certify that the report reflects the conditions on campus and that the university programs are of a quality that warrant reaccreditation. The second role of committee members is to serve as expert witnesses who bring the authority of the Southern Association and the vantage point of outsiders to bear on the change process. In the Southern Association, this is particularly true since there is one member of the team to evaluate each major component of the university program (including one librarian).

The role of the expert is particularly useful. If the institution is relatively secure, that person can be a change agent or at least the external part of the internal-external change agent team. The expert is in a position to provide a voice to support changes that have been proposed earlier and a vehicle for the generation of new ideas. To do either, the evaluator must be someone who understands libraries of the type being studied. According to the literature, the person and the evaluation that is conducted should have certain characteristics (Havelock, 1972; Kells, 1980; Baldridge, 1971). They can be summarized as follows:

1. *The evaluator on the visiting team should come from an institution that has at least as much prestige as the institution under study.* Since univer-

sities are generally very aware of their own images, they tend to prefer comparisons with institutions that they view either as peers or as role models. Therefore, evaluators from "lesser" institutions are at a disadvantage when they suggest programmatic changes.

2. *The library evaluator on the visiting team must understand the values of the institutions visited and operate within those values.* Much has been said about the political nature of accreditation. No visiting team report is ever likely to note all of the problems in the library, and it is important for the chair of the visiting team and the librarian on it to determine which ones are most important. That person must also decide which problems the university can effectively address and to focus on those issues. The library visitor must ensure that the problems that are addressed during the visit and in the team's report are treated in a way that makes sense in the context of the university.

3. *The library evaluator on the visiting team should make every effort to understand the organizational climate in the library.* The report that is produced should center on changes that can be accomplished and around which support can be built in the library and the university.

4. *It is better if the evaluator on the visiting team is someone who has been identified by the institution under study for inclusion on the team.* If there is no fear of disaccreditation, the library director is more likely to get the kind of evaluator who can be effective if the person on the team is known and respected.

5. *Throughout their time on campus, all members of the visiting team should be given free access to information about the library.* Again, the best evaluation is one that is based on openness.

The success of both the self-study committees and the visiting team depends on the degree to which there is general satisfaction with these evaluation processes in the university community. The capacity of accreditation to influence decision makers and to gain acceptance for change is contingent on the ability of those charged with carrying it out to combine objectivity and integrity with the kind of political sense that infuses new ideas into the decision-making process.

ISSUES IN THE ACCREDITATION PROCESS

While almost any issue can be treated in the accreditation process, the ones that will get the most attention are those that relate to direct services to the public. The issues that are dealt with should relate to the values of the institution and the library, should have administrative support, and should be issues behind which support can be built in the university and in the library. Some characteristics of the kinds of issues that can be treated most effectively by accreditation are described below:

1. *Change is most likely to occur when the need for change can be expressed within the value set of the university.* The use of peer grouping and themes that are of concern to senior administrators and the faculty are most effective.
2. *The need for change is stated most effectively in quantitative rather than qualitative terms.* While decisions are often made based on qualitative evidence, it is far easier to defend them if quantitative support can be produced.
3. *Change is more likely to occur when the self-study committee, the library administration, and others in the university community agree on the importance of the issue.* Consensus is critical, particularly between those who propose a change and those who will be asked to carry it out. Administrative enthusiasm is necessary in the adaptive process.
4. *Change is most likely to occur when it can be demonstrated that the effect of the change is clearly preferable to the existing state of affairs.* When the self-study can present an alternative to a situation that is generally agreed to be less than optimum, the change is more likely to be implemented.

In short, the issues that are likely to be dealt with most effectively are those that are of interest to the larger community and that are relatively easy to understand for people who are not intimately involved in the internal operations of the library. Recommendations about buildings, collections, and salaries are far more likely to get attention than those concerning the structure of the library catalog or classification systems.

Accreditation is at its best when it is viewed as a process designed to convince decision makers to make changes in their own interest. To do that, the process must appeal to their values and develop the kind of consensus that is required to raise a powerful voice for change. Good arguments skillfully presented with few surprises for the decision maker will lead to the kind of changes that make the accreditation process worthwhile.

APPLYING ACCREDITATION IN A UNIVERSITY SETTING

To understand how this model works in practice, it is necessary to look at its impact on two institutions. The process used for the reaccreditation of both institutions reflected many of the characteristics of the accreditation model listed above. It also provided the opportunity to determine the degree to which both preexisting conditions in the libraries and the issues that were treated influence the capacity of the study to promote change.

Case 1

The first case took place in one of the leading state-supported educational institutions in the Southeast. The university is governed by a president who reports to the head of a statewide system. Although advised by a thirteen-member board of trustees, the president has virtual autonomy in administrative matters relating to the campus. When the self-study began in 1972, the president was new to the post, and major changes had recently taken place in the structure of the university system. Only a year earlier, legislation had been passed to expand the university system from a six-campus organization to one including all public institutions in the state offering baccalaureate degrees. The university campus has a relatively small enrollment by national standards. In 1972 it had a student population of 20,000, including about 5,000 graduate students.

The University and Its Library

The library system of the university was overseen by the university librarian, who was responsible for the administration of the main library, an undergraduate library, and eleven other branch libraries serving various departments on the campus. The law and medical libraries were administered separately. The university librarian had an associate librarian, who, in turn, worked through an assistant librarian for management, a personnel librarian, and eleven department heads. The entire library system administered by the university librarian employed a full-time staff of 80 professionals and 141 support personnel. In addition, there were large numbers of graduate assistants and student workers. The total operating budget for the library system was just over $3 million, and the library's collections totaled almost 2 million volumes. At the time of the Southern Association visit, the library was one of the fifty largest academic libraries in the United States and Canada.

Authority over the university libraries was shared between the university librarian and a faculty library board. The board had a faculty chair, and it had substantial policymaking powers. It consisted of fifteen faculty members elected by the faculty council of the university, as well as two student representatives. The dean of the graduate school and the library director sat as ex officio members. This body advised the library director on matters relating to the operation of the library; formulated, with the advice of the library director, the basic policies governing the acquisition and use of library materials; and allocated the book funds that were not designated for specific purposes. The board was also expected to review library budgetary requests prior to their submission to the president. And, in addition to the advisory responsibilities given most other bodies of this sort, this board had responsibility for and authority over all matters relating to the collections, as well as some responsibility for some administrative details relating to the use of the library facility.

The time of the self-study was a difficult one for the library. The library director had had a long history of conflict with the library board, the library staff, and a number of other people in the community. Part of the problem stemmed from personality, and part stemmed from long-standing problems relating to the library building and the structure of the library organization. In any case, the librarian asked to be reassigned in the university just as the self-study process began, and much of the work was done under an acting librarian. The new director was hired just before the visiting team came to campus.

Relations between the University Library and Its Community

A survey conducted during the course of the self-study indicated that there was respect within the university community for individual services in the library, for the quality of the reference staff, and for the library collections in particular. Some personality problems and concerns about the cancellation of serials due to financial constraints were noted, but these had not undermined the university's recognition of its need for a first-rate library and its appreciation for the services rendered.

At the beginning of the self-study, one problem was considered to be of critical importance to both the library staff and their clients. The main library facility dated to 1929 and was built to support a much smaller institution. Even with an addition (completed in 1952), it was hopelessly inadequate. The lack of space made access to library collections difficult, and the service problems that resulted inconvenienced library users. A second addition was on the university's proposed list of new buildings, and a special collections building had been one of the library director's major priorities.

The Library Staff

The two issues that most concerned the staff were money and professional status. Staff members felt that the pay scales for professionals and support personnel were not adequate to retain good people unless they were tied to the geographic area for other reasons. This problem was particularly acute with support personnel. Although the community offered a large pool of qualified personnel for library jobs, the salaries offered by the library were too low to keep them in a career track. As a result, the library had a high rate of turnover. This made it more difficult to maintain continuity in library programs.

The other common concern focused on the status of librarians within the university community. Librarians did not have faculty status, and they felt that they were being excluded from consideration in decision making that affected their professional activities.

These two problems combined to lower the morale of the library staff. In fact, a 1975 survey of the attitudes of the library faculty and staff found that overall satisfaction with the quality of library services had declined across the board from 1969 to 1975.

The Southern Association Self-study

On April 7, 1972, the university's president appointed a steering committee to supervise the decennial self-study leading to reaccreditation by the Southern Association. The president was new to his position, and the SACs self-study provided an opportunity for a close examination of the university's program at a particularly appropriate time. Mechanisms that might begin a planning process for the university were high on the new president's list of priorities, and a larger committee than might otherwise be required was appointed so that a study could be produced that could form a baseline for future planning efforts. A critical analysis of the university and its program was specifically requested. The president's support for the process provided an incentive for the committee, for its members knew that, when the final report was completed, they would not be "talking to an empty hall." The committee was chaired by an influential member of the faculty and was charged with making a close examination of the campus.

After deliberating through the summer of 1972, the steering committee for the self-study appointed a number of subcommittees. These committees would produce 147 preliminary reports by the end of the study in January 1973 and involve the work of over 600 faculty members. Two separate committees were appointed to evaluate the library, one representing the library staff and the other representing the larger university community. The library staff self-study was chaired by a senior member of the library administration and reflected an official picture of the library. It was compiled as a staff report and was largely descriptive in nature. The conflict that existed between the library director and various constituencies of the library tended to discredit this report. As a result, the more important report was the one compiled by the external faculty committee.

Deliberations of the External Faculty Self-study Committee. The university-wide self-study committee on the library was appointed on September 15, 1972, and work began shortly after. Its chair was a faculty member who had been a member of the library board and who had a personal relationship with the chair of the university self-study committee. To provide data, a questionnaire was sent to all faculty, and copies were put in all study carrels in the main library facility. Copies were also distributed to users of the branch libraries. Major concerns were expressed by the respondents to the questionnaire about the condition of the library building and its collections. Concern about lighting, furnishing, organization, and, above all, space pervaded the results. A second set of concerns surfaced about funding levels, particularly as they related to collection development. Longer hours were requested, and concern was expressed about the need for better service in circulation, about stacks maintenance, and about the difficulty of accessing library collections. Many of these could be traced directly to the space problems of the library.

In addition to the data produced in the questionnaire, efforts were made by the committee to get information from a variety of users about the quality of library services. Library department heads and members of the library staff were interviewed. A general meeting with the library staff was also held. Staff concerns mirrored many of those expressed in the survey, but they also indicated a need for the development of more clearly defined goals for library programs. The space problem was also discussed, and the staff raised questions about the centralization of services, relations with other libraries, and the reclassification of the library's collections.

The analysis of the data gathered by the committee developed along with the actual gathering of the data. The degree to which data from various sources led to similar conclusions allowed committee members to reach consensus quickly. Along with the pressures placed on the committee by the tight deadlines set by the steering committee for the completion of the work, this consensus greatly facilitated the decisions relating to what should be included in the final report.

A Look at the Self-study Process. The process used by the faculty committee to evaluate the university libraries had many of the qualities of an ideal self-evaluation. The interest of the president in developing the planning process for the university was clearly advantageous. It is unlikely that the results of a study that expended this kind of energy could avoid having some impact on decision making. In addition, the committee's capacity to work as a unit was exemplary. Members of the committee respected each other, and the presence on the committee of two librarians provided much needed expertise in its deliberations. The openness of the process and the degree to which various components of the library's clientele expressed themselves provided an excellent example of how these phases of an evaluation should have been handled.

Some limitations in the methods used are also evident, however. Little effort was expended to define the role of the committee after the charge of the steering committee was received. Although planning for the entire self-study took place during the summer, the subcommittees were required to produce their reports quickly enough to preclude their spending time developing sophisticated plans for the conduct of the self-study. And little effort was made by the external faculty committee on the library to secure information about its operations from library files or to develop contacts with the library board, the internal library study committee, or members of the library administration. Other problems related to the timing of the process (for example, while the director's chair was vacant) and to low library staff morale.

Results of the Self-study. In some respects, the report of the self-study committee surprised those who received it. The report focused on the need for more books and journals and for assistance in the finding of materials already in the collections rather than on personality. The chairman of the steering committee commented that the initial reaction to the report was that it was too critical, but that, after closer reading, it was determined that the report was an accurate reflection of the conditions in the library.

From a political standpoint, the document was presented in a way that could be expected to get the attention of its audience. It was relatively short and used statistical data from the user survey and from other sources to good effect. Comparisons with other libraries were also used to impress upon the reader the need for the library programs to keep pace with those of its peers. Comparisons to a nearby rival library were used often to point up the weaknesses at the university. All of the problems identified were tied directly to the prestige and reputation of the campus as a center for research and graduate study.

Recommendations. The report of the university-wide self-study was decidedly negative in tone. Although the committee found evidence of goodwill and gratitude toward the librarians and high respect for their accomplishments, they felt it was their responsibility to focus on the needs of the program. The recommendations can be divided into three categories: space, money, and service.

The space problems in the library stemmed primarily from the inadequacies of the main library. It was found to be overcrowded, poorly lit, oddly laid out, and difficult to use. The committee noted that a decision had been made by the university to add to the stack area of the library, but it concluded that this addition would not be adequate. The collections would outgrow the new area shortly after it was completed, and even the momentary relief that the new area would give could not be expected for several years. A new special collections facility was also being considered, and $1 million had been raised from private sources for its construction. But the committee members felt that this building would not meet the space needs of the academic programs of the university. It suggested that a new central library should be built and that the old library facility be converted for use as a special collections facility.

In conjunction with these recommendations, the committee encouraged the library to seek funds for an automated circulation system and for the development of other computer applications. Circulation in the undergraduate library was already automated, and funds had been requested, without success, for a similar installation in the main library. The committee also urged the library to consider membership in the Southeastern Library Network (SOLINET) as both a move into automation and to cooperate with other libraries.

Money was an important theme throughout the report. The committee noted that the acquisition budget had once ranked among the largest in the Sougheast but that the university had fallen dramatically in relation to other libraries in the region by 1972–1973. They also noted that with 3 percent of the university's operating budget devoted to the library, the library ranked toward the bottom in this category among the forty members of the Association of Southeastern Research Libraries.

Space problems complicated use of the library, and the only way that appeared to be available to make the library usable was to enhance services. Library services also provided a focus for the study. The salary scale for staff was among the worst in the region, and this retarded efforts to attract competent staff; additional staff positions were also needed to enhance services. The committee also noted the long-standing conflicts between the library and the campus, and its report expressed a desire that the new university librarian should take an active role in the improvement of communications with the campus and in planning for the future of the university. To facilitate this, it was suggested that staff be added at the associate librarian's level to handle more of the daily routines in the library. Other suggestions for better service aimed primarily at improving the quantities of materials in the collections and the access to those collections. The collections were singled out for both praise and concern. Faculty and students were generally satisfied with the materials available to support their efforts, but concern was expressed about their continued capacity to do so. Funding limitations had not allowed the library to keep up subscriptions to as many periodicals as desired, and the rigid structure of allocations to teaching departments impeded the building of appropriate collections. It was felt that this could best be remedied by allowing for library participation on faculty committees and by putting more money into the hands of the librarians for the purchase of materials. It was also felt that records were not being included in the main catalog for some collections housed outside the general stacks; that it was often difficult to find materials even after a call number had been determined; that the use of both Dewey and Library of Congress classification numbers was cumbersome; and that stacks maintenance should be improved. Many of these problems related directly to space inadequacies and to funding limitations.

From the beginning, the report of the committee was designed to ensure that "the library should be recognized by the administration as an essential unit of the university, not merely as a repository of printed materials and a source of information, but as an important unit of the teaching, research, and planning process." It commented that "the library has drifted away from its central place in the university and has lost the high priority proper to it." The goal of the committee was to present ways in which this could be corrected. It succeeded in producing a politically useful document to support its objective.

Conclusion of the Work of the Self-study Committee.   Early in 1973, the reports of the individual self-study committees were completed and submitted to the Steering Committee. All of the individual reports were eventually bound for use, but the committee also saw the need for a shorter version of the findings that could provide a general overview of the campus. As a result, a self-summary report was developed.

This report integrated the findings of the two library committees into a single chapter. It developed a forty-page summary, including much of the descriptive data from the internal library report along with the more interpretive findings of the library committee. In areas where the conclusions of the two committees on libraries conflicted, both opinions were offered. The report is particularly important because it is a manageable document. While the multivolume analysis of the university is more thorough, the shorter form distilled the findings so that the substance of the report could be digested more easily by decision makers. It is a model of a politically sensitive document that can be read and understood. In fact, the president of the university read only the shorter version of its entirety and apparently read only parts of the larger report for clarification.

The Visiting Team

The visiting team appointed by the Southern Association to evaluate the university came to campus in the spring of 1974. It consisted of thirty-nine people under the chairmanship of the president of a similar institution.

The formal recommendations produced by the team mirrored those of the self-study committees. They included recommendations and suggestions calling for increased participation of librarians in collection development; a redefinition of the role of the administrative board; more money for library collections; more administrative personnel; a definition of the role of branch libraries; an upgrade in the status of the librarians; an extension of the collections into media other than print; and a call for a new building. Some of the suggestions were very specific (such as, replace worn phonodiscs). Others dealt with more pervasive issues (for example, the need for space). Most supplemented and emphasized earlier comments made in the course of the self-study (for example, the need for more travel funds, for planning, for cooperation with other libraries in the state and region, and for the inclusion of the faculty and the library staff in the decision-making process).

The Search for a University Librarian

At the same time that the self-study process was going on and before the arrival of the visiting team, the campus was entertaining candidates for the position of library director. Several concerns were expressed by the candidates. These included:

1. The level of compensation for the library staff and their status on campus.
2. The role of the administrative board in library decision making.
3. The space problems of the library, including concern about the current situation and an opinion that the proposed stack addition would meet the problem for only a short time.
4. The need for automation in the library.

The degree to which the observations of these people complemented those of the self-study reinforced these results and encouraged the university to address them.

Results of the Accreditation Process

One unfortunate coincidence seems to have limited the degree to which the report of the visiting team was effective. The library visitor came from a less prestigious institution and had been a candidate for the post of university librarian. Some of the specificity of his remarks during the visit and the fact that he had been an unsuccessful candidate for the directorship affected the degree to which his suggestions were taken seriously. On those occasions where his suggestions corresponded with those of the self-study committee, any effect that they had was credited to the internal committees.

Changes began in the library even before the end of the self-study process. Soon after the director stepped down, the acting director began to shape the program. Although she commented in her annual report that major changes in the program would be deferred until a replacement was found, she began dealing with problems that either required immediate decisions or whose resolution might be expected to prepare the ground for the new director.

Her first move was to begin to develop a relationship with the faculty library board. Both the acting director and the members of the board were concerned that the power vested in that body and its poor relations with the library administration might cause problems in identifying suitable candidates for the director's position. The acting director also began a program to keep library staff members and others informed of decisions made by the administration and to encourage participation in those decisions. A library newsletter began to appear regularly. In addition, where the former director believed that good decisions could not be made by committees and seldom used them, the acting director set up committees of library staff members to study storage facilities, the library guide book, reclassification issues, and automation.

Another change that took place early in 1973 was the decision of the library to join SOLINET beginning in fiscal year 1974. This was a major step in efforts to automate the library and to project it into the interlibrary cooperation efforts in the region.

In February 1973, the acting director was asked by the provost office to begin planning for a new stack addition. This had been raised in priority for capital funding in the university budget for the 1973–1975 biennium, and the decision was made to begin the architectural work as quickly as possible.

Planning and the New University Librarian

A new library director was hired beginning in the summer of 1973. Prior to assuming his post, he was asked by the university president to undertake a major planning effort concentrating on matters relating to collection development, space planning, and library staffing. As part of this effort, he requested that the board encourage faculty to participate in the process of identifying "the gaps between university needs and library realities and . . . to have these gaps documented and related to the academic programs of the university."

The planning process began in earnest in the fall of 1973. Three committees were established to study problems relating to the buildings in the library system, library collections, and staff. Each committee included both teaching faculty and library staffers. A plan for library services through 1980 was completed in October 1974, and an extended plan for the library through 1995 was published the following September. The issues raised reflected those mentioned in the self-study reports. A call was made for a new research library facility and for the remodeling of the main library to house the special collections. Expanded facilities for the branch libraries were also seen as needs, and more money was needed to retain the level of quality of the library collections. The need for additional staff and for the reorganization of that staff was also seen as a requirement if the library system expected to meet future challenges. By 1975, the administrative plan called for two associate librarians to aid the university library in the administration of the library program.

The effect of the planning process was to offer additional participation in library decision making to the library's clientele. It opened the communications process further and built upon the information in the self-study. Efforts were made to ensure that the planning continued through the establishment of a permanent committee for planning under the faculty library board. In short, the planning committees in the library continued the work of the self-study in tailoring the library program to meet changing times and in developing the appreciation of the university for library programs.

Changes in the Library Program

The coming of the new library director was accompanied by a number of major improvements in the condition of the library. Funds for collection development came almost immediately. Supplementary money was added to the base budget in September 1973 with a promise of more for the next year. The result was almost a doubling of the base budget. The library's relative standing among the libraries represented in the Association of Research Libraries rose dramatically in the years following the study.

In regard to the relationship of the faculty library board and the library director, discussions about the role of the board continued for the first year of the new director's tenure. Efforts were made to develop a clearly defined place for the board in the governance of the library. At the director's request and with the support of board members, substantial changes were made in the authority of the board in order to restore the autonomy of the library director in the daily operations of the library program.

Staffing in the university libraries improved as well. The number of professional staff members increased from 80 in 1972 to 107 in 1978, and the support staff increased in number from 141 to 190 over the same period. This was not accompanied by significant changes in salaries, however.

Perhaps the largest change related to the main library building, a change often attributed directly to the events surrounding the self-study. Following the recommendations of the faculty self-study committee, funds were found for a new library building. Ground was broken for the new central library facility in the summer of 1979, and the facility opened for use in the spring of 1984.

Not all of the problems were solved. Salaries remained low, and the question of the status of the professional staff remained unchanged after the reaccreditation. The need for better facilities for branch libraries was caught between the desire of faculty to keep these collections close at hand and the limitations in space in the buildings in which they were located. But, despite these lingering problems, it must be concluded that many of the major problems discovered during the course of the study were addressed and resolved in succeeding years.

While the caveat must be made that causality cannot be established with certainty between changes made and the accreditation process, it is clear that the self-study provided information that was used by later efforts. It is important to note in this case the degree to which the findings generated by accreditations and other studies occurring on campus in this period supported each other. And, in examining the impact of the self-study, the relationship of its recommendations to the changes that took place was either a significant coincidence or the study had a significant impact on administrative thinking.

Case 2

The second case studied involves the accreditation of a land grant institution. With the ascendancy of a new president of the institution in 1962, this university began a transition from an institution of technical education to a comprehensive university. Over the decade that followed, it underwent dramatic changes. It broadened its curriculum; began to admit women to its main campus on an equal basis with men; ended compulsory military training; reorganized its administration into colleges; and expanded rapidly. By 1970 the university was recognized as one of the two comprehensive state-supported universities in its state. When that president resigned in 1975, the school had 16,000 students studying in over seventy undergraduate programs in seven colleges, and 2,600 of those were graduate students in a variety of disciplines. And the university provided extension programs throughout the state. In terms of the quality and composition of its student body, the undergraduate students were above average though not outstanding. While the university had a reputation for quality in its technical programs, the newness of its other curricula tended to reduce its standing in those areas. Its goal, as summarized in its self-study, was to maintain and improve its newly found place among the top one hundred universities in the United States with teaching, research, and service programs designed primarily to fit the needs of its state.

Governance of the University

Responsibility for the university's governance was in the hands of a fourteen-member governing board, who, in turn, appointed the president of the university. The presidency had developed into a strong position. A new president was installed in 1975. He had been part of the administrative team since 1966, serving first as the head of the extension program, then as the vice-president for finance, and finally as the executive vice-president of the university. The change in presidents at this time was accompanied by the appointment of a new vice-president for academic affairs, three new deans, and a variety of other key administrative changes.

At the time of the self-study, authority for the day-to-day operation of the university was delegated to four vice-presidents (one each for administration, special projects, academic affairs, and student affairs). The academic affairs vice-president was responsible for the programs of the various colleges of the university and the basic activities supporting the teaching process. This included the libraries. In November 1976, the title for this position was officially changed to provost.

The University Libraries

The university libraries consisted of the main library and two branch libraries. The university had a strong tradition of centralized library services. Prior to 1965, only architecture had been allowed to set up an official library branch, and that was done at the insistence of the accrediting body for that discipline. In the decade that followed, several branches were proposed, but only the geology library was approved despite continuing space problems in the main library.

Just as the university had changed dramatically in the ten years preceding the self-study, its library had evolved from a small college library to a major university collection. In 1964, the library had a collection of fewer than 300,000 volumes with about 3,000 journal subscriptions. It employed a staff of 23 librarians and 28 support personnel and had a budget of less than $400,000. In 1975, the library held over 1 million volumes and subscribed to over 16,000 serials. Its staff consisted of 53 faculty and 103 classified workers, and the budget had risen to $3.3 million. By fiscal year 1976, the library was adding approximately 100,000 volumes yearly, and in the fall of 1975, it was accepted for membership in the Association of Research Libraries. Between 1965 and 1975, the portion of the total operating budget of the institution devoted to library resources rose from 1.8 to 3.9 percent.

While growth of this sort has many rewards, it is not without complications.

The main library facility had been constructed in 1955 to accommodate a 5,000-student campus. In the 1965 self-study, recommendations had been sent forward to enlarge it. But capital funds were not provided for this purpose, and by 1975 the library was badly cramped. Space for collections, users, and staff was at a premium, and off-site storage had been leased to house some of the library's materials.

Organization of the Library

The library was organized according to a divisional concept that included five departments (reference, acquisitions, serials, preparations, and user services), each of which administered a number of divisions. The administration consisted of the director, a single assistant, and a research office. The director of libraries was new to his post. He had come to the university two years earlier as an assistant director and succeeded to the post in 1975 when his predecessor left the university. While the departing director had been controversial, particularly as a result of rapid changes made in the library, the new director was generally respected.

Relations between the University Library and Its Community

To assist in the operation of the library and to ensure that library policies fit within the context of the university program, the faculty senate of the university had established a library committee to advise the director. It had two faculty members from each of the seven colleges, one graduate student, and one undergraduate student. The library director sat as an ex officio member. Unlike the faculty committee described in the first case, this committee was purely advisory. Its primary function was to ensure that the teaching faculty had a mechanism to communicate effectively with the library. In addition, many of the colleges and departments of the university had their own library committees to work with the various subject librarians.

The relationship between the library and its users at the time of the self-study was relatively good. Service improvements and enhancements in the efficiency of library operations begun in years preceding the self-study did much to improve the image of the library. Faculty and students respected the library staff and appreciated the quality of the service being offered. The overcrowding of the main library facility was almost universally considered to be a problem, and this provided a target for discontent. Most users agreed that service had actually improved over the years despite crowded conditions and staff shortages.

On the negative side, faculty were not satisfied with the collections of the library or with the accessibility of those collections. Both of these shortcomings can be seen as functions of the inadequate library building and of the rapid growth of library collections. It should be remembered that of the approximately 1 million volumes in the library collections, 300,000 had been acquired in the three years prior to the self-study. Acquiring materials at this rate is difficult, particularly when one is unaccustomed to doing so, and, even if it is done well, faculty perceptions of the quality of collections tend to lag behind the efforts to correct these limitations.

As for the servicing of the collections, the crowded building made it difficult to find materials in the collections. Work space was also at a premium. The acuteness of the problem and the length of time it had been a major concern of the administration had focused much of the attention of the university community on the shortcoming of the library building.

The Library Faculty

By 1975, efforts had been made to improve the compensation level and status of the library faculty substantially over what they had been ten years before. In the 1965 self-study report, the lack of faculty status for librarians and the low salaries offered for these positions were cited as a major concern. As a result of that study and of other documents that followed, librarians were given full faculty status and privileges in 1969. By 1971, they were also represented in the university's faculty senate, and administrators pressed for the inclusion of libraries in faculty committees. With this upgrade in status came substantial improvements in salary, and by 1975, they were competitive.

But the speed with which the library faculty and its role grew and the changes that took place as it tried to meet the new challenges being placed before it made it difficult for the staff to become comfortable with their situation.

Decision Making in the Library

The decision-making structure for the library was designed to accommodate broad participation within a traditional hierarchy. Policy decisions were made by directors, department heads, and divisional heads as appropriate. Various councils of administrators were established to provide formal communication devices for exchanging ideas between them. In addition, eleven library faculty committees were established to handle a variety of concerns, and library faculty and library staff associations had developed to discuss matters relating to the operation and to encourage socialization in the organization. Nevertheless, problems existed in the communications flow into the library from the outside and from the lower levels of the organization to those above them.

The Southern Association Self-study

In May 1975, the university president appointed a university self-study committee, and the process began in earnest that summer. A steering committee for the self-study was appointed, and eleven self-study committees (one for each of the Southern Association standards) were appointed early in the fall.

The timing of the study was significant. The new president wanted to use the self-study to help continue the change process on campus. In his charge to the steering committee, he expressed strong support for the self-study process and urged the members to develop a realistic plan for the university. It should be noted, however, that the impact of this study was not expected to be as dramatic as the decennial study that had preceded it. In 1965, the mission of the institution was changing, as was the whole temper of the campus. In 1975, the university had grown accustomed to change and required direction for continuing change rather than an impetus to initiate changes.

Two library self-study reports were produced, representing, on the one hand, the views of the library staff and, on the other, a broader campus view. The internal self-study was designed to encourage maximum participation on the part of the professional library staff. Individual librarians were asked to evaluate the area of the library in which they worked and to asses the effectiveness of the larger organization. These individual comments were cumulated into a divisional report from which departmental reports were developed. Finally, the institutional planning office of the university assimilated the five departmental reports into a single report for the study of the entire library.

The university-wide committee on the library consisted originally of six faculty members and three graduate students. The director of libraries served as a resource for the committee.

Deliberations of the Self-study Committee.   The work of the university-wide library committee began almost immediately. Two early decisions shaped the process. The first was a request from the chair of the steering committee that each department and nonacademic area conduct its own self-study. As a result of this request, the library self-study was generated, and each of the teaching departments generated reports that commented on library support for their interests. Another result was that a great deal of information was made available to the primary study committees by the end of March 1976.

The second decision was that only one questionnaire would be circulated on campus in the self-study effort. It was felt that a single instrument asking about all elements of the university program would be seen as less of a burden by members of the community and that the return rate might be higher. Institutional research was charged with compiling questions, and it published the results of the survey on March 29, 1976. Data collected simplified the study process.

In early 1976, the committee on the library began to compile its report. The whole committee met infrequently, but three subcommittees (one each for facilities, collections, and services) met often, and each compiled its own findings. Information was extracted from the sources available, and individual subcommittee reports were filed. These were completed by May 1, and the final report of the committee was developed through the summer. It was officially presented to the steering committee on September 1, 1976. The report was then edited and abridged for inclusion in the final report for the university. The steering committee decided early in the study that the final report should consist of only one volume, so brevity was extremely important in keeping the various recommendations in context.

Results of the Self-study.   Before commenting on the recommendations of the committee on the library, it is necessary to comment on the results of the internal self-study. The report that came forward from the library was a heavily edited version of staff concerns. The concerns expressed by individuals in the various departments on specific operational problems within those departments and on concerns relating to the internal operations of the library tended to be diluted as they went up the hierarchy. Divisional reports confirmed most of these concerns. But at the department level, most of the negative comments were filtered out, and the focus moved to more general problems relating to space constraints and the collection. The final library report continued this filtering, and it was, in the main, a more positive document than the support documents produced at lower levels.

The first part of the report of the library staff self-study was a discussion of the changes made between 1965 and the initiation of the new self-study. The earlier self-study was seen as a point of departure marking the beginning of a period of change in the library. The new report moved to a consideration of the resources available to support library activities. The major successes noted were those of collection building and automation. The major failures related to a building that was too small and growing security problems. The report recommended that the building be expanded from 100,000 to 451,000 square feet.

In terms of library organization, statements made in individual assessments relating to communications were reflected in the comment that "the librarians as faculty demand a high level of internal responsiveness to change and flexibility in addition to freely available channels of communication," but little was said beyond that. Personnel concerns were restricted to comments about turnover, particularly turnover among civil service workers.

The recommendations that came out of this study generally reflected old concerns or a need for the continuation of change in areas where change had begun. In terms of collections, the report suggested that the library continue to add 100,000 new volumes annually to fill gaps in its collections. The need for continued close contact with the university community and close scrutiny of the devices used to allocate funds and to acquire and process materials were also encouraged. Concerns relating to library services centered around the continued development of an automated circulation and catalog system and expansion of library orientation programs. As for the library organization, the study recommended that new divisions be established for serials and general reference; that policy manuals be developed throughout the library; that increased participation in decision making be encouraged among the faculty and staff; and that efforts be made to enhance communication within the organization and between the organization and its constituency.

The organization section was the most critical portion of the study. It reflected an appreciation of the needs of the library to develop its staff as a team better prepared to meet its challenges. Space planning was also addressed, with appropriate attention given to the need for new space for materials and users. Finally, the report commented on the need for continuing the development of library automation projects.

The report of the faculty committee on the library relied heavily on this internal self-study in many respects. Its first three recommendations related to space. The committee said that 50,000 square feet of off-site storage should immediately be found to alleviate space concerns, that the main library should be air-conditioned, and that a library addition should be constructed as soon as possible. As for collections, the committee had been advised that there was a feeling among the teaching faculty that too little effort had been spent in selecting and acquiring foreign materials for the collections. It was also recommended that the budget for library materials should not fall below the 1975–1976 level and that at least 100,000 volumes should be added annually.

Service concerns related primarily to the need for additional staffing, further development of automated systems for the library, better security, and increased hours during university breaks and holidays. The committee felt that the staff was both competent and helpful but recommended that more people be added to meet student and faculty needs for assistance. The self-study urged the library to develop new security measures and to continue development on its online catalog. Longer hours during break periods were seen as a significant need for those who wanted to use the library for research.

A concern was also expressed about communications problems between the library and its users. While the committee noted that the university library committee was expected to ensure that communication took place, the self-study committee felt that the process would work better if formal relations were established between the university library committee and the individual college and departmental library committees. Committee members also noted a lack of coordination between the library and academic departments when new programs were being explored and recommended that departmental library committees be told at regular intervals about the status of their book and periodical allocations. It was also suggested that greater effort be expended in exploring networking arrangements with other libraries, in general, and membership in the Southeastern Library Network, in particular.

Most of the problems identified in the report relating to the library and its services were not new, and most had been identified in the internal library report. In some areas, efforts were already underway to correct them. The budgetary recommendations reflected a fear that the purchasing power of the library for collections might be reduced, and the new funds requested were merely designed to keep pace with inflation. While a new building addition was noted as a major priority for the university, the request for more library space had been on the boards since at least 1965, and plans had been submitted to the legislation for funding the addition as early as 1970. The major difference was that the additional space needs projected in 1976 were substantially larger than those in the various planning documents. That report suggested that 351,000 square feet be added as opposed to the 150,000 square feet that had been requested ten years earlier. In general, the committee report was a conservative one reflecting a need for continuing the process of change that had begun ten years before.

The Visiting Team

The visiting team appointed by the Southern Association came to the campus in April 1977. Unlike the visitors in case 1, the library director was well acquainted with directors in the region, and he recommended the person who eventually was to evaluate him. While he was not personally acquainted with that person, he knew him by reputation and admired the institution from which he came.

The visitors were distressed by the library building. They pointed out in their report, "It is tragic that the talented and dedicated staff . . . and the rich and broad collection that has been gathered have had their educational effectiveness so severely limited by a grossly inadequate building." The major recommendation made by the visiting team relating to the library program was that vigorous efforts should be made to obtain funding for the expansion of the central library.

In terms of resources, the visiting team report spoke of the need in the library for continued financial support as it sought to provide the materials needed in an expanding educational program and also noted that the university had made a strong commitment to library collections, further suggesting that additional attention should be paid to the equipment that would be required to support the growth of the library program. The visiting group also echoed the self-study committee's recommendation that the institution join the Southeastern Library Network as part of its commitment to interlibrary cooperation.

The final set of suggestions related to the external relations of the library. It was suggested that the nonvoting status of the library director in the university council be upgraded to that of a full voting member. This suggestion was made on the premise that the vote would make the director's role more effective in the council. It was also suggested that membership in the university library committee include representatives of the library committees of the various colleges and that the director of libraries be included in discussions of new academic programs at the university level. These suggestion related directly to the need for improving communications between the library and its users.

The visiting team's report closely paralleled the report of the library self-study. But there was one area in which the visiting team expressed more concern than the committee on the library. The team pointed out that structural problems inhibiting communications in the organization existed and should be remedied, noting that the organization was shorthanded at the top. It is interesting that these concerns reflected sentiments expressed in the individual assessments of the library program but that were toned down as the self-study progressed. Team recommendations tended to emphasize structural concerns in the library and its administration. The final report emphasized the need for a tightening of the administrative structure and for additional support for the operation while re-emphasizing the dramatic need for space.

Change in the University Library

Tying specific changes to the accreditation process is perhaps more difficult in this case than in case 1. Changes had begun several years earlier as the institution began to emerge as a major institution of higher education. Rather than being a starting point, the reaccreditation process of 1975–1977 marked a reassessment of what had been accomplished over the previous decade and what was left to be done. While no formal planning process was in place between the two self-studies, it is evident in the degree to which the new report referred to the older one that the view taken by the self-study committee was that the 1975–1976 study was a continuation of the one completed in 1965.

Still, it should be noted that changes did take place during the course of the self-study and the accreditation visit and in the period following the reaccreditation studies that appear to relate to them. Although most of the work for the institutional self-study was completed by the beginning of spring 1976, the library produced departmental updates to the study the next year. By the time the update appeared, a number of the problems that had been addressed in the self-study had already been remedied. In early 1976, the library received its own computer for the further development of its automated system. It joined the Southeastern Library Network in the late spring of 1976. New services became available in July of that year through a new General Reference Division, and improved control over serials became a reality when the Serials Division was established in the Acquisitions Department. To address the communications problems within the library and between the library and its users, department chairs talked in their update about the development of written procedures.

But in the period directly after the self-study, signs began to appear that were ominous for the future of the library. For the first time in a decade, the library received no increase in its materials budget, and the intent of the study that the library continue to add volumes at a rate of 100,000 per year was placed in jeopardy. While the library did add 100,000 volumes in 1975–1976, this figure dropped to 68,000 the following year and stayed below 80,000 for several years thereafter.

But by the summer of 1977, major changes had been made in the library. The library had acquired and outfitted some 15,000 square feet of off-site storage and moved 200,000 volumes to that location. While this was far short of the 50,000 square feet requested in the self-study, it provided for two years' growth in the library collections. In public services, the new General Reference Division expanded the orientation function for underclassmen and moved to improve services for a larger population. The acquisition of foreign library materials was stepped up, and the library committed to enhance holdings of this sort as part of its cooperative arrangements with other universities. The replacement of missing materials was also given priority, and the process for doing so was streamlined. In order to meet its service commitment, twenty-three new library faculty positions were added under a state formula for the 1976–1977 school year, and two new civil service positions were created. Interlibrary cooperation increased as the library increased its lending to other libraries. Development of the library's automation program continued.

Several of the suggestions and recommendations of the self-study and of the visiting team were not dealt with in 1977 or in later years. Concerns relating to deficiencies in some areas of the collections had been received from the affected departments. Efforts were initiated to define these more precisely. For instance, the library also said that it did not understand the comment that additional copies of textbooks should be purchased since it had a formal policy excluding the purchase of textbooks. No new assistant directors were added, and the relationship between college and departmental library committees and the university library committee remained informal.

An attempt to deal with the limitations of the building was made in the fall of 1977, but even then, the solution was not altogether satisfactory. In a speech to the Board of Visitors in August 1976, the self-study chair noted that the most important problem facing the university was space and that the number one space problem was the library. A plan had been developed after the 1965 self-study to expand the library by 120,000 square feet. It had been in the hands of state government for a number of years, but funding had lagged. By the time of the 1975–1976 self-study, the need had grown to 351,000 square feet, and in the 1975–1976 annual report, the director asked that the plans for the addition be revamped. But the university felt that any alteration of the original plans might further delay construction, and it was decided that they should proceed with these specifications. In November 1977, the state passed a capital bond issue for new construction. The university's library addition and remodeling project was at the top of the priority list. Construction began almost immediately, and the expanded facility opened to the public in 1981. But by the time the facility was completed, it was at capacity.

It is difficult to conclude that major changes can be directly related to the reaccreditation process. The administrative changes recommended by the visiting team were not implemented, and although the building was expanded in the period after the study, the expansion was based on plans that predated reaccreditation. Still, the self-study appeared to serve as a communications device in bringing into the open problems that existed within the organization. The results were used as a benchmark to show what the library needed to continue being a viable part of the university community.

Evaluation and Planning at the University

In some respects, the self-study and visiting team reports represent an almost unconscious example of Kells's model for institutional evaluation. It is obvious that certain parameters had been developed in the 1960s as to where the institution was going and how it might get there. The 1965 self-study of the library was a major benchmark in this development, and the new study built on the old. The recommendations that emerged reflected the continuing adherence of the institution's view of the future and outlined plans for continued growth. The study of the library may not have had the impact of the earlier study, but it clearly helped the library identify the concerns that were limiting its capacity to adapt to a changing world and to communicate those concerns to policymakers in the university community and beyond.

CONCLUSIONS

This study was designed to show how regional accreditation as practiced in the South can be used as a catalyst for change. In pursuing this objective, it has presented a model of how accreditation is supposed to be applied to university programs in general and to the library in particular. The model described the background of the claims made for accreditation and provided a theoretical basis for properly assessing the impact of the process. It separated the idea of accreditation as a change agent from the role it plays as a regulator of higher education in order to allow a clearer view of the impact of the progress. An effort was then made to show how evaluations following this model could affect decision making within the library.

To act as a change agent, the accreditation process must help library leaders persuade key decision makers of the need for change and mobilize staff members and users of library services to support desired improvements. At its best, accreditation is a tool that provides a fresh view of the status of programs and suggests ways in which change can enhance their capacity to support the university.

It is fair to conclude from the cases examined that accreditation can in this way have a significant impact on decisions made by and for libraries. When the process is tailored to meet the specific needs of the institution, it can influence change. But if library managers are expected to use accreditation, they must have confidence in it. That requires a fuller understanding of what the process can and cannot do. The concluding comments of this study will address this requirement.

The Library as Part of the University

The first general comment about the reaccreditation process is that accreditation must always view the library as a component of the larger university. The people who are likely to oversee this kind of evaluation are more likely to be users of the library rather than those who work in the facility. User interests and understandings of library functions are limited to those that relate to the points at which the library meets its public. In both of the cases cited, this relationship had a substantial impact on the outcome of the self-study and visitation. The results of the program focused on issues like buildings, collections, and finances and spent less energy on concerns relating to the internal operations of the library. In both cases, the internal self-studies prepared by the library staff raised organizational issues that were primarily of concern to themselves. In each case, these were not given the emphasis in the reports of the committees of teaching faculty that they received from the librarians. Only in areas where the evidence could be quantified or in those in which nonlibrary personnel had a particular interest did this not hold true. (For example, the expression of concern about the salaries of librarians and library support staff; salary concerns are easily understood by those outside the library, and they receive a sympathetic hearing if presented as unfavorable comparisons with peer institutions. They can be expressed in quantitative terms, and data for comparison with other institutions is easily available).

Other issues relating to internal operations fared less well in the accreditation process. Consider the concerns expressed about communications patterns in the library in case 2. While the visiting team report and other documents produced in the course of the reaccreditation review identified problems here, no concrete changes were made to deal with them. The same is true of the visiting team suggestion that the size of the administrative staff should be increased. "Failures to communicate" and concerns about the span of control are problems rooted in differences in management style that are open to interpretation. Efforts to foster change in these areas require a strong understanding of the internal operations of the library and an appreciation of organizational procedures and staff perceptions of those procedures. It is unlikely that any accreditation study or any other evaluation managed by nonlibrarians will be able to gain enough of an understanding of these kinds of problems to allow them to influence changes of this sort unless they have been previously identified as problems by the university administration or unless they are extremely acute. Perhaps the greatest limitation of accreditation is its incapacity to exert influence on more subtle problems.

Another factor of great importance to the effectiveness of the reaccreditation process at both institutions in fostering change was the emphasis placed on the study by the central administration of each university. Central administration determines the kind of resources to be made available for the study and the goals that the evaluation is expected to pursue. If the institution's president thinks the study should produce substantial results and makes those expectations clear to those charged with conducting the evaluation, it is likely that others will expend the resources required to make this happen.

The same kind of support must also pervade the structure of the library. Given the charge for the self-study, the library director and other administrators must support the spirit of the evaluation wholeheartedly. This kind of support raises the stature of the process in the organization and ensures that those who assist with it pursue information for the self-study as if it matters. But even the most enthusiastic administrators are not likely to understand at the beginning of the process what that process will bring to the organization. Successful administrators tend to focus on results, and, for many, the aim of the study will be a report that will supply suggestions for internal improvement while meeting a requirement established by the accrediting agency. They are less likely to see the process as a means of communicating the concerns of the organization up and down the organizational hierarchy in a meaningful way. While the report is part of this communications process, the proceedings of the self-study committees, conversations between faculty, administrators and librarians, study procedures, and all of the other data gathering that goes on at this time may be more important in communicating library problems to those who can help solve them.

To some degree, this was the case at both of the universities studied. In both cases, the chief administrator on campus asked important members of the faculty to develop a report that reflected the true state of the university. These people were given the authority and resources to comply with this request. From the beginning, everyone understood that the power of the central administration stood behind the study. The self-studies on both campuses were expected to produce information for local consumption. However, senior administrators at both campuses said in later conversations that accreditation self-studies done on their campus were done for external consumption and that they had little impact on the views of the internal campus. The provost of one institution said that, in his view, accreditation required virtually nothing of the institution; anything that the institution received from the process was strictly the result of additional requirements placed on it by people in the institution. This same sentiment was expressed repeatedly by administrators in the libraries and in the central administrations in both institutions. It is not unreasonable to say that the impact of the accreditation process is based primarily on the importance placed on it by the school under study. But the idea that this is a flaw in the process reflects a misunderstanding of what accreditation hopes to accomplish. This is particularly true on campuses that have no fear that they will lose their accreditation. If the process is to be used well in these kinds of institutions, the decision makers must begin to consider the process as a self-improvement mechanism as well as a toll for quality assurance.

Preaccreditation Planning

Preparation for accreditation on both campuses followed a similar pattern. The primary responsibility for planning lay in the hands of a prominent faculty member who spent considerable time determining how best to carry out this activity. Planning at the lower level was given less attention. Patterns for faculty investigations of the programs of the university were clearly in place on both campuses, and in both cases these were followed. Every effort was made to ensure broad participation in the process.

In the first case, the relations of the library administration with the library's administrative board and the rest of the university were strained. The university librarian had actively discouraged his staff from making independent judgments about administrative matters. The internal self-study was produced largely as an exercise within the library office. As a result of this kind of management style and the lack of confidence on the part of the faculty committee in the willingness of the library to supply information, the external faculty study committee paid little attention to anything produced by the library hierarchy. Emphasis was placed on the collection of new data rather than on the use of information that had been developed in the internal self-study of the library or the faculty committee overseeing it. Even when the faculty committee sought to find out more about the library operation, it chose to use hearings or interviews with people in the library organization rather than printed sources. The role taken by the committee was that of a mediator trying to wind its way between prejudices raised in a long feud.

In the second case, the committee relied on existing data. Good relations between the library staff and library users were the rule of the day. While some of the faculty expressed a dislike for the former director, the new director was generally well thought of on campus and was credited with building up relations with the university community. The presence on the campus of a number of departmental and college library committees provided channels for interaction between librarians and the teaching faculty. When the self-study began, the effort put into the internal library self-study produced wide participation and a wealth of documentation. As a result, most of the effort expended in analyzing the library came from the library faculty and staff. The efforts of the external faculty committee were limited largely to the use of existing documents and the efforts of the library staff. The library director was active in the work of the external committee, at least as a resource, and he enjoyed its confidence. All of this simplified the data-gathering process and led to the creation of a report by the committee on the library that closely paralleled that of the library faculty.

This is not to say that these two libraries were without similarities. In each case, an administration that was committed to the idea of change developed procedures that they expected to form benchmarks for their efforts. On both campuses, new central and library administrators used the self-study processes and the documents that they produced as political mechanisms to achieve objectives in the library that they considered important (such as more space, salaries, and collection funds). In the final analysis, the difference in the way the accreditation process was used was a contrast between a conservative organization that saw the need for substantial change and an organization that was more dynamic and wanted to continue to change as it had for a number of years prior to the study. The requirements for change in these two cases were different, and the processes used to bring about change had to be modified to meet these requirements.

Issues Treated in the Accreditation Process

There are limitations to the kinds of issues that can be treated by a committee from outside the library organization. The library is unique in the university in that it has many of the components of a business office and many of those of the teaching faculty. It must also maintain close working relations with all elements of the university community if it is to function. It is unlikely that technical issues will ever be addressed in a self-study led by library users because the expertise to evaluate these issues is lacking. Even at a university where the make-up of the study committee was such that almost all of the members had long-standing working relationships with the library through library committees, the self-study committee declined to deal with these kinds of problems. The ones that generally prove most interesting to these committees are those relating to collections, specific services, and, in these two cases, space planning.

When a major problem is so obvious that it obscures others, it appears to have a major impact on any assessment of the library. It is perhaps inevitable that major problems (like space or personalities) will tend to mask more subtle ones in the deliberations of self-study committees. Examination by a group dominated by library users is not likely to have the time or expertise required to trace all of the problems of the library organization to their precise roots. In each case, the building situation was so serious and so long-standing that every other concern was related to space in the minds of the evaluators. One must wonder what would have been in the self-study report had the addition to their buildings been completed. The contrast between the focus on this aspect of the program and the change of focus with the departure of an unpopular leader in case 1 provides a useful contrast.

There are also important questions relating to the relationship between the timing of the evaluation and its capacity to induce change. Since accreditation takes place at regular intervals, however, the timing of self-study and the visit will not always occur when most needed. While accreditation does ensure that some evaluation will take place regularly, it cannot ensure that interim examinations of the library program will take place as a part of a larger planning process as the need arises. Plans must be in place for supplementary evaluations for this purpose.

The Rhetoric of the Accreditation Reports

The report of the self-study committee in case 1 was well suited to influence decision makers. Its use of statistical data and comparisons with rival institutions was designed to have a maximum impact on and to bring to the surface in a forceful way problems that had not previously been given much attention. The report was designed to convince the university that significant changes had to be made. As a result, it succeeded where the internal reports generated by the library staff did not. The chair of the committee used the credibility of his committee and the data that they compiled to create a compelling document to be used as the basis for library planning.

The document in case 2 is not as detailed or as forceful a report. The decision was made early in the process that reports of major committees should be relatively short, and the library report's analysis of the situation was largely qualitative. It was more a statement of the state of the library than a reasoned plea for change. The contrast is particularly striking when one considers that change resulted from both studies. This can be explained through an examination of the situations surrounding the self-studies. The first committee did its work at a time when the university and the library felt the need for change but had not yet developed an idea of what direction these changes would take. They had to sell their idea for potential improvement to the central administration. On the other hand, the second committee was speaking to an audience that had become accustomed to innovation. As a result, the committee could assume that the library and the university were willing and able to adapt to changing situations and that all that was required was a presentation of suggestions as to where the library should go next. While a more thorough assessment of the library and a stronger report might have been useful, the one produced met the need and encouraged the university to continue the change process.

The Self-Study Committee and the Implementation of Its Recommendations

In neither of the cases examined were members of the faculty committees co-opted into the process of selling innovation to the university community. In the first case, the chair of the campus-wide steering group worked to authenticate the findings of the library self-study committee, and the library committee cooperated in this process. However, the new librarian was expected to sell the needed changes to the university community and the administration. In the second case, the committee did even less. There are several possible explanations for this.

Librarians have a long tradition of fending off intrusion by faculty, and mistrust of faculty influence has grown as librarians have attempted to gain greater control of library affairs. This was particularly true at this university. There is also a problem in maintaining faculty interest in the project once their charge has expired. Faculty members had spent long hours on this project, and many felt the need to move on to other things.

Accreditation as a Component of Institutional Planning

At both universities, the accreditation process was used as the basis for institutional planning. In the first case, it served as the benchmark that began a transitional period and resulted directly in the development of a long-range plan for the university. One of the first missions given by the president to the new library director upon arrival was to develop a plan for the future of library services and collections extending, first, to 1980 and, then, to 1995. Many of the recommendations that came out of this process mirrored those that the self-study had produced earlier. The number of times the self-study was later cited in library documents is clear evidence of the importance of this process as a benchmark for the program.

In the second case, the process was less formal. No real long-term plan was produced, but it can reasonably be argued that the 1975 study was just another part of a planning process that had begun ten years earlier. The degree to which the new self-study relied on the older one as a benchmark indicates a sense of continuity that is critical to institutional planning. Planning is a dynamic exercise, and the role that this particular evaluation played in that process is attested to in the annual reports that were produced in the next few years.

Accreditation, Change, and the Academic Library

It would be ideal to end a study of the impact of accreditation on academic libraries with a strong affirmation that accreditation, or indeed any other substantial evaluation, automatically leads to change. But that is not possible here. One can certainly assert that the Southern Association visits and self-studies that preceded them in these two cases led to change. One can also add that in each case the evaluation was a substantial event in the life of the library and a very positive one. Yet one should remember that these two institutions were chosen for study specifically because of changes that took place in the library at roughly the same time as accreditation. The purpose of the study was not to determine whether accreditation led to change in all cases but to find out how this evaluation process assisted these institutions in determining what kinds of changes were appropriate and in building the support required to begin to implement these changes.

The accreditation process is viewed here as part of the life of the library rather than as a single event with direct causal relations to specific changes. Accreditation, like any other evaluation process, is merely a tool that is available to the library if the institution chooses to use it. The fact that the Southern Association decennial study is scheduled in a university provides no assurance that change will result. However, if the institution decides to use the process to foster change, it seems reasonable to infer from the literature and from these two cases that it can assist in helping the institution to change. The key is a desire on the part of the library and the university administration to invest resources in the process.

There appear to be several limitations to the capacity of accreditation to effect change, at least in the library. The first has to do with timing. Reaccreditation comes once every ten years, and the timing of the study does not necessarily correspond to specific needs for change in the organization. This is particularly true when one looks at the library in the context of the whole university. Since the study has a broad focus, it is likely to come to the university at a critical time for some areas while, for others, the crises requiring remediation may have passed. Further emphasis should be placed on the need for the library and other parts of the university to look upon the process as part of a continuing evaluation of its operations and services. After all, it is good management practice to develop the capacity to understand where the organization is at any given time from as many perspectives as possible.

The second limitation seems to be the failure of campus administrators to perceive that reaccreditation should be undertaken primarily for internal use. In both of these institutions and in the literature, the Southern Association and other accrediting agencies are perceived to act primarily as policemen. But their capacity to serve this function in the more prestigious universities is very limited. Further consideration should be given to convincing administrators and others of the role accreditation can play as facilitators of change as opposed to considerations of the possible external consequences that might result from the enforcement of standards. This is not as easy as it sounds. The concept that the Internal Revenue Service is there to help the taxpayer has little credibility; the same is true of any plea of helpfulness by a regulatory agency. As long as it maintains its functions of quality assurance, it is unlikely that regional accrediting bodies will ever be able to portray themselves entirely as helpful friends of their members so long as they hold the keys to governmental funding and the attraction of students. But more effort should be placed on the importance of using this tool along with others in the effort to keep institutions of higher education and their libraries in tune with their constituencies.

It seems appropriate to urge that further research efforts relating to accreditation center on the development of refinements to the process using the many evaluative techniques that are available in the institutional environment. The model outlined here provides a start in the development of a true picture of the accreditation process. Further research will be needed to refine that model.

BIBLIOGRAPHY

Ashworth, Kenneth. *American Higher Education in Decline*. College Station: Texas A&M University Press, 1979.

Baldridge, J. Victor. *Power and Conflict in the University*. New York: Wiley, 1971.

Baysore, Gerald Carl. "The Selection, Training and Evaluation of Examiners in Selected Accrediting Associations." Ph.D. dissertation, University of Denver, 1971.

Clark, David, and Guba, Egon G. *Effecting Change in Institutions of Higher Education*. Bloomington, Ind.: National Institute for the Study of Educational Change, 1966. (ERIC Document Reproduction Service No. 028 685)

Davis, Howard R., and Salasin, Susan E. "The Utilization of Evaluation." In Elmer L. Struening and Marcia Guttentag, eds. *Handbook of Evaluation Research,* vol. 2. Beverly Hills: Sage, 1975.

Dressel, Paul. *Handbook of Academic Evaluation*. San Francisco: Jossey-Bass, 1971.

Ferster, Herbert Vernon. "Criteria for Excellence: A Content Analysis of Evaluation Reports by a Regional Accrediting Association." Ph.D. dissertation, State University of New York at Buffalo, 1971.

Gelfand, Morris A. "A Historical Study of the Evaluation of Libraries in Higher Education Institutions by the Middle States Association of Colleges and Secondary Schools." Ph.D. dissertation, New York University, 1960.

Grant, George Calvin. "Attitudes of Higher Education Library Administrators Toward Adequacy of Middle States Association Library Evaluation Criteria and Processes." Ph.D. dissertation, University of Pittsburgh, 1982.

Havelock, Ronald G. *The Change Agent's Guide to Innovation in Education*. Englewood Cliffs, N.J.: Educational Technology Publications, 1972.

Houle, Cyril O. *The Design of Education*. San Francisco: Jossey-Bass, 1972.

House, Ernest R. "The Politics of Evaluation in Higher Education." *Journal of Higher Education* 45 (1974): 618–627.

Johnson, Edward R.; Mann, Stuart H.; and Whiting, Carol. *An Assessment of the Management Review and Analysis Program (MRAP)*. University Park: Pennsylvania State University, 1977.

Kells, H. R. *Self-study Processes: A Guide for Post-secondary Education*. Washington, D.C.: American Council on Education, 1980.

Kells, H. R., and Kirkwood, Robert. *Analysis of a Major Body of Institutional Studies Conducted in the Northeast, 1972–1977*. State College, Pa.: Association of Institutional Research, 1978. (ERIC Document Reproduction Service No. 010 540)

Ladd, Dwight R. *Change in Educational Policy: Self-studies in Selected Colleges and Universities*. New York: McGraw-Hill, 1970.

Levinson, Harry. *Organizational Diagnosis*. Cambridge, Mass.: Harvard University Press, 1972.

Lindquist, Jack. *Strategies for Change*. Berkeley: Pacific Soundings Press, 1968.

List, Marilyn Kaplan. "A Study of the Relationship between Twenty-seven Educational Innovations and the Accreditation of Public Secondary Schools." Ph.D. dissertation, New York University, 1969.

Lynch, Beverly P. "Libraries as Bureaucracies." *Library Trends* 26 (1978): 259–267.

Miller, Jerry W. "Organizational Structure of Non-governmental Post-secondary Accreditation." Ph.D. dissertation, Catholic University of America, 1972.

Morein, P. Grady. "Assisted Self-study: A Tool for Improving Library Effectiveness." *Catholic Library World* 50 (1979): 422–423.

Pfinster, Alan O. *The Future of Voluntary Accreditation*. San Francisco: Annual Meeting of the American Association of Colleges, 1973. (ERIC Documents Reproduction Service No. 071 559)

Poppenhagen, Bert W. *Institutional Accreditation and the Private Liberal Arts College.* Washington, D.C.: ERIC Clearinghouse, 1977. (ERIC Documents Reproduction Service No. 138217)

Raffel, Jeffery A. "From Economic to Political Decision-making." *College and Research Libraries* 35 (1974): 412–423.

Rossi, Peter H.; Freeman, Howard E.; and Wright, Sonia R. *Evaluation: A Systematic Approach.* Beverly Hills: Sage, 1978.

Southern Association of Colleges and Schools. Commission on Colleges. *Standards of the College Delegate Assembly.* Atlanta: The Association, 1977.

Stubbs, Kendon, and Buston, David. *Cumulated ARL University Library Statistics, 1962–1963 through 1978–79.* Washington, D.C.: The Association, 1981.

Studer, Sharon. "Evaluation Needs Assessment: Can They Make Evaluation Work?" *Bureaucrat* 9 (1980): 15–22.

Troutt, William Earl. "The Quality Function of Regional Accreditation." Ph.D. dissertation, George Peabody College for Teachers, 1978.

Webster, Duane. "The Management Review and Analysis Program: An Assisted Self-study to Secure Constructive Change in the Management of Research Libraries." *College and Research Libraries* 35 (1974): 114–125.

Wholey, Joseph. *Evaluation: Promise and Performance.* Washington, D.C.: Urban Institute, 1981.

Who's Who in America, 1980–81. 41st ed. Chicago: Marquis Who's Who, 1980.

Yates, Dudley. *The Impact of Regional Accrediting Agencies upon Libraries in Post-secondary Education.* Knoxville, Tenn.: Biennial Conference of the Southeastern Library Association, 1976. (ERIC Document Reproduction Service No. 135 337)

Young, Kenneth. "New Pressures on Accreditation." *Journal of Higher Education* 50 (1979): 132–144.

In addition, internal documents from each of the two libraries studied were consulted freely.

COLLEGE AND UNIVERSITY LIBRARIES:

TRADITIONS, TRENDS, AND TECHNOLOGY

Eugene R. Hanson

INTRODUCTION

College libraries in the United States began as small, donated collections of monographic materials. Once received by the institution, these collections were housed with other educational items, such as scientific specimens, numismatics, and art objects, in a relatively inaccessible room. Classroom instruction during the early period centered around recitation and lecture. The use of supplementary sources, which would have consisted of a meager number of available titles, was not widely recognized as an important adjunct to the instructional process until a later period.

Over one hundred years ago, Justin Winsor eloquently suggested a more elevated role for the library as an adjunct to the classroom:

Advances in Library Administration and Organization,
Volume 7, pages 209–244.
Copyright © **1988 by JAI Press Inc.**
All rights of reproduction in any form reserved.
ISBN: 0-89232-817-7

The proposition then is to make the library the grand rendezvous of the college for teacher and pupil alike, and to do in it as much of the teaching as is convenient and practicable. This cannot be done with a meagre collection of books, indiscriminately selected, with an untidy, ill-lighted, uncomfortable apartment. The library should be to the college much what the dining room is to the house—the place to invigorate the system under cheerful conditions with a generous fare and a good digestion. It may require some sacrifice in other directions to secure this, but even under unfavorable conditions the librarian can do much to make his domain attractive. As he needs the coopration of his colleagues of the faculty, his first aim is to make everything agreeable to them, and himself indispensable, if possible. College faculties are made up much as other bodies are—the responsive and sympathetic with those that repel and are self-contained. A librarian shows his tact in adapting himself to each; he fosters their tastes; encourages their predilections; offers himself directly where it is safe, accomplishes it by flank movements when necessary; does a thousand little kindnesses in notifying the professors of books arrived and treasures unearthed. In this way suavity and sacrifice will compel the condition of brotherhood which is necessary and is worth the effort.

With the student also the librarian cannot be too close a friend. He should be his counsellor in research, supplementing but not gainsaying the professor's advice. It would be a good plan to take the students by sections, and make them acquainted with the bibliographic apparatus, those books that the librarian finds his necessary companions, telling the peculiar value of each, how this assists in such cases, that in others; how this may lead to that, until with practice the student finds that for his work he has almost a new sense.[1]

By the end of the nineteenth century and the beginning of the twentieth, a number of developments took place that substantially improved the position of academic libraries. First, college faculty began to recognize that the library should be something more than a source for limited consultation and should serve in a capacity much like a laboratory in providing information to support the instructional process. This philosophy was slow to develop, however, in spite of the continuing lip-service acknowledging the library as the heart of the institution. Successful classroom instruction is dependent upon a variety of information, which supports and expands the activities of the classroom. Second, the development of technologies such as improved printing methods and electricity was a major force. As the demand for books and, later, periodicals burgeoned after the middle of the nineteenth century, this new technology was able to produce materials in large numbers at reasonable costs. The invention and use of the electric light exerted a favorable influence upon the extension of hours as students were no longer forced to curtail library activities at sundown because of poor lighting and the fear of fire. Third, library personnel prior to the establishment of library science education at Columbia University in 1876 were primarily limited to custodial activities carried out on a part-time basis. In 1893, it was estimated that only one-third of the colleges had full-time librarians whose chief duty was to direct the library.[2] Fourth, financial support for the library steadily increased as its role in higher education demanded improvement, expansion, and attention to the curriculum and research needs. The well-established private college and the larger universities were frequently able to obtain a specified appropriation from the institutional budget, as well as endowments from outside donors. This permitted trained library personnel to expand and enrich collections and to employ specialized staff who could develop and implement suitable techniques.

Today's libraries are at the crossroads as the electronic age has provided a means to accomplish the many labor-intensive processes more efficiently, quickly, and extensively. Libraries have an opportunity to restructure the majority of their operations in order to take the greatest advantage of expanded storage, remote access, and shared information and resources in more than printed formats.

Traditionally librarians have tended to be overly concerned with methods, procedures, and the status quo. The end product under these conditions was frequently of secondary concern as routines became ingrained and fixed. This in part accounts for the reluctance of many library personnel today, particularly those in the 40–50-year-old category, who have devoted little time to professional growth and development, to adjust to the changing methodologies. The format and delivery mode for information has changed radically as electronic publishing, online databases, telefacsimile transmission, and video discs become increasingly commonplace. The electronic age will provide a wide range of oportunities to automate many tasks that support the supplying of all types of information regardless of where it is housed. It will permit libraries to achieve better their stated objectives of supporting the instructional and research activities of the academic community. During the last seventy-five years, libraries have enjoyed a period of relative stability, only to be faced today with new technology that must be implemented side by side with traditional approaches. The size of the library will generally have considerable influence on the extent of automation, as the results of current surveys indicate that the larger university libraries have been involved in the process for some time and have developed integrated systems encompassing online catalogs, circulation, purchasing, and serials control.[3]

The application of computers in higher education expanded during the 1960s. Library schools began to incorporate courses in information science and the mechanized retrieval of information. In many instances the principal proponents of the application of computers in library processes originated among individuals who were "outside" the field of library science. Some of the pioneer libraries were Florida Atlantic University, the Library of Congress, Massachusetts Institute of Technology, the National Library of Medicine, and members of the University of California System of Higher Education. By the standards of today, the process was greatly inhibited by limited hardware, which was extremely costly, and by a lack of library personnel trained in systems analysis and automation in general. The batch process, which required that information emanating from the library be stored on cards or tape and then entered into the main computer during a nonpeak period, prevailed. It was not until the late 1960s and the early 1970s that libraries began to have time-sharing systems available to them. Unfortunately higher education was entering a period of austerity, and many libraries made hard choices in determining priorities. Some of the larger libraries chose to develop in-house systems utilizing the batch process and later the online or real-time approach. The principle disadvantages of these individual efforts were the high cost of developing suitable software and adapting hardware to individual library needs. In spite of the "rugged individualism" of libraries as expounded by many librarians, it was readily apparent that most library activities were done in a similar rather than in a unique manner in the majority of libraries. Frequently the greatest differences were not in the uniqueness of the process but rather in the complexity and magnitude of its relationship to the overall operation. Faced with high costs, a paucity of library personnel skilled in automation, limited budgets, and increasing amounts of materials being published, librarians sought to develop the availability of cataloging information so important to the compilation of individual library catalogs. The most logical approach was undoubtedly the further development of union catalogs.[4] The idea of union catalogs and lists was not a new one; it had been suggested in the thirteenth century when a registry of titles housed in English and Scottish monastic libraries was attempted.[5]

One of the most formidable and successful efforts was the National Union Catalog at the Library of Congress, which was begun in 1901 and consisted of catalog cards done by the Library of Congress and many other large libraries in the United States. By the 1960s over 1,000 libraries were contributing cards to the catalog.[6] Cataloging information or "copy" submitted by these libraries served as the information source for the shared cataloging project, which produced catalog cards for sale to all types of libraries. Between 1930 and 1960, many regional union catalogs were established, forming an important tool for the so-called bibliographic centers. These centers maintained union catalogs and lists and aided in verifying the locations of materials, routing interlibrary loan requests, preparing statistics, promoting uniformity and standardization in cataloging and loaning procedures, ensuring equalization of requests for loans, and ideally promoting the development of resources within the region.[7]

Although in a card or book form, union catalogs and lists were important, their usefulness was hampered by their confinement to a single location and high compilation and maintenance costs. Although methods of duplication were devised, the ability to access the union catalog and/or list through a computer terminal was revolutionary not only in speeding up the process but also in making many more titles available. The major value of a union catalog or list is to determine the location of material in other libraries so they may be judicious and efficiently borrowed through interlibrary loan. Second, they allow for the coordination of resources among participating libraries because the holdings of neighboring libraries are now readily available. Third, the provision of bibliographic data in the form of a stylized entry such as a catalog card, a periodical record and holding statement, and the newer computer screen data has aided substantially in the standardization of bibliographic information and in its recording and use by many libraries. This provides a very important source of information not only for processing but also for libraries that have purchased the same title and now want to catalog and place an entry in their manual or online catalog or list. Fourth, union catalogs and lists encourage research once the material is known to be available. Finally, they assist in appraising the scarcity and rarity of materials for reprinting purposes.

A survey of the fifty states in 1974 revealed that twenty-eight states had some form of union catalog, and union lists of serials had been compiled within thirty-nine states.[8] The majority of the catalogs and lists included the holdings of academic, public, and special libraries and provided an excellent source for interlibrary loan and for cooperative collection development. By the late 1970s, the compilation of manually prepared union catalogs had slowed considerably because of the increasing difficulties and cost of compilation and maintenance.[9]

Although the union catalog in a card format was the dominant approach, five union catalogs were being issued in microform and two in a machine-readable format by 1974. The value of the union catalogs and lists was indisputably established; no library could possess all titles and must be able to access the collections of other libraries quickly and efficiently. The automated networks appeared to be a solution to the compilation and maintenance of online catalogs and lists. The inputting of information in a machine-readable form into local and union catalogs and lists was by a batch process utilizing punched cards, paper tape, and magnetic tape. Early studies cautioned against hasty conversions to the new format because of high costs for equipment and personnel. An early plan to computerize the state union catalog in Connecticut in 1971 was abandoned in favor of a combination of microfilm and printed cards because it was considered simpler and more economical.[10]

The application of the newer technology occurred first in the ready production of catalog cards, then book or printed catalogs and lists, and later in microfiche or microfilm catalogs and lists. All of the above have served as interim solutions to the problem of storing and accessing large amounts of bibliographic information. The application of computers went one step beyond all previous approaches; it not only vastly increased storage capabilities but also made the information accessible from remote locations.

The standardization of cataloging information played an important role in the cooperative compilation and dissemination of information. Continuing efforts by the American Library Association, since its founding in 1876, have promoted national and international agreements, which today guide the development and compilation of bibliographic databases. Without this common cooperative interest, libraries, particularly the large ones, could not survive the steadily growing amount of information.

Once the hardware and software were available, the problem of converting the existing manual records to a machine-readable format became formidable. As would be expected, individual libraries looked to the Library of Congress for assistance in the conversion project. In 1966, the Library of Congress began distributing machine-readable tapes containing bibliographic records for current books it was cataloging. Although few libraries were in a position to purchase and utilize the information, the initial step had been taken to ensure the distribution and continuing support for machine-readable catalogs.

The computer was particularly suitable for information formerly manually compiled and housed in the card catalog because of its many capabilities. A digital computer basically can be used to control processes, store and retrieve information, maintain files of information, perform computations on information, and arrange and rearrange information. In addition it can:

1. Perform large volumes of repetitive, time-consuming operations automatically and accurately over a long period of time.
2. Operate at high speeds, measured in one one-millionth of a second or less.
3. Direct itself in a predetermined manner once it is provided with information and a set of instructions.
4. Process one job at a time or several jobs almost simultaneously.
5. Receive an input of information and instructions from remote locations, process the input, and transmit the results back to a remote user.
6. Choose among alternatives in processing information in a way that is equivalent to making decisions.[11]

Computers do have a number of obvious limitations that must be taken into consideration in developing an automated system:

1. The computer cannot perform without sets of instructions; it must have a set of instructions for every application or job it is to perform. Every operation and decision to be made by the computer must be foreseen in advance by humans and the alternatives specified in the programs.
2. While it can perform at incredible speeds, a computer can do nothing that it is not programmed to do. Computers cannot perform any operation that cannot be performed by humans.
3. The computer can operate only on information, and that information must be in a form that it can recognize and then convert to a machine-readable form.
4. It can detect, but generally cannot correct, inaccurate information fed into it; the results of computer processing are only as accurate as the input placed into the system.
5. The computer is not capable of performing all necessary operations in a library system; in all cases, humans must specify which information is to be collected and how it is to be organized, stored, retrieved, arranged and rearranged, and disseminated.[12]

BIBLIOGRAPHIC UTILITES AND LIBRARY NETWORKS

The technology, although expensive and specialized, was in place so that large amounts of information could be stored in citation or catalog card style within a centralized database that could be accessed by many remote terminals. The time was right for the formation of the so-called bibliographic utilities.[13] The first of these utilities was the Ohio College Library Center (OCLC), which began in 1968 as a state cooperative and later expanded into a regional network.[14] Its primary purpose was to develop a union catalog through a shared online cataloging system that allowed many libraries to add and utilize information. The system was operational by 1971, being greatly enhanced by the MARC tapes produced and distributed by the Library of Congress. Up to this point, very few individual libraries had the financial resources and the computer hardware to store and handle them. Although a number of newly formed consortia or networks anticipated similar services for libraries on a regional basis, arrangements were made so that OCLC could function as a service center and contract for online cataloging services to libraries in many areas.[15]

By 1974, twenty-two distributive networks based on the sharing of information and resources in a regional (multistate) area were operating in addition to OCLC.[16] Frequently these regional consortia or networks functioned similarly to the former bibliographic centers in the support of union catalogs and lists, interlibrary loan, communications, verification and location of materials, joint cataloging, and cooperative collection building. Automation played a key role, however, as most of them promoted its development and application by serving as brokers for information, personnel training, and computer and online services.

Multitype library networks have continued to develop since the late 1960s and early 1970s and have been identified by many acronyms. A few of the better-known regional multistate networks in addition to OCLC are NELINET (New England Library Network, 1966); SOLINET (Southeastern Library Network, 1973); SLICE (Southwest Library Interstate Cooperative Endeavor); Bibliographic Center for Research, Rocky Mountain Region; PNBC (Pacific N.W. Bibliographic Center); PALINET (Pennsylvania Area Library Information Network, 1972); MIDLNET (Midwest Regional Library Network); and WLN (Washington Library Network, later Western Library Network). Both interstate and instrastate systems have been successfully planned and implemented. Because of the feasibility of loading information into a system through machine-readable tapes or directly online, the scope of the union catalog can be readily and economically adjusted to the needs of many libraries. Commercial vendors have become actively involved in developing and marketing software packages developed for regional or individual library system such as WLN, UTLAS, VTLAS, LIAS, and NOTIS. WLN is now marketed by Biblio-Techniques, Inc.; UTLAS (University of Toronto Library Automation Systems, 1963) is available from UTLAS, Inc. Library Automation Systems; VTLAS (Virginia Tech Library System) is available from Virginia Technical University; LIAS (Library Information Access System) is available from Pennsylvania State University; and NOTIS (Northwestern Online Total Integrated System, 1970) is available from Northwestern University.

A 1985 survey of thirty library systems, being marketed either by commercial turnkey vendors[17] or a library selling its own software, indicated the following diverse pattern of organization: fifteen private corporations, two private corporation/partnership; one private and public corporation; one public corporation; one private/nonprofit corporation; three nonprofit corporations, one individual owner; one by another public library; three by another library; and one by a private university.[18]

In addition to the multitype library network, specialized networks such as RLIN, which is a shared bibliographic service designed to meet large research library needs, have been successfully established and supported.

College and university libraries have readily joined the regional networks because of a number of reasons. Although the costs of contracting for services with the bibliographic utilities have not been lower, access to collective online data has proved very effective in supplying bibliographic information and in the sharing of resources by libraries regardless of location. The utilities have permitted libraries many of the benefits of the new technology and resulting information transfer capabilities through a relatively manageable annual fee and with a minimal amount of on-campus hardware. The utilities have been pioneers and supporters of research and development, employing staff members to update and expand services continually. They have developed online union catalogs and lists into efficiently accessible and timely tools. They have recently attempted to integrate the bibliographic or cataloging information with other library processes such as acquisition, serials control, authority control, and circulation.

Telecommunication has been and will continue to be a major concern for library systems and networks. All types of communication services are being considered in the quest for a more effective means than traditional telephone lines. Although the progress is slow because of costs, regulations, and the difficulty of mounting a coordinate effort, there is a clear recognition of the need for low-cost, high-volume communication capabilities. A variety of alternative methods such as microwave, cable, television, radio and television signals, satellites, and fiber optics are currently being tested and applied in library networks. The University of Pittsburgh was the first university to select and begin implementation of a campus-wide optic fiber information system, which appears to offer great promise for the future. Developed by AT&T, the optic fiber system can transmit voice (telephone), data (computers), and video (television) at a rate of 1.7 gigabits per second throughout its main and branch campuses[19] and has interface capabilities with other systems. It utilizes a highly focused laser beam transmitted over low-loss, glass fiber light guides. Some of the advantages of fiber optics over wire are decreased space for transporting lines or guides and minimal regeneration of signals and interference by power lines and surges of lightning.[20]

In spite of the role of the bibliographic utilities in the development and extension of automated services, there will undoubtedly be a lessening of dependence upon them for those services not requiring shared information as found in the union lists and catalogs. As library systems are improved, storage capacities enhanced, and costs lowered, libraries will seek to develop integrated systems utilizing the best available technologies, broad communication capabilities, and expanded remote access to all types of information regardless of location. Most systems being developed and marketed today attempt to supply an integrated, multifunction local system that can operate on a more reasonably priced minicomputer rather than sharing a mainframe computer with other academic and administrative units. Once the information is in a machine-readable format, it can be readily added to the local database, where individuals may edit and search it without concern for communication costs and network delays and interruptions. One author commented that the use of the bibliographic utilities for locating material to be borrowed on interlibrary loan has changed as some libraries now utilize network interlibrary loans subsystems to locate titles available only from out-of-state sources.[21] It is extremely important that libraries building machine-readable records closely adhere to nationally and internationally accepted standards such as the full-length bibliographic record of the MARC II format, which was developed by Library of Congress, and the OSI Standards for automated systems.

The achievement of total integration for heterogeneous systems has been an elusive goal because of residual variations in machine-readable records, incompatible language, and a variety of hardware. At this time, libraries seeking to provide users with full and direct access to automated systems in other libraries can join together, select and install a single shared system, and live with the high telecommunication costs. Two (or more) libraries, separated by longer distances and seeking easy access to each other's systems, can reach agreement on common database standards; select, install, and coordinate identical systems; and support telecommunication linkage between the two systems.

Because of high communication costs, limited storage capabilities, and the need to separate information of value to other libraries from that pertinent to only a single library, the bibliographic utilities have become involved in developing communication links and local microcomputer interfaces. Up to this point, the computer industry lacked standards and an interest in developing them. Each vendor was largely satisfied in achieving compatibility with the supplied or specifically designated equipment for its system. The International Standards Organization (ISO) has fostered the development of an international network architectural model based on an open system of communication. Designers of the model began by defining all of the tasks necessary to permit two users to communicate within the network and then organized the tasks in such a manner so that they were linked together for efficient interaction. The result is the Open Systems Interconnect (OSI) Reference Model. It comprises seven layers forming a framework of standard interconnected procedures and permits diverse users to interconnect and share information in spite of varying equipment and network specifications. Each of the layers consists of discretely defined tasks, which build upon other levels in defining operations of greater complexity. The OSI

Reference Model requires that a system or device be connected to a physical means of communication by which access can be made to one or more other systems. The means or medium of communication may vary from a simple line from one point to another to a more complex interconnection of private, local, and packet-switched networks. A computer terminal or other electronic apparatus capable of information processing and communication can be used as the linking device.

OCLC is implementing a packet switch network that will support the OSI Reference model:

> It allows for data transmission not just over telephone lines but by additional transmission media such as wire, satellite or microwave. It permits message traffic to be controlled at several distributed switching centers instead of a single central location.
>
> It is an open, rather than closed network that gives user access to not just the OCLC system but eventually other host systems.[22]

A breakthrough on the linkage problem is imminent; several vendors are now marketing networking products that would connect stand-alone systems acquired from different vendors. One example is the Irving Network, which is being used to link three public libraries in Colorado that use three unique computer systems supplied by different vendors. It was estimated that each additional computer system would cost approximately $40,000.[23] Although unit costs remain high, the network has provided interconnection at a somewhat reduced cost.

The Irving Network has a number of benefits worth noting. First, it does not require changes to existing hardware, software, or data bases. Second, it links the bibliographic information permitting the sharing of resources among libraries. Any number of libraries could be linked together, forming not only a union catalog but also accessing information pertaining to status, location, and borrowing of specific items. Third, the users would utilize the same CRT screen they were accustomed to in their home library regardless of the system they chose to access. Fourth, the network can be installed on a modular basis, permitting additional libraries to be interconnected and new functions to be added later.[24] Another, the Library Systems and Services Inc. (LSSI), was developed for libraries in Massachusetts and currently connects local systems acquired from different vendors.

By making use of the OSI model, the network would eventually be able to interconnect a number of other networks supporting the Linked System Project Network, which includes the Library of Congress and several other large libraries.

Although costs of the two systems are high and their application is at an early stage, the potential of such linkage is impressive. Undoubtedly greater attention will be given to the standardization of equipment, databases, language, and interconnection capabilities as automated library systems continue to develop and to be implemented in additional libraries. Because of the inseparable relationship of linkage and communication, it is hoped that continuing research and development will permit libraries to deal with the problem of incompatibility and rising financial costs in their efforts to expand the availability of materials for library patrons:

> The implementation of OSI standards will provide a smooth, well-lit highway between the "doors" of the different systems, but system vendors and users will still have to follow certain internal standards and practices to permit the "key" to the door of one system to unlock the doors of other, different, systems. At a minimum, those involved in library automation will need to develop a common command language whereby an instruction such as "AU ABCDEFG" is universally recognized as a command to search for the occurrence of "ABCDEFG" as an author in a bibliographic record. Each different system vendor will have to develop software that will permit this common command to be translated into the specific author search command required by the vendor's system. Such an interface will need to be bidirectional—to be able to process both incoming and outgoing commands.[25]

The bibliographic utilities will be radically restructured in view of changing technology. The new OCLC system, the Oxford Project, seeks to utilize the rapidly changing technologies, "including the interrelationships of computers [mainframes and microcomputers], terminals, software, networks, telecommunications, imaging and printing and high density optical disks and other locally accessible storage devices."[26] The redesigned system will make maximum use of the microcomputer to perform tasks at the appropriate local, regional, national, and international levels. The new system will have four distinctive environmental features:

1. It increases the power, flexibility, and availability of the OCLC online system.
2. It supports distributed processing, including access to distributed optical disk or other high-density memories as they become available.
3. It enables OCLC to control its telecommunication environment in order to ensure users the most cost-effective service.
4. It sets the stage for electronic delivering of the contents of books and other library materials.[27]

The LS (Local Systems) 2000, as now being developed and marketed by OCLC, is an example of the above as it retains information of value to the local library at its source while linking the library to a centralized database for broad information needed for bibliographic control.

In addition to the many improvements in communication and the linkage or interconnection of library systems, the problem of storage has been radically alleviated by recent developments. Of particular interest to libraries will be the optical and video disks (CD-ROM),[28] which will provide increased capabilities for the distributive processing of union catalogs and commercially produced databases. The Ramapo Catskill Library System of Middletown, New York, recently created and made available a union catalog that contains over 600,000 unique titles and 1.8 million physical items in both a videodisc and COM (micro-fiche) format.[29]

> In the near future, American libraries, corporations, and other organizations will become populated by CD-ROM drives or players attached to a variety of personal computers, work-stations, and (even) communication terminals. Non-volatile databases will be distributed on these laser discs. Instead of expense of accessing online databases, CD-ROM's will provide a cost effective alternative by permitting entire databases to be distributed for local use. Major online database publishers will experience cost savings and the opening of new markets. Hybrid systems will be developed that will search locally stored laserdisc databases, and, for information not found, will automatically dial up and extract additional data from online utilities.[30]

This new technology has already caused one producer of three medical data-bases, Microdex, Inc., to discontinue its online search services in favor of microfiche and optical media editions only. The reason given for this change was the high connect time cost, the lack of menu-driven software for inexperienced users, the inability to integrate graphics within the text, and the insufficient revenue generated by the online services.[31]

The application of a combination of mainframe storage facilities at local and remote locations used in conjunction with this high-density storage will permit considerable flexibility, further expanded access, and decreased costs for com-munication and storage. The future of technology in libraries appears to be dependent on the availability of financial resources, an informed body of library personnel, and the recognition and acceptance of its value by students and faculty.

ONLINE CATALOGS

The impact of the bibliographic utilities on the development of the online catalog has been substantial in providing ready access to cataloging information. Al-though only a few hundred local online catalogs are now operational, they will be commonplace by the end of the century. Access to the library catalog will no longer require that the patron be present at the physical catalog as the terminal now connects the user to the database in one or more locations. Although the book and the microfilm or microfiche catalogs permitted decentralization through the placing of copies in several locations, these forms were slow to use and in most cases even more costly to compile and maintain than the traditional card catalog.

Efforts by the larger libraries such as the Library of Congress fixed the feasi-bility and importance of machine-readable cataloging information. The Library of Congress was one of the first to close its card catalog and to produce all catalog records from that point on in a machine-readable form. During the mid-1970s, a few larger academic and public libraries planned and developed online catalogs. Some of the leaders were Northwestern University, Ohio State University, University of Illinois at Champlain Urbana, and the University of California System of Higher Education.

Today it is safe to assume that most large college and university libraries have or are in the process of developing plans for an online catalog. In fact, it is difficult to imagine that any major automation project today would not include an online catalog as its focal point. The commercial vendors invariably develop the online catalog module first by using cataloging information that has been produced and stored on magnetic tape. This is generally followed by other functional modules, such as circulation, and later by purchasing, serials control, and other library processes that utilize the bibliographic information of the library catalog. Many of the microcomputer-based systems being developed for libraries with fewer than 100,000 volumes are using a similar modular approach beginning with the public access catalog. The online catalog will not only decentralize and speed up access to bibliographic information but will also permit the searching of an increased amount of data through more access points than possible in the traditional catalog. The use of Boolean logic, with its relational or conditional characteristics, will permit quicker and more productive searches. The online catalog terminal will expand the user's capabilities beyond the monographic or book-dominated card catalog; now the user will be able to interact with larger amounts of stored bibliographic data. Government documents, special collections, serials or periodicals, and commercial databases will be accessible to the user of the online services. The user will be able to determine the location of the material, information about status, and even request that it be sent to a special location. Finally, patrons will be able to search large union catalog databases such as the one maintained by OCLC, which contains approximately 13 million records contributed by over 4,800 libraries.[32]

A recent survey, *Using Online Catalogs*,[33] indicates that patrons in general had no difficulty in accepting the online public access catalog. As would be expected in view of earlier user studies of the card catalog, subject access was considered of major importance. Keyword and term searching are relied upon heavily, and patrons felt a need for lists or a thesaurus of subject terms used in the system. The menu-driven approach was sufficiently easy to use, but as patrons became more experienced, they expressed a preference for a combination of menu and command capabilities. In addition to screen instructions, assistance from public service staff proved to be a valuable asset. The graphic displays indicating commands and other summary information should be placed near each user terminal, serving as a reminder to infrequent users. Printers were welcome adjuncts, particularly if they were easy to use. Sufficient space for note taking and books and paper was also needed. Terminals should be located in conspicuous locations on the main level and supplemented by others in more out-of-the-way locations, depending upon the capacity of the computer selected.

The online patron access catalog, however, is not without problems. The more obvious are the initial capital investment in computer hardware and software and the continuing cost of maintaining them, the need for a continually functioning system, the conversion of records to machine-readable format, and the need to instruct users.

The online catalog will become commonplace in the twenty-first century. It will revolutionize accessibility, compilation and maintenance procedures, and the extent of potential coverage. The actual storage of the bibliographic data will probably be in one or a combination of two forms: traditional computer processing units and/or the new easier storage disks.

ONLINE DATABASES

The online databases that began in the 1970s form an important aspect of the information-gathering resources of academic libraries. Today over 2,000 online databases are available, with approximately forty to fifty being added annually. The once-labor-intensive tasks of locating, verifying, and recording bibliographic citations sought by faculty and students have radically changed as the online databases cover a wide range of topics from chemistry to library science. They have greatly improved accessibility to information in remote locations, speeded up the searching process, and made information more quickly available than through traditional printed or microform indexes. Electronic publishing will undoubtedly continue to expand, with a greater number of the former printed indexes being available online or in a stand-alone disc format, although serious problems could occur if machine-readable formats are the only forms produced for distribution. The development of the CD-ROM, with its large, compact storage capacity, offers a promising medium for catalogs and indexes because it can be distributed directly to libraries, where it can be searched by library staff and patrons without incurring communication charges. The situation facing libraries today is analogous to the period when microprints were being purchased by libraries in an effort to increase access to titles and to reduce storage space requirements for periodicals, reports, and other research materials. Speed in searching, however, was not attained during that period, for the optical and mechanical devices that were developed to assist the user in locating the position of the material on rolls of film remained slow. The most prolific producers of machine-readable information are government agencies, professional associations and societies, and a growing number of commercial firms. Although some online database producers market directly to libraries and individual use, the majority are contracted for through a sort of database vendor who offers access to a number of databases. Many vendors are promoting services to individual users at off times. Communication costs are a key factor in providing online database services; it is estimated that over a million hours of connect time (actual time used to search the database) were used in 1982.[34]

College and university libraries have been slower in using and promoting online database services than research and special libraries because many faculty members lack knowledge about the available services and are reluctant to venture beyond the traditional methods of assembling citations. In addition, the question of funding searching services for students and faculty has undoubtedly caused librarians to be cautious about promoting something that could become a drain on already strained budgets. Most libraries today charge some sort of fee, although total cost recovery is not sought and would not be financially feasible for users because of the higher total cost from vendors' fees, communication costs, print-out costs, equipment purchase and maintenance, and staff time. One library reported changing its major budget catagory from library materials for the collection to information resources in an effort to emphasize that information comes in formats other than books and periodicals that were actually owned by the library.

Many·librarians maintain that only librarians should search the databases; however, current literature indicates a growing number advocating end user searching. If one of the major advantages of online searching, speed, is to be retained, librarians may have no other choice than to devote less time to the actual process and rely more on trained paraprofessionals and end users among faculty and students. As library patrons gain more experience in using online catalogs, database searching will become more natural. Self-help programs and access through personal home computers will undoubtedly greatly increase end user capabilities.

PERSONNEL AND LIBRARY MANAGEMENT

Because of their relatively minor role in the intellectual life of the early colleges and universities, the need for specially trained library ·personnel did not exist until the latter part of the nineteenth century. Up to this point and in the minds of some academicians today library personnel should be trained on the job without the benefit of formal course work in library science. As the role of the library became recognized more fully, the demand for trained librarians led to the establishment of library economy and later library science programs. The distinction between a baccalaureate and master's degree in library science was not of particular concern until the mid-1940s.

The graduation of the first "librarian" undoubtedly began the long-standing controversy over which tasks should be done by the trained librarian as opposed to those done by the library staff. Because of the relatively unimportant role of many early librarians and the predominance of labor-intensive tasks carried on by them in support of acquiring, processing, storing, and circulating printed materials, responsibilities were generally commonly shared by all personnel, particularly in the small libraries. A number of studies of library education prior to 1960 called attention to this shortcoming, resulting in an attempt to improve the curriculum by including both pragmatic and theoretical concepts in it. Some progress was made, but unfortunately in the small and medium-sized libraries, the distinction between so-called clerical and professional tasks continued to be blurred. From a professional point of view, librarians retained the task-oriented and information-locating processes and assigned the housekeeping functions to support personnel. Contact between students and faculty varied among librarians and support staff, with librarians theoretically primarily involved in those situations requiring the application of a body of knowledge (reference, collection development, preparing bibliographies, and so on).

The continuing problem in library science education has been

> the difference between training (the teaching of specific operations and procedures aimed at "the threshold of entry") and education (the development of a critical approach to current practice with the awareness that the future needs of the profession will change).[35]

Many educators feel that students in library schools should be prepared for not the first but rather the last job in order to ensure professional development necessary for the upper-level positions.[36]

The ratio of librarians to support staff has steadily decreased from a predominantly professional staff in small and medium libraries in the 1940s to a recommended one librarian for every two support persons. With static budgets, increasing demands, and rising personnel costs, the ratio of support personnel has slowly increased, particularly in the technical services and other routine dominant activities such as cataloging, purchasing, and circulation. Although automation is occasionally viewed as a means of reducing personnel costs, it most frequently creates a shifting of more of the task-oriented activities, such as acquisition, cataloging, serials control, and circulation, to the support staff. This shift illustrates the social phenomenon referred to as *technological imperative*, which denotes that once a newer technology is applied in order to accomplish a "very complex, routine mental work, that work is driven downward in the work hierarchy, away from the professionals."[37] Supposedly those librarians caught in the technological imperative will be reassigned to a "much more clearly definable professional responsibility."[38]

An investigation of staffing patterns and work assignments in all public and private colleges and universities in Texas noted a significant trend in

> that the larger libraries generally delegated more tasks to paraprofessionals than the small libraries do. Specific areas in which this trend was observed were in cataloging with LC copy [printed cards obtained from the Library of Congress], adaptation [such as variant editions, translations or title changes] and member copy [done by contributors to union catalogs], terminal processing; revisions and conflict resolution; and authority work.[39]

The author believed that although the bibliographic utilities have had some impact on assigned tasks, other changes could be initiated. It appeared that librarians and administrators who seriously want to streamline in order to utilize the most cost-effective methods and to increase efficiency would benefit from an analysis of cataloging task assignments in libraries and then be able to formulate realistic and objective job task guidelines free from traditional and personal likes and dislikes.

The new emphasis on access to information sources will undoubtedly open up many opportunities for those librarians who are flexible and willing to adapt. In some cases, additional training will be necessary in order to interact favorably with computerized databases and students and faculty engaged in research. Specialized training in library automation must be included as a major component for all librarians. In addition, emphasis should be placed on greater knowledgeability about the materials and methods of scholarship and research. During the 1960s and 1970s insufficient attention was given by library schools in general to the theoretical aspects of librarianship; to sound administrative practices to be used in planning, organizing, coordinating, controlling, staffing, budgeting, and evaluating; to a broad perception of the library in relation to the parent college or university; to the similarity of all types of libraries; and to the necessity of developing networks and cooperative relationships.

Library schools, supported by the American Library Association, must recruit the best possible people. The idea that anyone can be a librarian should be discouraged; this philosophy has resulted in many positions being filled by individuals who were unable to reach their original, primary professional goals and turned to librarianship as a second career. Many of them lack motivation to develop essential skills. Librarians who lack professional motivation and intellectual curiosity and seek the sheltered life among the books are next to impossible to weed out because of the same tenure held by teaching faculty. All library personnel must be actively supported in developmental programs, including formal course work, attendance at regional and national conferences, and experience in other departments and other libraries.

The preliminary results of a study designed to identify ''knowledge needed and possessed by university librarians during the first ten years of their careers'' indicated that management knowledge needs—specifically in the areas of planning, personnel, and training—ranked very high in importance but low in knowledge possessed:

In addition, the results indicated that certain knowledge was perceived by these university librarians to be relevant only when associated with certain positions. These knowledge areas included writing skills, systems analysis, program evaluation techniques, and inferential statistics. This result is particularly troubling, because how can any librarian be effective without the ability to think analytically or to write well? How can professionals be effective if they are unable to evaluate services and activities using program evaluation techniques or to conduct operational studies using statistics? This is a brief summary of the study that we undertook, but it suggests that deficiencies may exist among academic librarians in aspects of knowledge that are important for effective performance and professional leadership.[40]

College and university librarians need much more than the traditional technical skills taught in library schools if they are to function successfully in an academic environment. The four kinds of knowledge needed are

> a knowledge of the history and development of higher education, an appreciation for the history of scholarship and learning, the way knowledge is obtained in various disciplines, and an ability to evaluate research.[41]

The question of faculty status for libraries is a continuing issue, which has been debated for many years. One of the problems has been the inability of most librarians to define who they really are in a manner that is understandable and believable by themselves and by others.[42] One author suggested that the idea of librarians' being teachers is fiction intended to improve the stereotyped image of librarians, support their need for status, which has been inordinate among many academic librarians, and project their role to others in spite of their general lack of understanding that libraries are part of an educational system rather than a separate educational agency.[43] In comparing librarians and teachers, she pointed out some major dissimilarities:

> The librarian's dissemination of the graphic record differs from that of a teacher. The librarian does not disseminate content and does not disseminate by teaching but by means of a library process, by means of a librarian's behavior—by creating, operating, and maintaining a library and providing library services through the myriad behaviors that they require.[44]

She continued by pointing out that librarians sometimes teach when teaching is the best method to provide the patron with efficient and effective access to graphic records. Although library instruction has been receiving renewed attention in many libraries today, she believed the actual commitment to the teaching function bv most librarians was minimal and suggested:

> Perhaps much, and maybe most, library-use instruction would be better thought of as informing rather than as teaching. If it were, that fact would not change or diminish the role of librarians in the institution of education. That set of behaviors or role called "librarian" is an educational role, and it remains one whether or not teaching is a part of it.[45]

She cautioned that librarians as teachers is an inconsistent self-image and that an understandable and believable professional identity "cannot be developed on such a base," calling for librarians to "come to terms with themselves and their work."[46] She concluded optimistically that ample opportunities exist within a crucible of change where knowledge continues to grow, the number of publications increases, and the developing technology opens up many new and improved methods for handling information.[47]

As academic libraries expanded, new skills were needed by administrators and librarians in planning, developing, coordinating, and evaluating human, material, and physical resources. The library schools and professional leaders began to look to business administration for guidance in managing libraries. As a result, management theories have been the subject of a continuing debate for the last twenty years. Considerable attention has been given to management styles in libraries similar to what has been done in industry and business. As professionalism increased among librarians in a pattern reminiscent of other semi-professional groups, tension in the administration of college and research libraries heightened. The situation was complicated by some librarians who had faculty status and sought to assume the egalitarian and nonbureaucratic role of the teaching faculty.[48] One author, in describing the university library of the twenty-first century, suggested that the uniform movement of librarians toward faculty status will undoubtedly accelerate the recognition of the Ph.D. rather than the master's as the terminal degree.[49]

Librarians and library administrators have for some time been interested in the latest management techniques, particularly the more participative or consultative approaches. A review of the results of many articles and research studies indicates that although "enthusiasm for participatory management continues, the experiment of some institutions and the research of librarians have tempered the more extravagant claims of its early proponents."[50] Most librarians and library administrators agree on the obvious benefits of participatory management; the point of major controversy is the extent of participation in view of the ultimate responsibility resting with the library administrators. Moran pointed out that she found few advocates of participatory management who have suggested that the library "be run by majority rule or that the administration should abdicate responsibility and allow the staff to do whatever they please."[51] Librarians must understand the limits of their involvement and participation, for extreme position will not resolve all problems and ensure happiness in every decision nor will it guarantee increased commitment to goals or to higher production levels:

> Finally, librarians will have to accept that participatory management is no substitute for individual responsibility and leadership. There will likely always be library directors and just as likely they will be paid considerably more than the rest of the non administrative staff. Directors receive such salaries not because they are older, more intelligent, or harder workers than other professionals, but because they are accountable for the operation of the library. It is the director who most often will set the parameters within which staff participation will operate.[52]

The management of college and university librarians has become increasingly complex in larger institutions. In addition to duties with regard to personnel, the director must continue to bear the major brunt for providing both manual as well as automated services; coping with crowded reading rooms and stack areas; managing static budgets further diminished by ever-present inflation for materials and services; rising personnel costs; conforming to student and faculty demands for longer hours and expanded services; setting overall priorities and adhering to them in spite of political pressure; justifying and advocating the needs of the library; financing, planning, and implementing automated procedures; cooperating with other libraries in networking and revenue sharing; being politically visible; dealing with aging library personnel who have found a safe, secure home; dealing with the preservation of deteriorating paper; and being all things to all people. He or she must be knowledgeable but receptive to every idea suggested by librarians, faculty, staff, and students; strong but gentle and conscious of all problems; able to work with all members of the academic community but always open-minded and free from bias; willing to discuss every problem and decision with the majority involved but never become involved in details; able to provide adequate resources for all departments and services but never question the methods used by personnel in utilizing them; committed to the expressed missions and objectives of the institution but frequently standing alone when dissatisfied personnel appeal to a higher authority; active in professional organizations in spite of limited financial support; involved in continuing educational growth but thinking first of other library personnel; and involved in producing articles for publication that adds rather than detracts from the professional expertise of others.

A number of recent studies have identified a growing turnover of library directors because of mounting pressures from all segments of the academic community. Some of the problems identified were difficulty in successfully planning and implementing cohesive long-range plans; inability of the institution to accommodate the necessary change; and the haunting reality that library goals are continually subjugated to selfish individuals and group pressures.

During this current age of collegiality and consultative management, the responsibilities and duties of the director should be delineated in writing. This statement should be statutorily based and a clear depiction of the scope and nature of the duties and power of the director.[53]

In addition to being thoroughly trained in library science, management theory, personnel practices, budgeting methods, and evaluative techniques, the library director of today and tomorrow must know the role of the library as an adjunct to education, support consultative management and seek a consensus when it provides a sound and responsive solution to current and future needs, assume active responsibility for identifying appropriate avenues for library development, and do everything possible to pursue clearly defined institutional goals and client interests.[54]

ORGANIZATION

A hierarchical organization was the dominant pattern in academic libraries until recent years. Library organization began as a highly centralized structure in view of their limited and ineffective role in the early colleges and universities. As new services and activities were implemented, small functional departments, such as shelflisting, cataloging, library extension, acquisition, and reference, developed. By the 1940s and 1950s, these smaller units were being merged into two large divisions, technical services and public services. Although still hierarchical in structure, this organization supposedly shortened the chain of command of the director, improved coordination among the departments, and utilized the expertise of a divisional director. Technical services were comprised of routine tasks normally done out of the sight of the public, such as cataloging, photoduplication, acquisitions, serials control, and occasionally circulation. The public services were made up of those activities where there was considerable interaction with the public, such as reference, interlibrary loan, circulation, government documents, and library orientation and instruction.

Some library administrators, however, supported a decentralized structure of divisional libraries organized around broad fields of knowledge, such as science, humanities, social science, and education. These divisions frequently assumed the functional activities, such as collection development, circulation, and cataloging, within a specified subject area. In most cases, trained library personnel with a strong subject background assumed responsibility for the activities, as well as serving as reference librarians and subject bibliographers. As would be expected, this type of organization proved most popular in several larger universities, such as the University of Colorado and the University of Nebraska.

Branch libraries in addition to a centralized main library were popular in large universities. The decentralized branches provided specialized subject support to schools, colleges, or departments of the university. These were physically separated from the central library, being supported and administered frequently by the entity it served. As in the case of the large subject divisional libraries, many types of relationships existed between the central and the branch libraries. A separate undergraduate library was another approach used by the larger institutions. This was either a totally separate building or simply a special area of the central library designed to accommodate the needs of undergraduate students. Generally they housed a modest collection of appropriate materials supporting the undergraduate curriculum and specialized reference service personnel.

Recently, the reforming of libraries into more logical units other than by function has been successfully adopted by Columbia University and other large and medium-sized universities. Basically these systems utilize large divisional-type units staffed with bibliographers or librarians who have a subject expertise or special training. Collection development, reference, and other means of accessing information are handled by members of the work unit assigned to special subject areas. The technically oriented operations, such as purchasing, check in, record keeping, processing, and the majority of the cataloging, are done by a unit specially trained to handle these largely routine tasks. Various forms of this organizational pattern exist as libraries attempt to lessen the functional aspects while accentuating the informational access approach. A recent study of the effects of automation on the organization of university libraries predicted a similar pattern, only it is now referred to as *matrix management*. Staff members possessing special subject expertise are organized into groups according to special fields of knowledge, such as humanities, social science, and natural history, which in turn can be further subdivided by discipline. Each group is responsible for providing reference services to assist in accessing information sources in their particular area of study.[55]

Today the coexistence of a dual structure of governance, hierarchical and collegial, exists when librarians are recognized as faculty in collective bargaining agreements. The situation will vary widely from one institution to another according to the degree with which librarians are recognized and accorded rights and responsibilities similar to those of teaching faculty. Conflict and instability can result whenever hierarchical and collegial structures are somehow linked or paralleled, particularly if the terms of the collective bargaining agreement do not specifically define authority and responsibility, not only in personnel matters such as tenure, promotion, and evaluation but also in administrative or management aspects traditionally assigned to the director.

According to Brown, collegial models have three dimensions of influence or control:

1. *The degree of control.* This may refer to the amount of influence a collegial committee has on any decision. The amount of influence, or the degree of control, depends on whether the recommendations of the committee are advisory or are binding by virtue of tradition or agreement. For example, a committee of peers exercises control when it decides who will receive merit increases.

2. *The issues subject to control.* Here, for example, search, promotion, and tenure committees, with the majority of members elected, may determine who will join the staff, who will be promoted, who will be rewarded, and who will receive tenure.

3. *The level at which control is exercised.* A collegial governance structure in coexistence with a hierarchy can exercise control or influence at any level from individual library department to the senior university administration.

In unionized organizations, representatives of the collegial processes as well as individuals can expect to influence their union. In turn, the union has legitimate power in dealing with senior university administration.

These three dimensions, the degree, the issues, and the level at which control or influence are exercised can range from perfunctory through advisory to full decision-making power. In a unionized university all three dimensions are matters for negotiation.[56]

Brown pointed out the indisputable fact that the support staff members would be excluded from the collegial process. Because of a higher percentage of support personnel than librarians, she believed that "a research library cannot operate with only a collegial structure"; therefore a hierarchical or a similar structure must be in place in order for the library to achieve its goals.[57]

Brown continued by discussing a number of problems arising in institutions with coexisting hierarchical and collegial structures.[58] The first four are largely understandable without explanation: accountability, lack of organizational flexibility, large amounts of time and resultant expense, and communication between structures. The fifth suggested there was ambiguity among university librarians in committing themselves to managerial functions. Some consider nonmanagerial positions intellectually superior and may seek other employment if management responsibilities are required. In addition,

> Many of them find it completely and unalterably unacceptable to take directions from non-librarian professionals or support staff. In my [Brown's] judgement librarians cannot adopt the view of some faculty that they will neither manage nor be managed.[59]

The last problem alluded to was the potential role conflict for librarians with management responsibilities who are members of the faculty union when they must deal with such issues as cutting services, resulting in a reduction of fellow library faculty.[60]

In a recent article, one author suggested that as the role of university librarians expanded and a greater number were given faculty status, "some delicate blend of hierarchy and collegiality will probably work best."[61] Change will undoubtedly be difficult, but experimentation is necessary.

There will undoubtedly be closer interaction among all of the functional departments and their personnel once an integrated automated system is operational. In many cases, there will be total interdependence of the former functional units, and departmental personnel will no longer be relatively isolated but will be under the scrutiny of their peers and the library patrons. Library faculty and support staff must have a greater awareness of activities in other areas because small problems or errors in one can block the work flow, causing slowdowns throughout the system. Workloads will shift, paperwork will be reduced, and a "blending and reorganization will occur."[62]

College and university libraries have experimented with a number of differing organizational structures. Today they follow many patterns depending on tradition, the size of the library, the kind and size of the parent institution, the available physical facilities, the prevailing administrative philosophy of the director, the geographical composition of the campus, the strength and political power of academic disciplines or areas, and the relationship to other academic support agencies on the campus.

The amount and extent of organizational change that may be attributed to the new technology is open to conjecture. Because of the ability to access the catalog and databases in remote locations both within and outside the library, there will undoubtedly be greater decentralization of services. Many library activities will no longer have to be done in an area adjacent to the catalog and other files because these will be available in most cases online. It appears that "libraries may at last be able to provide their users with the decentralized, individual services they have always preferred."[63]

Academic libraries continue to experiment with different organizational patterns in attempts to balance the desire to bring the best service possible to users with the reality of a finite amount of funds to be spent on those services. To date, the perfect organizational structure has yet to be developed, and surely no one perfect organizational structure would suit all libraries. The new technologies will undoubtedly have a major effect on the organizational patterns of libraries, but at this point one can merely speculate about what their impact will be.[64]

FINANCIAL SUPPORT

Financial support for libraries has slowly evolved in the United States. Because the first colleges were private institutions, it was expected that the library collection would be comprised primarily of donated books and pamphlets. The practice of endowing the parent institution, with the library singled out as recipient, began quite early and continues today. Both private and public colleges and universities frequently required each student to pay a library fee in order to ensure some viable and continuing form of support. As the role of the library became more directly tied to the curricular and research needs, institutional budgets included specific allocations for the library. Unfortunately, the amount, then as well as now, was frequently determined by the remaining amount of money available once the fixed costs had been drawn off. A study of the historical development of financial resources for academic libraries revealed that the accrediting agencies had a considerable influence in developing the standards for "judging" financial support. Eventually these standards were frequently used as a means of determining the amounts to be apportioned for the library.[65] Unfortunately this resulted in the use of a number of purely arbitrary standards that measured inputs rather than outputs.

1. Total amount expended for library (first method employed)
2. Total library expenditure per full-time student enrolled
   a. Expenditures per student for books, periodicals and binding
   b. Expenditures per student for salaries (librarians)
   c. Expenditures per student for wages (clerical staff and student assistants)
   d. Expenditures per student for miscellaneous expenses
3. Total library expenditure per faculty (infrequently used)
4. Total percentage of institutional (Education and General) budget expended for library purposes
   a. Total library budget may be in turn divided by percentage distributions within budget categories such as library materials, salaries and wages, miscellaneous
   b. Further divisions may be made with separate categories for books, periodicals and binding

c. Internal distribution by percentages indicates administrative well being of institution. For example 60% for personnel, 30% for miscellaneous.[66]

During the early period, librarians, as well as most academic administrators, knew and used only rudimentary budgeting procedures. With the application of management principles to library administration during the 1950s and 1960s, a wide variety of the newest, most sophisticated methods, such as performance budgeting and planning programming budgeting systems, were suggested and applied. Although many library directors laboriously prepared lengthy budget documents, few believed the results justified the effort.

The use of formula budgets has become popular in many public-supported systems. California, Texas, and Tennessee have developed and used them not only to determine annual financial support for the college or university but also specifically for the library. Frequently major consideration is given to academic programs, size and projected annual growth of the collection, and number of faculty and students.

The continued use of standards, particularly by the accrediting agencies and library associations, provided some arbitrary guidelines. Today many of these groups have limited quantitative amounts, replacing them with qualitative measures that attempt to examine the role of the library in supporting and fulfilling the overall institutional objectives.

Frequently expanding college and university budgets have not resulted in increased amounts being available for the library, nor have the needs of the library caused substantial fluctuations from one year to the next. It appears that library financing is based not on need but rather on available funds. Because of their role in the academic environment, libraries are responsible for supporting not only instructional but also widely varying individual research needs. Frequently these diverse demands from the faculty and students cannot be objectively defined and defended. This can inevitably create "an environment in which there are no absolute standards to be met, only relative or comparative ones."[67] In response to this situation, libraries have judged their worth by standards and statistical (input) information consisting of expenditures, volumes held, and staff size. Unfortunately, such an approach does little for the development of a rationale for articulating library needs and matching them to the resources required to fulfill them.[68]

Today the bulk of the library budget is expended for personnel costs. It appears in view of prevailing situations in most colleges and universities that little can be done to lower these costs unless services are curtailed or done by other means. An increase in the proportion of support staff to librarians would be another possible solution, but it would surely be adamantly opposed by librarians and the library association. It may be that the development of the electronic library will fall prey to preliminary inadequacies. As might be expected, a recent survey of expenditures in college and university libraries in 3,104 institutions indicated considerable variation in the expenditure for library operations.[69] The average amount expended per student during 1981–1982 was $215.63. In comparison, a similar study in 1965–1966 reported an average per student expenditure as $54.23.[70] An analysis of twenty surveys completed between 1923 and 1966, revealed a low of $9.52 per student expenditure in the teachers' colleges to a high of $61.97 in 147 colleges and universities.[71] Private institutions today as a whole expend more for their libraries than public. Federal contributions to all institutions consisted of approximately 1 percent of all library expenditures. Almost one-third of the federal grant monies were received by private institutions, resulting in 137.8 percent more federal grants per full-time student equivalent.

It is clear that there is considerable deviation in the amounts expended for library support by various institutions. Expenditures have continued to rise, although they have not advanced substantially enough to compensate for the supposed new role of the library, periods of increased enrollment, the ever-present inflation, and certainly not in most instances to support a major automation project. If automated library systems are to be planned and implemented, campus funds must be diverted or outside sources tapped.

Probably the most appropriate means of comprehending the necessary financial outlay is a review of the cost components of an automated system that would normally be an important part of the preliminary planning process. Final determination of the cost for each of the components, however, will require considerable time and the application of varying methodologies. Some of the major cost components for startup are:

Central site processing equipment
Data storage
Terminals
Telecommunications hardware
Software, including operating system license
Installation, profiling, and training
Site preparation
Records conversion (bibliographic, item, and patron)
Supplies (including removable disk packs if required)
Performance bond (if required)
Legal and consulting fees
Project coordinator for six or more months

Ongoing cost components include the following:

Hardware and software maintenance
Telecommunications charges
Supplies
COM backup (if required)
System manager

System operators
Programmer/analysts (if required)
Reserve fund for future upgrades
Insurance (if required)[72]

The following rules-of-thumb provide a general estimate for cost projection:

- Estimate 5,000 characters for each bibliographic record if the system is to include a patron access catalog with up to 30 indexes and authority control. This formula supersedes the earlier convention of estimating 3,000 characters per record that was common before libraries began to specify many indexes and authority control. [Cost of conversion is $1.10 per each bibliographic record.]
- For circulation, calculate one terminal per service point for every 100,000 annual transactions or significant fraction thereof. [Record conversion costs: 30 cents per item- or copy-specific conversion including both labor and the labels, and 50 cents per patron records to be created including the labels.]
- For acquisitions, estimate one terminal for every 10,000 titles acquired annually, or significant fraction thereof.
- For serials, estimate one terminal for every 50,000 issues checked in, or significant fraction thereof.
- For the patron access catalog, estimate one terminal for every 100 persons coming into the library each day.
- Add sufficient terminals for the reference staff.
- Add ports for dial-up access from outside the library system; consider at least one port or a minimum of five percent of the total number of ports.
- Estimate $12,000 for each terminal to be supported on an optimally configured system. An optimally configured system is one that has half of the total number of terminals it can support.
- Estimate hardware and software maintenance at one percent of the initial purchase price per month.
- Assume that vendor maintenance charges will increase by ten percent per year.
- Miscellaneous costs such as site preparation, shipping, and performance bonds normally do not exceed 20 percent of the system purchase price.[73]

As in any other labor-intensive operation, success is dependent on human thought and attention. In a situation such as this, a gain in productivity normally fails to offset the increased amount for salaries. The hope that the decreasing cost of hardware will make expenditures for automation more relative to conventional methods has failed to materialize because the declining cost of "computer hardware has increased the proportion of software and other labor-intensive components in the total spent for computer operations."[74]

It does not appear at this time that electronic publishing and the accompanying online databases will reduce the cost of accessing information because of database fees, communication charges, hardware and software, and library personnel doing much of the searching. The greatest benefit will be in the increased amount of material available to researchers and the speed with which it can be accessed. The further development of the CD-ROM may eventually decrease online searching through stand-alone systems.

The question of where the funds for automating the library will originate is a difficult one. Reduction in personnel costs will undoubtedly not materialize, nor will the expansion of electronic publishing alleviate the situation. If additional funds are not provided, libraries will have to rely heavily on existing cooperative ventures, which will provide joint usage of computer systems, hardware and software, and library materials. As a whole, librarians recognized some time ago that it is impossible to go it alone. College and university libraries cannot hope to possess every title or scrap of information their patrons may have an occasion to use. The variety of cooperative ventures aimed at ensuring access to all possible materials is a tribute to the efforts of many farsighted administrators and librarians. Union catalogs were and shall continue to be a major factor in knowing what is available and where it is located. The cooperative purchasing and storing of materials has been greatly enhanced by a variety of plans proposed and carried out primarily by large institutions. Some examples of these are the Farmington Plan, the Latin American Co-operative Acquisition Plan, the Center for Research Libraries in Chicago, Hampshire Inter-library Center, and the Research Library Group (RLG). Each of these recognized the need for libraries to cooperate in the purchasing and the sharing of resources. In addition, the revitalization of the bibliographic centers in the form of networks and consortia has permitted the ready cooperation among all types of libraries not only in the sharing of bibliographic data and resources but also in the development of automated projects. The next step will be the linking of the many individual systems, regional networks, and commercial databases.

Financial support for libraries will continue to be a pressing issue. The electronic library will undoubtedly achieve reality only by the influx of additional funds and the employment of automation specialists or retraining of existing library personnel. The sharing of resources, aided by the new technology, will play an even greater role in achieving the goals of individual libraries. The local library will rely heavily on a collection of printed as well as the newer formats, carry on local functions, and further expand its ability to supply all types of resources and information through a more sophisticated automated approach.

SUMMARY AND RECOMMENDATIONS

The academic library has slowly evolved from its rudimentary beginnings to a position of importance in the instructional and research program of most local institutions and in a developing national system of libraries. The common problems and goals that at one time were attacked in a parochial manner are now being alleviated through increasing cooperation, which has been greatly enhanced by the application of newer technology.

It is clear that the manual systems employed in libraries for generations have reached and in many cases exceeded the limits of their effectiveness in view of the burgeoning amount of information and personnel costs. In addition, each library cannot economically and efficiently exist as a self-contained entity but should continue to utilize cooperative methods that will promote the standardization and sharing of bibliographic information, the exchange of all types of graphic materials and other data resources, and the improvement of modes of communication. "Paradoxically libraries will be able to fulfill their local responsibilities only if they are able to design and develop effective cooperative systems."[75]

The electronic age has ushered in a period of unprecedented change for libraries in institutions of higher education. The traditional concept of the library as a storehouse of books must be radically changed if libraries hope to remain relevant adjuncts to classroom instruction and student and faculty research. The ability to access the contents of other libraries readily will cause a reconsideration of which items will be acquired for local storage and what should be the extent of faculty and student querying and utilization of other collections and information sources. All of this will require application of a variety of computers, terminals, software, networks, telecommunication, imaging and printing, and locally developed or purchased stand-alone systems. Just as libraries in the early days used printed book and card catalogs that were exchanged among each other, the availability of an electronic linkage with a substantial number of networks and individual libraries will support cooperative and coordinated efforts never before possible. Automated systems at all levels will move beyond primarily bibliographic control toward more sophisticated interconnected databases housed in many remote locations.

Bibliographic utilities and commercial vendors will continue to be active in the research and development of automation. Increased attention will be given to systems that are flexible and are able to combine both online and stand-alone components. Bibliographic control, which will rely heavily on online union catalogs, will be greatly augmented through general access to information assembled by commercial or nonprofit groups. As optical disks and other high-density memories become more economical and readily available, they will replace printed indexes, abstracts, lists, and catalogs.

The size of the library will undoubtedly continue to be an important factor in the extent of automated activities. Lower hardware and software costs and increased interest in cooperative ventures will permit greater participation, particularly by the small libraries.

Because of their key role, government and state libraries will play an important part in overall development and growth of automation and networking.

The degree of success that will be achieved will be to a large measure dependent on the ability of libraries to plan adequately for change in the light of the available technology and instructional and research needs; the allocation and commitment of financial resources; and the willingness of colleges and universities to join and support overall cooperative and distributed efforts, though it may require a lessening of individual autonomy for most libraries.

The amount of material indexed and available online will be greatly expanded as libraries and commercial firms continue and expand efforts to share the work of cataloging, indexing, and other bibliographic information. Emphasis will be placed on the role of the end user in the searching of all types of online data files. Printed instructions and self-help programs will provide some direction, while paraprofessionals and librarians will assist in solving more difficult individual problems. New access points or methods of searching, such as subject headings and classification numbers, will be included. In addition, new search qualifiers, such as type of materials, country of publication, and others, will improve the end results of the search and speed up the process. Online catalogs will be available in many remote locations, particularly faculty offices, classrooms, and laboratories.

Personnel will continue to be the principal ingredient in bringing about change and the application of technology. Librarians as a professional group must recognize the need for a revamping of the library science curriculum in order to prepare individuals who are knowledgeable, flexible, and professional in the handling of information. The controversy between training and education in the library schools will undoubtedly continue. The innovative programs will concentrate on preparing students who are able to develop and apply a critical approach within a changing environment. One possible solution may be to increase the number of credits required for the master's of library and information science degree so that students may be adequately educated and not simply trained. Perhaps the American Library Association should accredit only the programs graduating generalists and turn the specialized areas over to other groups.[76] Whatever approach is undertaken, it is apparent that the librarian of the future should be more sophisticated and knowledgeable about all forms of information and their use rather than only printed materials and methods of processing. Narrow-minded individuals motivated by selfish vested interests and parochialism should be discouraged from remaining in library positions. Only those willing to change and adapt to new strategies and technologies will be able to alleviate the real problems of the future. Greater responsibility should be assigned to support personnel for routine tasks and procedures, while librarians with master's degrees become more actively involved in research, planning, and evaluation. Professional librarians should extricate themselves from the day-to-day operations of acquisitions, cataloging, circulation, and the locating, handling, verifying, and manipulating of common bibliographic information. Other labor-intensive tasks that do not require the application of decision making, based upon the theory and principles of librarianship, such as serial check in, shelf listing, shelf maintenance, binding preparation, and inventory, should be cooperatively planned by librarians and paraprofessionals and carried out primarily by the latter. Every effort should be made by all personnel to accept and utilize standardized bibliographic information from traditional online services. The application of both manual and automated procedures at the same time will cause problems with those who are unable to let go of the time-honored traditional approach and have become more concerned with the methods rather than the desired results or goals. In addition, backup systems must be secured and maintained in order to continue services in case of mechanical and electrical failures. Continuing education, workshops, and meetings may suffice for many librarians, while others may need additional formal education as well as a change in professional attitude.

During this time of collegiality and job security, it is important that the overall goals of the institution and its components are not subjugated to personal desires and social pressures. For example, it is imperative that library personnel be accountable for their actions and be evaluated on a continuing basis not only by their peers but also by qualified managers who are ultimately responsible for the overall operation. Personnel policies and individual likes and dislikes will have to be reconsidered if maximum usage is to be made of expensive computer hardware and software. This will require the hours of employment to be radically changed from the traditional eight-to-five day. In the future, twenty-four-hour access from many remote locations will be a reality. Commercial database services have recognized and accommodated this constant need for information through the use of continuously available dial-up services.

During the last 110 years, since the founding of the American Library Association, it has been difficult for librarians as a professional group to reach a consensus of opinion on many major issues and to shape the development and the cooperative growth of a national system of libraries. Undoubtedly this is caused to a large extent by the varied membership of the Association, which is comprised of librarians and laymen from all types and sizes of libraries. As a group, the Association frequently has been unable to marshal sufficient financial and political resources to resolve many continuing problems satisfactorily. The situation is complicated by the many fragmented groups in the Association who may be organized into divisions or units by function, type and size of library, and activities or interests. In many instances, the Association has been unable to act responsively, quickly, decisively, and efficiently in meeting the changing environment.

In spite of a long history of experimentation with many organizational structures, the hierarchical structure is most widely encountered in academic libraries today. Collective bargaining will undoubtedly bring about an unstable combination of collegial and hierarchical structures wherever librarians have full faculty status. If the collective bargaining agreement mandates a dual structure for the library even though faculty activities differ substantially from their associates in the teaching departments, it is essential that a written document or statement be prepared that defines on a statutory basis the responsibility and authority vested in the office of the director. It would be extremely difficult to operate within a situation where the library director was not fully cognizant of his or her responsibilities in the direction and coordination of the staff, services, collection, buildings, and external relations.[77] One major problem in any dual system of this type is the tendency for an adversative relationship between management and librarians to develop. In many cases; this frequently places paraprofessionals in a position of choosing sides, with personal and social pressures being applied by the long-established force. A second is the slowness of a totally democratic governing body to react to problems and needed changes. Frequently the inertia caused by prolonged discussion and consensus-reaching bodies will lessen the efficiency and effectiveness of the library program, particularly in areas of overall development, support, services, and resources for faculty and students. Frequently a lack of experience, limited insight into the overall problems, and many egocentric viewpoints cause majority rule to produce less than the desired results over time.

In spite of limited success with newer management techniques and organizational innovations, librarians and directors must continue to utilize them whenever they can effectively aid in fulfilling stated goals and objectives, improving financial support, and contributing to library services and resources at a local, state, regional, and national level. In view of the cyclic interest in library organizational structure, it appears highly unlikely that a single lasting pattern will be applied that ensures ultimate attention to the overall needs of the library. Undoubtedly a successful organization will require mutual trust and commitment among all parties involved; attention to continuous planning, goal setting, and evaluation; knowledge of and concentration on faculty and student needs; and a recognition of the total information-supplying responsibilities, not just departmental or individual perceptions or notions. Technology demands flexibility and change, which have never been easy for the library profession. Personnel and services will no longer need to be grouped by function around major library components like the card catalog, the serials check-in file, the reference desk, and the loading and receiving dock. The terminal brings all of these file components to every possible location. The problem will be the willingness of personnel to accept and adjust to these radical changes.

The problem of financial support will continue to exist in most libraries as they strive to continue their roles as repositories of archival resources and assume a more universal role as information brokers. In view of the competitive demands for already limited financial resources among all colleges and university departments, libraries must consider every alternative for improving the efficiency and containing the cost of their operations. It will probably be necessary to redistribute existing resources from some of the more traditional areas into the newer automated information services. Parent institutions must assess the present and potential roles of the library and allocate sufficient financial resources to permit adequate development of cost-effective, integrated information systems. Before any change is made in current and future resources, it is essential that adequate short- and long-range plans be developed. These must reflect the current state of the resources of the library, the overall and specific goals and objectives for instruction and research, and a realization that participation in realistic cooperative endeavors is a necessity. Planning for technological enhancement must objectively consider projected levels and phases of the system, initial and continuing equipment and operational costs, anticipated system life and replacement, site preparation, data conversion and furniture, auxiliary equipment, and supplies.

Budgeting formulas that as in the past have been based on arbitrary amounts will undoubtedly continue to be applied. Unfortunately, need varies greatly from one institution to another because of past library support and development, the attitudes of faculty and students toward using library resources in classroom activities and research, and the role and competency of subject-oriented librarians and faculty who selected and continually promoted a variety of resources. The newer technology will not reduce costs in the immediate future; in fact, it will probably increase them in view of the capital outlay for hardware, software, built-in obsolescence, communication charges, and physical requirements. It will undoubtedly necessitate a reassignment of personnel, resulting in apprehension among the more traditional employees, more extensive training and public relations, and greater recognition that the units of the library are not separate and isolated entities. On the other hand, the broad expansion of access to more information than ever before should greatly enhance the role of the library.

College and university libraries are at a crossroad. If they are to continue and improve their role as the information center of the parent institution and serve as a link to external sources of archival and current information, in all formats, it is imperative that adequate financial support and that the mechanism for change be top priorities. At this point it is not clear as to the willingness of institutions to respond to the financial need and how the "change will be controlled and guided."[78]

Although any vision of the future of libraries is obscured by traditionalism and personnel and institutional situations, it is hoped that

> the library of the twenty-first century will become much more diverse in its activities. Books will undoubtedly continue to exist througtout the new century, but the media available for recording and transforming knowledge will increase substantially, perhaps in ways not now foreseen. The proliferation of media, plus the increasing specialization and complexity of knowledge, suggests that the library will become a much more complex social institution. The keepers of the treasure house, the professional librarians, will also have to become both more of a generalist and more of a specialist in the many areas that will develop. In the next century the librarian will work almost entirely with the intellect. The tedious muscle work of yesterday and today will be done by machines and nonprofessional staff. Of course the librarian will have to administer those machines and staff. Thus librarians will become administrators of the science of knowledge, or, in short, *administrative/knowledge scientists*.[79]

NOTES

1.   Justin Winsor, "College Libraries As Aids to Instruction," United States, Bureau of Education, *Circular of Information*, No. 1, 1881 (Washington: Government Printing Office, 1881), pp. 8–9.

2.   Lodilla Ambrose, "The Study of College Libraries," *Library Journal* 18 (April 1893): 115.

3.   Maxine K. Sitts, ed., *The Automation Inventory of Research Libraries*, prepared by the Systems and Procedures Exchange Center, Office of Management Studies (Washington, D.C.: Association of Research Libraries, 1985).

4.   A union catalog is an up-to-date, open-ended, selective or comprehensive compilation of catalog entries whose primary function is to indicate the resources of two or more libraries. Union lists vary from catalogs only in bibliographic entry style and in the extent of coverage.

5.   E. Hanson and J. Daily, "Catalogs and Cataloging," in *The Encyclopedia of Library and Information Science*, ed. A. Kent and H. Lancour (New York: Dekker, 1970), vol. 4, p. 249.

6.   E. Hanson, "Union Catalogs," in *Encyclopedia of Library and Information Science*, ed. Allen Kent et al. (New York: Dekker, 1981), vol. 31, p. 407.

7.   Ibid., p. 414.

8.   *Resources and Bibliographic Support for a Nationwide Library Program*, Final Report to the National Commission for Libraries and Information Science by Vernon Palmour, Marcia Bellassai, and Nancy Roderer (Washington, D.C.: Government Printing Office, 1974), pp. 210–211.

9.   During the 1930s many manual union catalogs were compiled by using WPA (Works Progress Administration) workers. Regional catalogs were particularly popular and served for many years until replaced by the online computer-stored catalogs.

10.   "Computerized Union Catalog Abandoned in Connecticut," *Library Journal* 96 (May 15, 1971): 1662.

11.   John Corbin, *Managing the Library Automation Project* (Phoenix: Oryx Press, 1985), p. 18.

12.   Ibid., p. 19.

13.   A bibliographic utility is an organization that plans, stores, and maintains online files of bibliographic and other records, which are sold on a contract basis to many libraries.

14.   A library network is an organization comprised of two or more libraries, linked by an established means of communication for the expressed purpose of sharing or exchanging information and/or resources.

15.   Richard DeGennaro, "Research Libraries Enter the Information Age," *Library Journal* 104 (November 15, 1979): 2405–2410.

16.   *Resources and Bibliographic Support for a Nationwide Library Program*, pp. 205–209.

17.   A vendor who sells an automated package including hardware, software, development, and maintenance.

18.   Joseph R. Matthews, *Directory of Automated Library Systems* (New York: Neal-Schumann, 1985), pp. 12–13.

19.   Tommy Ehrbar, "Light Years Ahead," *Pitt Magazine* 1 (March 1986): 14.

20.   Ibid., p. 15.

21.   Richard Boss, "Technology and the Modern Library," *Library Journal* 109 (June 15, 1984): 1184.

22.   Martha Moses and Phil Schiever, "New Telecommunications Network to Set Stage for 24-hour System Availability," *OCLC Newsletter*, no. 161 (February 1986): 4.

23.   "Networking Product at ALA," *Library Systems Newsletter* 5 (September 1985): 66.

24.   "The Irving Library Network," brochure distributed by Minicomputer System, Inc. (MSI) in 1985, p. 1.

25.   "OSI Not a Panacea for Interfacing," *Library Systems Newsletter* 5 (October 1985): 79.

26.   "A Special Report, The New OCLC System," *OCLC Newsletter*, no. 161 (February 1986): 1.

27.   Ibid.

28. CD-ROM denotes compact disc-read-only memory. Laser technology makes it possible to store over 3 million MARC catalog records on four of these compact discs.

29. Alred L. Freund, "A Regional Bibliographic Database on Videodisc," *Library HiTech* 3 (2) (1985): 9.

30. Brower Murphy, "CD-ROM and Libraries," *Library HiTech* 3 (2) (1985): 23.

31. Microdex Prefers CD-ROM," *Library Systems Newsletter* 6 (February 1986): 12.

32. "Chronology," *OCLC Newsletter*, no. 161 (February 1986): 15.

33. *Using Online Catalogs; A Nationwide Survey*, as summarized in "PAC Survey Revisited," *Library Systems Newsletter* 5 (October 1985): 76–77.

34. Martha William, "Highlights of the Online Database Field, Statistics, Price and New Delivery Mechanism," in *National Online Meeting Proceedings*, ed. Martha Williams and Thomas Hogan (Medford, N.J.: Learned Information, 1984), p. 1.

35. Richard Budd as quoted in "Library Educators Ponder Future of Accreditation," *American Libraries* 17 (March 1986): 199.

36. Ibid.

37. Allen Veaner, "Librarians the Next Generation," *Library Journal* 109 (April 1, 1984): 623–625.

38. Ibid., p. 624.

39. Joan Kuklinki and Noreen Alldredge, "Staffing Patterns and Work Assignments," *Technicalities* 1 (November 1981): 8–9.

40. "Defining the Academic Librarian," reaction by Sheila Creth, *College and Research Libraries* 46 (November 1985): 472.

41. Edward Holley, "Defining the Academic Librarian," *College and Research Libraries* 46 (November 1985): 462–466.

42. Pauline Wilson, "Librarians as Teachers: The Study of an Organization Fiction," *Library Quarterly* 49 (April 1979): 146.

43. Ibid., pp. 150–152.

44. Ibid., p. 155.

45. Ibid., p. 157.

46. Ibid., p. 160.

47. Ibid.

48. Nicholas Burckel, "Participatory Management in Academic Libraries: A Review," *College and Research Libraries* 45 (January 1984): 25.

49. Clyde Hendrick, "The University Library in the Twenty-First Century," *College and Research Libraries* 47 (March 1986): 128.

50. Burckel, p. 32.

51. Barbara Moran, "Academic Libraries: The Changing Knowledge Centers of Colleges and Universities" (Washington, D.C.: Association for the Study of Higher Education, 1984 [ASHE-ERIC Higher Education Research Report, no. 8]), p. 52.

52. Burckel, "Participatory Management," p. 32.

53. "Standards of College Libraries, 1986," *College and Research Libraries News* 47 (March 1986): 198.

54. Thomas J. Galvin, "Beyond Survival: Library Management for the Future," quoted in Burckel, "Participatory Management," p. 34.

55. Hugh Cline and Loraine Sinnott, *The Electronic Library* (Lexington, Mass.: Lexington Books, 1983), pp. 174–175.

56. Nancy A. Brown, "Managing the Coexistence of Hierarchial and Collegial Governance Structures," *College and Research Libraries* 46 (November 1985): 479.

57. Ibid.

58. Ibid., pp. 479–481.

59. Ibid., p. 480.

60. Ibid.

61. Hendrick, "University Library," p. 131.

62. Remarks of John Corbin at the Integrated Online System Conference, Atlanta, October 18, 19, quoted in *Library Systems Newsletter* 4 (November 1984): 81–82.

63. Moran, "Academic Libraries," p. 35.

64. Ibid., pp. 33–34.

65. E. Hanson, "College and University Libraries, A History of Their Identity and Financial Support" (unpublished research paper written for H. E. 212, Research Seminar in College Administration, University of Pittsburgh, Winter 1968), p. 87.

66. Ibid., p. 44.

67. Richard Talbot, "College and University Libraries," in *The Bowker Annual of Library and Book Trade Information,* 29th ed. (New York: Bowker, 1984), p. 76.

68. Richard Talbot, "Financing the Academic Library," in *Priorities for Academic Libraries,* ed. T. Galvin and B. Lynch (San Francisco: Jossey Bass, 1982 [New Direction for Higher Education no. 39]), p. 37.

69. Betsy Faupel, "College and University Library Expenditures in the U.S., 1981–82," *College and Research Libraries News* 47 (February 1986): 114–117.

70. American Library Association, Library Administration Division, *Library Statistics of College and Universities, 1965–66,* Institutional Data (Chicago: ALA, 1967), table B.

71. Hanson, "College and University Libraries," p. 92, table X.

72. Richard Boss, "Projecting Library Automation Costs," a Forum Edited by Jon Drabenstott, *Library HiTech* 3 (3) (1985): 119.

73. Ibid., pp. 118–19.

74. Moran, "Academic Libraries," p. 39.

75. Ibid., p. 81.

76. "Library Educators Ponder Future of Accreditation," *American Libraries* 17 (March 1986): 198.

77. "Standards for College Libraries, 1986," *College and Research Libraries News* 47 (March 1986): 198.

78. Moran, "Academic Libraries," p. 81.

79. Hendrick, "University Libraries," pp. 127–128.

A REFERENCE CORE COLLECTION FOR A PETROLEUM LIBRARY

Nancy Mitchell-Tapping, Valerie Lepus,
Rashelle S. Karp, and Bernard S. Schlessinger

INTRODUCTION

In 1973, America found itself at the mercy of oil price and production manipulations by a group of nations joined together in the Organization of Petroleum Exporting Countries (OPEC). Because of OPEC's policies, the price of oil became prohibitive, and severe shortages were felt throughout the United States. Since 1973, we have become painfully aware of the critical role that oil plays in our economy and in the quality of our lives.[1]

Oil is this nation's primary source of energy. The *US Industrial Outlook* for 1987 states that in 1986, U.S. consumption of oil rose by 3 percent, while aggregate consumption of all other sources of energy remained virtually unchanged. This makes the petroleum share of total U.S. energy consumption a high 42.5 percent.[2] However, since the mid-1960s, the amount of oil discovered

Advances in Library Administration and Organization,
Volume 7, pages 245–260.
Copyright © 1988 by JAI Press Inc.
All rights of reproduction in any form reserved.
ISBN: 0-89232-817-7

in the United States has dropped each year.[3] Recently this has been partly due to OPEC's deliberate lowering of oil prices, resulting in an economics-based reluctance by U.S. businesses to invest money in discovering domestic oil sources. It is estimated that with oil priced at less than $16–18 per barrel, new investments in the more costly techniques of secondary and tertiary recovery cease. At less than $15 per barrel, stripper-well production, which is responsible for production of at least 1 billion barrels per day, is also terminated.[4] And at the low price of $10 per barrel, "US exploration could be cut by 60 percent, causing a production loss of about 2 billion barrels by 1990; [and] pushing US dependence on imported oil to 60 percent, as compared with 30 percent currently."[5] Many feel that within a relatively short period of time, this situation could severely threaten the economic and political security of the nation as oil-producing countries gain a dangerous stranglehold on energy.

The United States has already felt the beginnings of economic problems as the deliberate lowering of oil prices has resulted in failures of banks that had lent money to oil-producing countries that could not compete with OPEC. At one time, the United States was the world's lowest-cost producer of petroleum. It was also a substantial exporter. And although a large amount of oil still remains in the United States, the easy-to-find and inexpensive-to-produce oil has been exploited.[6] Finding and developing new techniques of producing it are the challenges American faces. And timely, accurate information is one of the keys to meeting these challenges. To this end, we have developed a core reference collection for a petroleum library.

The major resources included were identified by analysis of five major petroleum library reference collections, selection of candidates for the list, and review of the resultant list by thirty special librarians working in petroleum industry libraries. Items on the final list were then verified and annotated for this article. The core list is divided into three sections: reference materials, journals, and databases. Each section is alphabetically arranged by title.

The reference materials section contains dictionaries, handbooks, yearbooks, guides, directories, encyclopedias, atlases, statistical sources, indexes and abstracts, and government publications. In all, fifty-nine items are included. The approximate total 1987 price for the fifty-nine items in this section is $5,500, and all listed editions are the most recent as of 1987.

The journals section contains twenty-eight items. The approximate total 1987 subscription price for the twenty-eight items is $1,800.

The database section contains six databases, whose hourly costs range from $84 to $120.

REFERENCE MATERIALS

AAPG Bulletin Membership Directory and Annual Report. American Association of Petroleum Geologists. Tulsa, Okla.: AAPG. Annual. Free to members only. Not for sale.

Approximately 40,000 professional geologists registered with AAPG are profiled, including name, affiliation, address, type, and year of membership. Indexes by alphabet, geography, and division are present.

AGI Maps and Geological Publications of the U.S. William R. Pampe, comp. Alexandria, Va.: American Geological Institute, 1978. $3.
Publications are listed under each state with categories including general geology, guidebooks, maps, mineral resources, and bibliographies.

Annual Energy Outlook. Washington, D.C.: Government Printing Office. Annual. $10.
Projections are presented for energy production, consumption, and prices, both domestic and international. Topics discussed include the international context in which domestic markets may be expected to operate and the important underlying assumptions about the general state of the economy and its growth. Appendixes contain detailed tables, as well as a discussion of the forecasting methodology and assumptions.

Annual Energy Review. Washington, D.C.: Government Printing Office. Annual. $10.
Statistics are presented, both historical and present, for prices. Some international data are also given.

Annual Oil and Gas Statistics: Statistiques 80–81. Paris, France: International Energy Agency, 1983. $33.50.
Comprehensive statistics on oil and gas based on an annual submission of statistics by IEA member countries, mostly in Europe and American continents, are provided.

API Standards and Recommended Practices. Washington, D.C.: American Petroleum Institute. Series of booklets. Price varies according to booklet.
Each booklet contains recommendations for specific equipment in drilling and production of oil and gas.

Association of Desk and Derrick Clubs of America Standard Oil Abbreviator. 3d ed. Tulsa, Okla.: PennWell Publishing, 1986. $14.95.
More than 1,500 everyday abbreviations used in the oil industry are included.

Basic Petroleum Data Book: Petroleum Industry Statistics. Washington, D.C.: American Petroleum Institute, 1986. $100, members; $125, nonmembers.
Statistical tables are presented on reserves, exploration and drilling, production, financial information, refining, imports and exports, offshore gas, and natural gas.

Bibliography and Index of Geology. Boulder, Colo.: Geological Society of America, 1969–. Monthly. $925.

The literature of earth sciences (books, serials, reports, maps) is covered for the world. Subject and author indexes are included.

Bibliography and Index of North American Geology. Washington, D.C.: U.S. Government Printing Office, 1931–1970.

Each annual volume, until its cessation in 1970, is a comprehensive bibliography and detailed subject index for the year of publications about the geology of North America, including Greenland, the West Indies and adjacent islands, Hawaii, Guam, and other island possessions, but not the trust territories of the United States.

Canadian Oil Register. Calgary, Alberta, Canada: Southam Communication Ltd., 1984. Annual. $95 (Canadian dollars).

Entries for over 5,000 oil and gas companies and suppliers of goods and services for the oil and gas industry include company name, address, line of business, capital, date of incorporation, name of subsidiaries, number of employees, and landholdings. Arrangement is by line of business, with product/service and personal name indexes included.

Directory of Certified Petroleum Geologists. Tulsa, Okla.: Association of Petroleum Geologists, 1986. $40.

Entries for about 2,300 members include name, address, personal data, and information about education, career, and consulting availability. Indexes by alphabet and geography are available.

Dictionary of Earth Sciences. Sybil P. Parker, ed. New York: McGraw-Hill, 1984. $36.

Approximately 15,000 terms are defined, covering eighteen fields, which include geology, oceanography, crystallography, petroleum engineering, mining engineering, geochemistry, hydrology, petrology, and mineralogy.

Dictionary of Geologic Terms. 3d ed. Robert L. Bates and Julia S. Jackson, eds. Garden City, N.J.: Anchor Press, 1984. $7.95.

Written for nonspecialists, the dictionary contains approximately 8,500 of the most commonly used terms in geology and the related earth sciences.

Dictionary of Geoscience Departments in Universities in Developing Countries. Caracas, Venezuela: Association of Geoscientists for International Development, 1980. Irregular. $9.50.

Coverage of 130 departments, with an additional 90 in less detail. Includes the name of the institution, the department name and address, the names of faculty with ranks, highest degrees held, and principal areas of research, the programs and degrees offered, the language of instruction, and financial and job opportunities available. A personal name index is included.

Directory of Geoscience Departments of the U.S. and Canada. 25th ed. Alexandria, Va.: American Geological Institute. Fall 1986. $18.95.

Universities and colleges in the United States and Canada (709) that offer degrees and programs in the geosciences are listed with location, department name, and faculty names. Entries are indexed by alphabet, by faculty, and by coded specialty.

Dictionary of Petroleum Terms. 3d ed. Jodie Leecraft, ed. Austin, Tex.: Petroleum Extension Service, 1983. $16, hardcover; $9, paperback.

Written for the specialist, the definitions in this comprehensive dictionary are useful for nonspecialists as well.

EIA Publication Directory 1983: A User's Guide. Washington, D.C.: Energy Information Administration, 1984. Annual, free.

Detailed indexes and listings for all EIA publications are provided, as well as complete information on how to order them.

Elsevier's Oil and Gas Field Dictionary. L. Y. Chaballe and L. Masuy. Amsterdam: Elsevier, 1980. $138.50.

A six-language approach (English, French, Spanish, Italian, Dutch and German) is used for approximately 1,300 terms. An Arabic supplement is included.

Encyclopedia of Earth Sciences. Rhodes W. Fairbridge. New York: Reinhold Publishing Co., 1966–1982. 10 vols. $95 each.

a. *Encyclopedia of Oceanography*. 1966
b. *Encyclopedia of Atmospheric Sciences and Astrogeology*. 1967.
c. *Encyclopedia of Geomorphology*. 1968.
d. *Encyclopedia of Geochemistry and Environmental Sciences*. 1972.
e. *Encyclopedia of World Regional Geology, Part I: Western Hemisphere*. 1975.
f. *Encyclopedia of Sedimentology*. 1978.
g. *Encyclopedia of Paleontology*. 1979.
h. *Encyclopedia of Soil Science, Part I: Physics, Chemistry, Biology, Fertility, and Technology*. 1979.
i. *Encyclopedia of Mineralogy*. 1981.
j. *Encyclopedia of Beaches and Costal Environments*. 1982.

This ten-volume comprehensive series has been written for laymen and specialists. Extensive cross-indexing within and between volumes helps make this a valuable tool, as do the comprehensive reference lists.

Energy Information Guide. 3 vols. David R. Weber, ed. Santa Barbara, Calif.: ABC-Clio, Inc., 1984. $116 set. Volume 3, *Fossil Fuels,* $39.95.

Covers more than 3,000 reference works on energy and energy-related subjects. There are guides to organizations, government agencies, and print and nonprint sources on energy. Title index, subject index, and document number index are provided.

Energy Projections to the Year 20--. Washington, D.C.: U.S. Department of Energy. $5.50. Irregular, title varies according to year.

The publication provides projections to 2010 of energy supply and demand under various world economic and domestic energy supply assumptions with trends from 1960 and comparative projections from previous national energy policy plans. An appendix presents estimated probabilities of world oil acquisitions by U.S. refiners.

Energy Statistics Yearbook 1982: Annuaire des statistiques del'energie 1982. New York: United Nations, 1984. $60. Formerly *Yearbook of World Energy Statistics.*

A global framework of comparable data is provided on long-term trends in the supply and availability of mainly commercial primary and secondary forms of energy. Historical and current data are presented.

Gas Facts: 1982 Data. Arlington, Va.: American Gas Association, 1983. $30.

Detailed statistics for 1982, and summary statistics for 1960–1981, are included for varied aspects of natural gas production, distribution, and consumption.

Geologic Reference Sources: A Subject and Regional Bibliography of Publications and Maps in the Geological Sciences. 2d ed. Dederick C. Ward et al. Metuchen, N.J.: Scarecrow Press, 1981. $35.

This bibliographic guide to approximately 4,300 significant current reference sources in geoscience and its subdisciplines is intended as a ready reference guide. The sources are divided into three categories: General, Subject, and Regional. Formats include bibliographies, texts, treatises, serials, maps, and computer databases.

Glossary of Geology. 2d ed. Robert L. Bates and Julia A. Jackson. Falls Church, Va.: American Geological Institute, 1980. $60.

Written for the practicing geologist, the coverage includes approximately

36,000 terms in biostratigraphy, caves and karst, igneous petrology, plate tectonics, paleomagnetism, and others. A list of 100 common abbreviations and a list of references are included.

Handbook of Oil Industry Terms and Phrases. 4th ed. Tulsa, Okla.: PennWell Publishing, 1986. $29.95.

An alphabetical approach is used to technical terms and phrases used in the oil industry.

Handbook of Petroleum Exploration. Suzanne Taaken. Fort Worth, Tex.: Institute of Energy, 1978. $24.

The handbook is especially useful in obtaining formulas, economics, and other information for formulating petroleum negotiations.

Handbook on Petroleum Land Titles. Lewis G. Mosburgh, Jr. Oklahoma City, Okla.: Institute for Energy Development, 1981. $32.

Legal requirements of acreage acquisition in exploration and production are carefully covered.

Illustrated Petroleum Reference Dictionary. 3d ed. Robert D. Langenkamp. Tulsa, Okla.: PennWell Publishing, 1985. $55.95.

More than 3,000 entries and hundreds of illustrations are included in this standard tool, as well as Steven Gerolde's Universal Conversion Factors.

International Energy Annual. Washington, D.C.: Government Printing Office. Annual. $4.75.

Current data and trends are provided for production, consumption, stocks, imports, and exports of primary energy commodities in more than 190 countries, dependencies, and areas of special sovereignty.

International Petroleum Encyclopedia. 19th ed. Tulsa, Okla.: PennWell Publishing Co., 1986. $75.

All phases of the petroleum industry are covered in atlas format, country by country, including population, area in square miles, the name of the capital, the monetary unit used, and a statistical report. More than sixty countries are included.

Landman's Encyclopedia. 3d ed. R. L. Hankinson and R. L. Hankinson, Jr. Houston: Gulf Publishing, 1986. $69.95.

Comprehensive information is included on land measurements, lease agreements, deeds, letters of intent, letters of inquiry, scouting reports, drilling forms, disclaimers, and courthouse regulations. There are approximately 1,800 entries.

Latin American Petroleum Directory. Tulsa, Okla.: PennWell Publishing, 1983, $45.

Companies (about 1,700) active in Latin America, including those engaged in drilling, exploration, production, refining, marketing, transportation, and petrochemical manufacturing, are covered with brief histories or descriptions of their activities.

McGraw-Hill Encyclopedia of Geological Sciences. Daniel N. Lapedes, ed. New York: McGraw-Hill, 1978. $75.

This comprehensive treatment of the geological sciences includes geology, geochemistry, and geophysics, as well as articles about aspects of oceanography and meteorology essential to the understanding of the solid part of the earth. Approximately 560 articles and 700 photographs, maps, tables, graphs, and diagrams are included. An index and an appendix that lists properties of 1,500 mineral species add to the value.

McGraw-Hill's International Petroleum Review. Pauls York, ed. Washington: McGraw-Hill, 1980. $197.

This compilation of official U.S. government intelligence reports on the petroleum industry around the world analyzes the current state of the industry in selected developing countries and uses industry outlook reports and marketing outlook reports for petroleum-related equipment. All reports are prepared by U.S. officials and consultants.

Modern Petroleum Technology. Pts. 1 and 2. 5th ed. G. D. Hobson, ed. New York: Wiley Interscience, 1984. $225/set.

The scientific and technical aspects of the oil industry are comprehensively presented for students and newcomers in this field of the industry. Thirty chapters and indexes.

Natural Gas Annual. Washington, D.C.: Government Printing Office. Annual. $14.50

Contains national statistics on gas production and consumption.

Offshore Oil and Gas Yearbook, 1981–1982. 2d ed. Martin Beudell. London: Nichols Publishing, 1982. $130.

Up-to-date field statistics and leasing arrangements are presented here, including maps for countries, varying by the year.

Oil and Gas Directory. Houston: Geological Directory, 1984. Annual. $30.

About 200 companies involved in petroleum exploration, drilling, production, and supplies are listed. Entries contain name, address, phone, telex, and principal personnel by activity, company name, and personal name.

Oil and Gas International Yearbook. 74th ed. London: Longman Publications Service, 1984. $140.

Editions include a year-end report and reviews of the business, operating subsidiaries, property, and exploration of major oil companies worldwide.

Oil Economist's Handbook 1985. Gilbert Jenkins, ed. London: Elsevier Applied Science, 1985. $90.

This ready reference tool provides international coverage of the commercial side of the oil industry, including energy resources, energy production, transportation, petroleum refining, petroleum products, and storage. A chronology section lists events that have had a significant impact on the international energy field. The 180 tables are especially valuable.

The Penguin Dictionary of Geology. D. G. A. Whitten with J. R. V. Brooks. New York: Penguin Books, 1978. $6.95.

Especially useful for nontechnical personnel, the dictionary covers approximately 4,400 widely used terms, including some obsolete and popular terminology. An appendix contains a table of minerals.

PennWell Directories Tulsa, Okla.: PennWell Publishing.

a. *Asia/Pacific, Africa/Middle East Oil Industry Directory.* 1984. $70.
b. *Europe Oil Industry Directory.* 1984. $70.
   Set price for a and b, $120.
c. *Off-Shore Oil Industry Directory.* 1985. $85.
d. *Petrochemical Industry Directory.* 1984. $85.
e. *Petrosoftware Directory.* 1984. $95.
f. *Refining and Gas Processing Directory.* 1984. $85.
g. *USA Oil Industry Directory.* 25th ed. 1986. $95.

Petroleum Abstracts. 7th ed. Tulsa, Okla.: University of Tulsa Information Services Division, 1985. Subscription-based fee. Price ranges depending on size and type of library.

Abstracts cover the technical literature of the exploration and production segments of the petroleum industry. Included are the areas of geology, geophysics, geochemistry, drilling, well logging, reservoir studies, and transportation.

The Petroleum Dictionary. David F. Tver and Richard W. Berry. New York: Van Nostrand Reinhold, 1982. $18.95, paperback.

This comprehensive combination dictionary-handbook (about 3,800 items) covers many aspects of the petroleum industry, including geology, geophysics, seismology, offshore technology, and materials and techniques used in drilling and production of oil and gas.

The Petroleum Exploration Handbook: A Practical Manual Summarizing the Applications of Earth Sciences to Petroleum Exploration. Graham B. Moody, ed. New York: McGraw-Hill, 1961. $75.

Appendixes in this still-useful item provide geological material, mapping and surveying tables, mathematical tables, and tables of estimated and proved reserves in the United States and Canada.

Petroleum Marketing Monthly. Washington, D.C.: Government Printing Office, $47/year. Single copy, $4.25.

Data are included for the U.S. Petroleum Administration for defense districts and each of the fifty states for the current and previous month and for a corresponding month in the previous years, with some historical data. Included are sales prices, sales volumes, percentages of sales, and first sales for consumption, reported by type of seller and type of sale.

Petroleum Processing Handbook. William F. Bland and Robert L. Davidson, ed. New York: McGraw-Hill, 1967. $88.95.

Standard production techniques involving pipeline and refining data are described in this still-useful book.

Petroleum Production Handbook, vol. 2: *Reservoir Engineering.* Thomas C. Frick, ed. Dallas: Society of Petroleum Engineers of AIME, 1986. $28, members; $56, nonmembers.

Various technical principles of reservoir engineering and gas properties and correlations to properties of reservoir rocks and estimation of oil and gas reserves are treated.

Petroleum Supply Annual. Washington, D.C.: Government Printing Office, Annual. $20.

Summaries are presented for petroleum supply, refinery capacity, and stocks and deliveries of petroleum products, including a list of facilities and associated capacities in each state.

Petroleum Supply Monthly. Washington, D.C.: Govenrment Printing Office, $46.00/yr. Single copy, $3.75.

This monthly contains statistics for U.S. supply, disposition, and stock of crude oil and petroleum products, with monthly data for the most recent month. Explanatory notes are provided for the data collection methodology.

Platt's Oil Price Handbook and Oilmanac. New York: McGraw-Hill, annual. $125.

Provides a record of oil industry prices for the previous year. It reflects prices published in the daily *Platt's Oilgram Price Report,* and shows both crude and product worldwide prices as published by Platt's.

SPE Membership Directory. Dallas: Society of Petroleum Engineers of AIME, 1986. $25, members; $100, nonmembers.

Entries for approximately 50,000 petroleum engineers include data on name, address, affiliation, career, and education. Indexes are by company name and geography.

Twentieth Century Petroleum Statistics. Dallas: DeGolyer and MacNaughton, 1985. $35.

Started in 1945, this yearbook presents statistics for crude oil reserves and production prices, natural gas reserves, refining capacity, and total oil supply of the United States and the rest of the world.

The Whole World Oil Directory 1985. 2 vols. William J. Feinberg. Deerfield, Ill.: Whole World Publishing, 1985. $103.

Listed for approximately 18,000 entries are addresses, telephone numbers, and principal officers of oil and gas companies, drilling contractors, equipment, suppliers, consulting services, refineries, transmission, pipelines, companies, and transportation companies. Indexes of companies and personnel are included.

Who's Who in Engineering. 6th ed. Gordon Davis, ed. New York: American Association of Engineering Societies, 1985. $200.

Approximately 15,000 engineers are covered, with entries including address, positions, education, background, and personal data. There are indexes for societies and awards and indexes by specialization and by state of residence.

Who's Who in World Oils and Gas, 1982/83. 7th ed. London: International Publications Service, 1982. $96.

Biographical information on senior personnel (about 4,000) in the petroleum industry is presented, including nationality, current position, and personal data.

JOURNALS

American Association of Petroleum Geologists Bulletin. Tulsa, Okla.: AAPG, 1917–. Monthly. $70.

Book reviews and new publications from the world literature, as well as articles related to exploration, are included. Approximately 2,500 pages per year.

American Petroleum Institute Division of Statistics Weekly Statistical Bulletin. Washington, D.C.: American Petroleum Institute, 1965–. Weekly. $50.

Drilling statistics, rig counts, and drill footage are presented, together with technical discussions. Approximately 8,000 pages per year.

American Scientist. Washington, D.C.: Sigma XI, 1913–. Bimonthly. $24.

Scholarly articles concerning up-to-date research in all scientific fields are presented. Geology is well represented. Approximately 700 pages per year.

Bulletin of Canadian Petroleum Geology. Alberta, Canada: Canadian Society of Petroleum Geologists, 1953–. Quarterly. $17.

The *Bulletin* contains articles and reviews of petroleum geology, as well as reports of the association's activities. Approximately 300 pages per year.

Bulletin of American Paleontology. Ithaca, N.Y.: Paleontological Research Institution, 1895–. $27.50/vol. 2 vols./yr.

Scholarly articles concerning up-to-date research in paleontology form the bulk of this journal. Approximately 300 pages per year.

Canadian Journal of Earth Sciences. Ottawa: National Research Council of Canada, 1964–. Monthly. $140.

Highly specialized articles cover the fields of geochemistry, geophysics, paleontology, sedimentology, and stratigraphy. Approximately 3,000 pages per year.

Drill Bit. Denver: Hart Publications, 1953–. Monthly. $24.

Current information on exploration and production drilling may be found here. Approximately 1,300 pages per year.

Drilling. Dallas: Associated Publishers, 1939–. Monthly. $34.50.

Drilling completion, well servicing statistics, and articles concerning the petroleum industry are included. Approximately 1,600 pages per year.

Fossil Energy Update. Oak Ridge, Tenn.: U.S. Department of Energy Technical Information Center, 1976–. Monthly. $75.

Government statistics on drilling and pipeline activities are presented. Approximately 1,700 pages per year.

Geological Society of America Bulletin. Boulder, Colo.: Geological Society of America, 1888–. Monthly. $75.

The official publication of the society includes original research papers in such fields as geochemistry, geophysics, stratigraphy, and paleontology. Approximately 1,300 pages per year.

Geology. Boulder, Colo.: Geological Society of America, 1910–. Monthly. $47.
Technical reviews of current research, as well as abstracts of current research, are included. Approximately 1,700 pages per year.

Geophysical Prospecting. Oxford: Blackwell Scientific Publications, 1953–. 8/yr. $109.
The official journal of the European Association of Exploration Geophysicists contains research papers on geophysics as applied to petroleum and mineral exploration and other related sciences. Abstracts of papers presented in *Geophysics* are included, as well as society news and information. Approximately 1,000 pages per year.

Geotimes. Falls Church, Va.: American Geological Institute, 1956–. Monthly. $16.
Professional meetings in geology are listed chronologically. The short news reports of scientific meetings are especially valuable. Approximately 500 pages per year.

Gulf Coast Association of Geological Societies Transactions. Houston: TX: GCAGS, 1950–. Annual. $35.
Transactions of symposia held in various major cities in the Gulf Coast area are presented, as well as full papers on exploration ideas and techniques. Approximately 500 pages per year.

Journal of Foraminiferal Research. Washington, D.C.: Cushman Foundation for Foraminiferal Research, 1971–. Quarterly. $30.
Scholarly paleontological research reports are presented. Approximately 700 pages per year.

Journal of Geology. Chicago: University of Chicago Press, 1893–. Bimonthly. $45.
Academic reports of current research in geology are contained in the journal, as well as notes of future events. Approximately 700 pages per year.

Journal of Paleontology. Lawrence, Kan.: Society of Economic Paleontologists and Mineralogists, 1927–. Bimonthly. $65.
Research articles are presented in paleobotany, paleoecology, and paleobiogeography. Approximately 1,600 pages per year.

Journal of Petroleum Geology. Dallas: American Institute of Mining, Metallurgical and Petroleum Engineers, 1949–. Monthly. $18.
Current petroleum industry research is included. Approximately 400 pages per year.

Journal of Petroleum Technology. Dallas: Society of Petroleum Engineers of AIME, 1949–. Monthly. $24.

Engineering articles and reports of current industry activity comprise the bulk of the journal. Approximately 2,300 pages per year.

Journal of Sedimentary Petrology. Lawrence, Kan.: Society of Economic Paleontologists and Mineralogists, 1931–. Bimonthly. $95.00

Geological research on petrology and sedimentation is reported. Approximately 1,400 pages per year.

Marine Geology. Amsterdam, Netherlands: Elsevier Scientific Publishing, 1964–. Bimonthly. $400.

This international journal of marine geology, geochemistry, and geophysics publishes original studies and comprehensive reviews, as well as a listing of marine geology papers published in other journals. Approximately 2,100 pages per year.

Ocean Industry. Houston: Gulf Publishing, 1966–. Monthly. $15.

Offshore engineering construction and operations in domestic and international activities are reported. Approximately 1,400 pages per year.

Oil and Gas Investor. Denver, Colo.: Investor Publishing, 1981–. Monthly. $95.

Economic and investment sectors of the oil industry are covered, in addition to recent oil economic activity in the United States. Approximately 800 pages per year.

Oil and Gas Journal. Tulsa, Okla.: PennWell Publishing, 1902–. Weekly. $34.

Current news of energy businesses, both international and domestic, is presented, with statistics on drilling and footage in exploration. Approximately 8,200 pages per year.

Petroleum Engineer International. Dallas: Harcourt Brace Jovanovich, 1929–. 15/yr. $18.

Worldwide coverage of oil news and articles on reservoir management are contained here. Approximately 1,700 pages per year.

Petroleum Outlook. Greenwich, Conn.: John S. Herold Inc., 1948–. Monthly. $120.

International information about buying and selling oil companies, exploration notes, and stock market news are included. Approximately 900 pages per year.

Technological Papers of the Society of Petroleum Engineers. $5.00/paper, members; $7.50/paper, nonmembers. Must have name of specific paper when ordering. Proceedings volumes vary in price.

World Oil. Houston: Gulf Publishing, 1916–. 14/yr. $15.
   Exploration drilling and production are treated, plus international news in both the offshore and onshore sectors specializing in production. Approximately 3,400 pages per year.

DATABASES

APILIT. 1964–.
   Produced by the Central Abstracting and Indexing Service of the American Petroleum Institute, this contains information concerning literature relating to petroleum refining and the petrochemical industry. Citations only prior to 1978, abstracts since, with a growth rate of about 200 records per month. $100 per hour.

APIPAT. 1964–.
   A product of the API Central Abstracting and Indexing Service, this covers patents related to petroleum refining and the petrochemical industry. Citations only prior to 1980, abstracts since, with a growth rate of about 700 records per month. $99 per hour.

COMPENDEX. 1969–.
   Compendex covers engineering and technological literature worldwide. Citations and abstracts, with a growth rate of about 12,000 records per month. $99 per hour.

GEOREF.
   Comprehensive international coverage of geological literature is provided in this product of the American Geological Institute. The growth rate is about 7,000 records per month, with coverage in some regions back to 1785. $84 per hour.

P/E NEWS.
   Produced by the Central Abstracting and Indexing Service of the American Petroleum Institute, this includes references to articles from major suppliers of petroleum and energy business news. $95 per hour.

TULSA. 1965–.
   Produced by the University of Tulsa, this file includes Tulsa Abstracts and covers all aspects of petroleum information, including exploration, drilling, production, storage, and patents. $120 per hour.

NOTES

1. Fred L. Hartley, "Energy and America's Future," *Vital Speeches of the Day* 52 (May 1, 1986): 444–448.

2. *1987 U.S. Industrial Outlook: Prospects for over 350 Industries* (Washington, D.C.: U.S. Department of Commerce, 1987).

3. Richard Kerr, "Another Oil Resource Warning," *Science* 223 (January 27, 1984): 382.

4. Edward L. Morse, "After the Fall: The Politics of Oil," *Foreign Affairs* 64 (Spring 1986): 792–811.

5. Max Wilkinson, "Oil and the West," *World Press Review* 33 (June 1986): 43.

6. Philip Abelson, "Energy Future," *Science* 234 (December 5, 1986): 1169.

Editor's Note

Readers may find library developments in other countries, especially third world countries, interesting. The short papers that follow describe an effort in the kingdom of Jordan that resulted in the construction of a new public library with many modern features. The editors are indebted to Nahla Natour, a former graduate student in Clarion University's College of Library Science, for the two short papers that follow.

PRIVATE INSTITUTIONS AND COMPUTER UTILIZATION IN COMMUNITY SERVICE AND EDUCATION:

THE CASE OF THE ABDUL-HAMID SHOMAN FOUNDATION

As'ad Abdul Rahman

The future can only be an extension of the present, which, in turn, was a result of the past. The recent past will therefore have to be examined for trends and clues in order to arrive at the possible directions and scenarios of a better future.

What does the recent past of the Middle East, and in particular Arab countries, look like to a detached observer? What did independence achieve for those countries with a colonial legacy?

Advances in Library Administration and Organization,
Volume 7, pages 263–274.
Copyright © **1988 by JAI Press Inc.**
All rights of reproduction in any form reserved.
ISBN: 0-89232-817-7

Political and other social conditions notwithstanding, let us examine the social aspects most relevant to our topic:

1. Standards of living have risen manyfold, as in most other countries of the world, yet feudal and often tribal values still dominate most classes of Arab society.
2. Health has improved considerably, judging by life expectancy figures, which have doubled over the last fifty years, yet malnutrition-related diseases, not to mention famine, still exist in many areas.
3. Agriculture, once the main product of most Arab countries, can feed less than half the population.
4. Education in general has made impressive strides, yet illiteracy rates in the Arab countries still vary between 40 and 70 percent. In the past fifteen years, analphabetism has even increased in the most populous Arab nation, Egypt.
5. Science graduates, from over seventy Arab universities, exceed 3 million. Yet Israel, with a population under 3 percent of the total Arab population, produces twice as many scientific papers every year as all Arab countries combined.

With such a gloomy picture, what are the prospects for the future, and a better one at that?

The Abdul-Hameed Shoman Foundation (AHSF) accepts the following statement of the final report of the 1981 UNESCO Congress:

> It was unanimously agreed that science and technology, together with the teaching of them through the various types of formal and non-formal education, constituted an essential factor in improving the material and cultural conditions of people's lives and a priority objective of cultural development. It was emphasized that, in the world of today, mastery by a society of scientific and technical knowledge was an essential condition for the assertion of cultural identity and independence and for the promotion of effective participation by the people in determining and implementing collective action for development and thus ensuring better national control of its results.

A further proposal by the congress provided the stimulus. It urged "non-governmental organizations to contribute, each according to its sphere of work and speciality, in implementing the suggestions in the report."

Herein lie the major motivation for the AHSF endeavors: to improve the education of future scientists and to foster a greater and more relevant understanding of the nature and findings of science among the populace as a whole. In more recent times, a further dimension has been added to traditional education: information technology.

The AHSF addresses the bulk of its activities to some of the more pressing needs of Jordanian society and beyond. It has sponsored studies in agriculture, as well as encouraged science teaching projects and rewarded young scientists from all over the Arab world. It is at present engaged in creating the modern basis for disseminating scientific information through a computerized library in Amman and a more ambitious project of a bibliographic scientific databank in Arabic.

The AHSF is trying, in this way, to place as much emphasis on basic applied science and scientific education as on the emerging new field of information technology (IT). IT is becoming the most effective means for handling the present information explosion, especially in science and technology. IT is the merger of two fast-developing high technologies, computers and telecommunications. It allows the fast acquiring, storing, and distribution of information, as needed best by the user. IT, however, requires highly trained expertise, and it does not come cheap.

Even in a small third world country like Jordan, certain institutions can acquire and use advanced information technology. Banks, airlines, and the armed forces can afford to pay for high-caliber staff and buy the most up-to-date equipment. They can use this technology as efficiently as any others in the rest of the world. The sectors of society left behind in the race to modernize are often the ones that affect more people and whose actions have more impact on the future directions of society. Two such areas are public administration and education, and they tend to be the sectors least able to afford the new technology.

Nearly one-third of the 3 million people in Jordan sit at study benches every working day. Educated people are the main "export" product of a country with a high birthrate and limited natural resources. Children under 15 account for almost 50 percent of the population. They are going to spend most of their adult life in the twenty-first century. It is toward this group that the AHSF is addressing many of its activities. Seminars for computer awareness are being organized for the ministry of education and headmasters of schools. A special plan for teaching the teachers has been drawn with the help of the ministry and dealers of the chosen microcomputers. Further, a special section at the AHSF is open for computer literacy for all subscribers to the Abdul-Hameed Shoman library in Amman. Supporting material—books, journals, and audiovisuals—is also available. Trained staff are always on hand for helping users, and they participate in courses and seminars.

The official ceremonial inauguration of the new six-story site of the AHSF took place on January 8, 1986, under the auspices of the prime minister of Jordan. The foundation has already established a marked presence in the cultural and scientific life of the country, and in other Arab countries.

It is perhaps time to ask, What is the Abdul-Hameed Shoman Foundation? What are its objectives and achievements, its constitution and organization? Where does it draw its income from?

The AHSF was established in memory of the founder of the Arab Bank Ltd, the late Abdul-Hameed Shoman, in recognition of his great services to the Arab nation. In addition to his important contributions to the economic field in general and banking in particular, he was always driven by his national fervor and aspirations for the development of science and technology in the Arab world. The General Assembly of the Arab Bank Ltd., chaired by his son, Abdul-Majeed Shoman, resolved in its annual meeting on March 31, 1978, to establish the Abdul-Hameed Shoman Foundation, for the advancement of science in the Arab world, to be located in Amman, Jordan.

The AHSF has two primary objectives:

1. To contribute to the development of Arab scientific research, directly or indirectly, through institutions, organizations, or individuals, provided this research leads to an increase in knowledge and is of instrumental value to the Arab nation. The foundation's major areas of interest lie in the field of basic and applied physical sciences and technology, as well as humanities, according to the priorities of development in the Arab world.
2. To contribute to the development of a cadre of Arab scientists and specialists in the fields of natural, basic, and applied sciences. This objective stems from the Arab need for highly qualified scientists and researchers and from the important role science and technology play in the development of nations.

The AHSF adopts the following means for realizing its objectives:

1. Setting up a research center where Arab scientists will be invited to work.
2. Supporting existing Arab scientific institutions and sponsoring new research. It also includes the AHSF grants for Arab researchers and scientists.
3. Publishing results and disseminating information gained from Arab scientific research.
4. Producing scientific, cultural, and educational programs for the use of academic and technical institutions through Arab television networks.
5. Cooperating with other institutions and scientific centers to achieve common goals.
6. Holding seminars, workshops, and exhibitions whose themes correspond to the objectives of the foundation.
7. Establishing modern public libraries to serve the needs of researchers and students.
8. Publishing books and scientific periodicals to further the stated aims of the foundation.
9. Awarding annual prizes for young and prominent Arab scientists and researchers and for science school teachers who invent, innovate, or develop new scientific experiments or teaching techniques.

STRUCTURE OF AHSF

A board of directors is the body responsible for setting down the foundation's policy. It is invested with executive authority and administrative supervision. The present board of directors consists of:

Chairman	Abdul Majeed Shoman
Deputy chairman	Khalid Shoman
Member	Dr Constantine Zurayk
Member	Abdul Rahman Bushnaq
Member	Hasseeb Sabbagh
Member	Munib R. Masri
Member	Ibrahim Bakir
Member	Dr Usama Khalidi
Member	Farouk Kamal Jaber
Member	Abdul Hameed Abdul Majeed Shoman

The executive committee includes the chairman of the board of directors and his deputy, together with two members of the board and the director general of AHSF.

The Professional Advisory Committee, of selected Arab scholars and professional scientists, evaluates grant applications.

FUNDS OF AHSF

AHSF funds are made up of:

1. An annual grant of 2 percent of the annual net profit of the Arab Bank Ltd.
2. Personal donations of the Abdul Hameed Shoman family.
3. Other approved subscriptions and donations.
4. Income from proceeds of sponsored publications and projects.
5. Income from investment of foundation's funds.

ACHIEVEMENTS

Despite its relatively short existence, the AHSF can list some of its achievements.

Research in Pure and Applied Sciences

Food and Agriculture

Arab countries have been increasing alarmingly their dependence on food imports in the last two decades, despite possessing fertile land, water, manpower, and capital. The AHSF has sponsored several relevant research projects:

1. "An Analytical Study of the Problem of Food in the Arab Countries" by Dr. Subhi Qassem of Jordan University.
2. "Policy-Oriented Systems Analysis of Arab Agricultural Sections," as applied in Jordan and Sudan, undertaken by a team led by Dr. A. B. Zahlan, to be published in eight volumes. The findings were discussed in a special seminar in Amman in November 1984.
3. Research on residues of insecticides in vegetables and fruit, undertaken by the Royal Scientific Society of Jordan.

Industry

1. "Arab Construction Industry," by Dr. A. Zahlan. Research and publication were sponsored by AHSF.
2. "Hazards of Chemicals and Methods of Protection," conducted by the Royal Scientific Society.

Awards and Prizes

Abdul Hameed Shoman Prizes for Young Arab Scientists are part of a program to encourage scientific research. These nine prizes are intended as an incentive for young Arab scientists' achievement of discoveries, and inventions. They have been awarded since 1982 in the fields of medicine, agriculture, engineering, basic science, humanities, and social science.

The Abdul Hameed Shoman Prizes for School Teachers of Science in Jordan are five annual prizes open to preparatory and secondary school teachers who innovate or develop new methods of teaching science.

Writing, Translation, and Publication

Following are some of the works sponsored by the AHSF:

1. *Science and Technology in Israel,* a monograph compiled by Sameer Jabbour, IPS, Beirut, 1982.
2. "Ahmad Shawqui," by Dr. Irfan Shaheed.

3. *Jerusalem Historical Documents,* by Dr. Kamel Assali, AISP, Beirut, 1985.
4. *Handbook for Arab Researchers,* in various fields of science, starting with agriculture.

In order to increase the transfer of knowledge and to make new information accessible to Arabic-speaking people, the AHSF also sponsors the translation of science books, among them the following:

1. *Introduction to Embryonic Development,* by Steven B. Oppenheimer, translated by Ramses Lutfi.
2. *Introduction to Classical and Modern Optics,* by Jurgen Meyer-Arendt, translated by Dr. Omar Hassan El-Sheikh.
3. *Classical and Modern Physics,* by Kenneth Ford (in preparation).
4. *Pregnancy,* by Gordon Bourne, translated by Dr. Zeid Kilani.

Subscriptions to Scientific Societies and Institutions

This includes subscriptions, buying of Arab publications of science, donations for laboratory equipment, and sponsorship of the publication of research findings.

Scientific Conferences and Seminars

Two seminars have been sponsored by the AHSF. The first was held in November 1984 to discuss the findings of the research sponsored by AHSF on policy-oriented systems analysis of the Arab agricultural sectors. The second was a joint effort with the Center for Arab Unity, in Beirut, on Arab scientific research and the obstacles facing it. It was held in Amman in May 1986.

Sponsorship of a Scientific Magazine in Arabic

The first four issues of *Scientific Horizons* have appeared. Since July 1985, the magazine has been a bimonthly and will continue to be so until September 1987, after which it will appear on a monthly basis. *Scientific Horizons* is designed for nonspecialized readers and aims at spreading basic sciences and applied sciences among the broadest sectors in the Arab world.

Databank

This is a project to establish a scientific bibliographic databank in Arabic. This bank, together with a ''permanent exhibition'' of personal computers, has been rendering some service to the Amman community since early January 1986. It is designed to help in fighting computer illiteracy and providing extracurricular education through special programs and, in many cases, through computer games.

Abdul-Hameed Shoman Public Library

This project was completed in January 1986. Since then, this library (the only fully computerized public library in Jordan) has been open to the public. The library provides comfortable reading halls to its visitors. Thousands of books, journals, periodicals, and references have been made available to the Jordanian people. Members can borrow three books at a time for a renewable period of two weeks. To become a member, a symbolic refundable deposit of JD5 is required. In the first fifteen days (January 8–January 23, 1986), the Abdul Hameed Shoman Public Library received 1,840 visitors, of whom 234 became full members.

With such projects and services, we at AHSF hope to prove that private institutions (like the Arab Bank Ltd.) can be an effective tool in spreading and fostering modern and informal continuing educational projects for the community.

ACKNOWLEDGMENT

This paper was originally presented at the conference, "Education for the 21st Century: The Way to a Better Future in the Middle East," Istanbul Hilton, January 31–February 4, 1986, sponsored by the Professors World Peace Academy.

ABDUL-HAMEED SHOMAN PUBLIC LIBRARY

Nahla Natour

Recognizing the crucial role of libraries in providing culture and education to the general public, the Abdul-Hamid Shaman Foundation established the Abdul-Hameed Shoman Public Library in Amman in early 1986 to serve, free of charge, readers from all walks of life. The library has three main objectives:

1. To foster continuing education, supplement school and university education, provide up-to-date information, and encourage academic excellence.
2. To serve as a center for cultural activities and to promote the enjoyment and appreciation of arts through lectures, concerts, plays, exhibitions, and specialized courses.
3. To cultivate the pursuit of leisure and recreation.

Advances in Library Administration and Organization,
Volume 7, pages 275–278.
Copyright © 1988 by JAI Press Inc.
All rights of reproduction in any form reserved.
ISBN: 0-89232-817-7

Special features of the library include:

1. Emphasis on reference works and professional journals, particularly in science and technology.
2. A wide range and carefully selected collection of periodicals in all branches of knowledge. Special attention is given to periodicals in pure and applied sciences because of the considerable demand for such services.
3. A computerized reference system, the first of its kind in Jordan.
4. Highly developed services for students and researchers, including indexing, abstracting, and state-of-the-art information storage and retrieval.
5. Multimedia aids, including records, tapes, slides, microfilm, and microfiche.

DATA BANK

To answer a long-felt need for up-to-the-minute information and research support, the foundation is in the process of establishing a computerized databank that will allow speedy access to information from Jordanian, Arab, and international sources. To this end, the AHSF Information Department has undertaken several projects:

1. To computerize the functions of the AHS Public Library, including acquisition, classification, cataloging, abstracting, circulation, and retrieval.
2. To computerize the union catalog in Jordan, in collaboration with the Department of Libraries, Documentation and National Archives and the major public libraries in Jordan.
3. To establish a bibliographic databank of scientific and technical works published in the Arab world since the middle of the nineteenth century.
4. To compile a who's who of Arab scientists.
5. To monitor scientific research in progress in the Arab world and make it available in specialized databases.
6. To provide online links with selected databanks around the world, ensuring access to information from a variety of sources.
7. To provide information-retrieval facilities for users.
8. To disseminate computer literacy through the provision of personal computers for the users of the AHS public library.
9. To organize seminars, conferences, and courses relating to the various uses of information technology, especially in education.

10. To communicate with other databanks and information centers in the Arab world in order to exchange experience and information and minimise duplication of effort.

SCIENCE MAGAZINE

Due to the increasing awareness of the importance of science and interest in scientific and technical information in a simplified form, the AHSF is sponsoring the publication of a science magazine in Arabic aimed at students and the general public. The magazine seeks to promote scientific thinking and enquiry.

The magazine is published by the Institute for Arab Research in Beirut on a three-year AHSF grant of U.S.$212,500 under the title Afaq Ilmiyyah. The zero issue appeared in March 1985. *Afaq Ilmiyyah* is published bimonthly and will eventually be published monthly. It contains regular features, including a cover feature, selected scientific issues of general interest, news, features about our scientific heritage, Arab research centers and outstanding scientific personalities, book reviews, and scientific entertainment.

In addition to an editorial board, the magazine has a science advisory committee made up of over twenty noted Arab scholars and scientists in a variety of fields.

SCIENTIFIC CULTURAL CENTRE

The Scientific Cultural Centre is one of the recent additional functions of the foundation for the implementation and attainment of its goals. It aims at encouraging the cultural and scientific movement in Jordan by promoting participation between professionals and laymen and by providing the necessary facilities for the acquisition of needed skills and exchanging scientific expertise.

It also aims at maintaining strong relations between Jordanian and other Arabic cultural and scientific centers. It organizes seminars, cultural and scientific meetings, poet gatherings, artistic exhibitions, film showings, and book fairs, and its hall is often used as a training workshop.

The Scientific Cultural Centre's activities in 1986 included nine seminars, four training courses, two lectures, six poetic and literary gatherings, three exhibitions, and one book fair. All of these activities were held free of charge, indicating the encouragement offered by the management of the foundation to various cultural and educational bodies and nonprofit organizations and societies in Jordan.

In addition to its current activities, the center will adopt two new approaches:

1. A Jordanian panel discussion series by Jordanians, or Arabs residing in Jordan, centering on communal, scientific, and cultural issues.
2. An Arab cultural season for the AHSF, where distinguished and highly reputed Arab scholars and celebrities will be invited to give lectures in their own field of specialization.

BIOGRAPHICAL SKETCHES OF THE CONTRIBUTORS

As'ad M. Abdul-Rahman is Director-General of the Abdul-Hamid Shoman Foundation. He is a former professor of political science at Kuwait University. He was a visiting professor at American University, Washington, D.C., in 1980. An active lecturer and author, he has written three books: *The Palestine Liberation Organization: Genesis and Development 1964–84; The World Zionist Organization: 1882–1982;* and *Nasserism: Role and Developments in Internal Construction.*

Barbara I. Dewey is Director of Admissions and Placement at Indiana University School of Library and Information Science. Among her recent publications are *Library Jobs: How to Fill Them, How to Find them* (1987), and "Job Evaluation Systems in Academic Libraries: Current Issues and Trends," *Journal of Library Administration* 6 (4) (Winter 1985–86). A former reference and interlibrary loan librarian, she lectures at professional meetings on topics related to job seeking and employment.

Raymond K. Fisher is librarian of the Extramural Library of the University of Birmingham, England. In 1986, he was a member of the planning team and a speaker for the Off-Campus Library Services Conference III held in Reno, Nevada. Earlier that year, he was a British Council visitor to Czechoslovakia to examine library services to university external and part-time students. A full-time librarian who publishes in professional literature, he maintains a strong interest in the classics and has published *Aristophanes Clouds: Purpose and Technique* (1984).

Joy M. Greiner, Assistant Professor in the School of Library Service, University of Southern Mississippi, was formerly head of branch services, Jackson, Mississippi, Metropolitan Library System. She has served as a consultant to the Mississippi Library Commission. She is the author of "A Comparative Study of the Career Development Patterns of Male and Female Library Administrators in Large Public Libraries," *Library Trends* 34 (Fall 1985): 259–289.

Eugene R. Hanson teaches library science at Shippensburg University of Pennsylvania. He has had extensive experience in small and medium-sized college libraries as a cataloger and a director. He is the author of "Union Catalogs" in the *Encyclopedia of Library and Information Science,* edited by Allen Kent et al. (1981).

Rashelle S. Karp is Assistant Professor in Clarion University of Pennsylvania's College of Library Science. Her past experience includes being State Librarian for the Blind, Rhode Island, and service as a children's librarian in Connecticut. One of her professional interests is library services to disabled persons and other special groups. A recent publication of hers is "Public Library Unions: Some Questions," *Public Library Quarterly* 7 (4) (1986).

David Kaser is Distinguished Professor, School of Library and Information Science, Indiana University. He has consulted to more than 100 academic libraries in Africa, Asia, the Middle East, and North America. He served as Director of Libraries at Vanderbilt University for several years and later at Cornell University. He is the author of several books, most recently *Books and Libraries in Camp and Battle* (1984).

Valerie Lepus is a graduate student in the College of Library Science, Clarion University of Pennsylvania. Her professional interests lie in children's services. She has prior service as an assistant librarian for Arthur Andersen and Company, Denver.

J. Louise Malcomb is acting head of undergraduate library services, Indiana University, and prior to that was Public Services Coordinator in Government Publications. Her professional interests include teaching library science courses in government publications, information services, and Indiana official document sources.

Nancy Mitchell-Tapping, School of Library and Information Studies, Texas Woman's University, worked in public libraries in Dallas while pursuing a master's degree in library science.

Nahla Natour is a librarian at the Ministry of Planning, Amman, Jordan. A former graduate student at Clarion University, she is working to automate library functions in the ministry library. Earlier she organized a documentation center for that library.

Judith L. Palmer is a doctoral student in library science at North Texas State University and Public Services Librarian at the Irving Texas Public Library. She is active in professional associations, holding memberships in the American Library Association, the Texas Library Association, and the Dallas County Library Association.

Bernard S. Schlessinger is Professor and Associate Dean, School of Library and Information Studies, Texas Women's University. He has served as chair of the American Library Association's Publishing Committee and as a consultant on automation in Arkansas and has conducted a seminar on planning and evaluation in Chicago. He is co-editor of *The Who's Who of Nobel Prize Winners* (1986).

P. Diane Snyder is an Assistant Professor in Clarion University of Pennsylvania's College of Library Science. She was Media Specialist/Librarian in the Spring Cove School District where she planned and developed library/media programs and facilities. Her professional interests center on this area of library service.

Delmus E. Williams is Director of the Library at the University of Alabama in Huntsville. He is an active *American Library* member with current service on the Planning and Evaluation Committee of the Library Organization and Management Section of the Library Administration and Management Association. He is the author of "The Second Generation: Planning for the Replacement of Automated Systems," *Resource Sharing and Information Networks* (Fall 1986).

Priscilla C. Yu, University of Illinois Library, is Assistant History Librarian and Associate Professor of Library Administration. She lectured at Peking University Library and Nanjing University Library in 1985 while on a visit to China. Active in the American Library Association, she has served as chair of the Books to China Committee and the Duplicates Exchange Union. She has published before in ALAO, and her paper "National Library of China: The Acquisition of Foreign Language Materials," appeared in *Library Acquisitions: Practice and Theory* 8 (1) (1984).

INDEX

Advances in
Serials Management

Edited by **Marcia Tuttle,** *Head Serials Department,*
University of North Carolina at Chapel Hill and **Jean**
G. Cook, *Serials Librarian, Iowa State University*

Change has always been characteristic of serials, and now
the nature and speed of that change have altered with the
development of electronic technology. Inflation, research
in preservation methods, and changes in publishers'
practices and vendors' reservice all make their mark on
serials librarianship. Advances in Serials Management will
present essays on current issues in the topics, emphasizing
response to change and clear communication among those
who work up with serials as producers, processors and
users.

Volume 1, 1986, 238 pp.   Institutions: $56.50
ISBN 0-89232-568-2   Individuals: $28.25

CONTENTS: Introduction, *Marcia Tuttle and Jean G.*
Cook. **Serial Agent Selection in Research Libraries,** *Jan*
L. Derthick, University of New Mexico Library and
Barbara B. Moran, University of North Carolina at Chapel
Hill School of Library Science. **CONSER: The Role of**
OCLO, *Mary Ellen L. Jacob, Vice President, Library*
Planning, OCLC. **Serials' Place on the Organizational**
Chart: A Historical Perspective, *Jean G. Cook, Iowa State*
University Library. **The Integrated Serials Department,**
Joline R. Ezzell, Duke University Library. **Decentraliza-**
tion of Serials Functions, *Ruth C. Carter, University of*
Pittsburgh Library. **Serials Prices,** *Ann L. Okerson, Simon*
Fraser University Library. **Annotated Serials Biblio-**
graphy, 1982-1985, *Marcia Tuttle, University of North*
Carolina at Chapel Hill.

JAI PRESS, Inc.
55 Old Post Road - No. 2
Greenwich, Connecticut 06836-1678
or call: (203) 661-7602

DATE DUE

GAYLORD			PRINTED IN U.S.A.